MEDITATIONS TO
TRANSFORM THE MIND

MEDITATIONS TO
TRANSFORM THE MIND

The Seventh Dalai Lama

Translated, edited, and introduced by
Glenn H. Mullin

Snow Lion Publications
Ithaca, New York

Snow Lion Publications
P.O. Box 6483
Ithaca, New York 14851 U.S.A.
Telephone: 607-273-8519
www.snowlionpub.com

Printed in Canada on acid free, recycled paper.

ISBN   1-55939-125-1

Library of Congress Cataloging-in-Publication Data

Bskal-bzaṅ-rgya-mtsho, Dalai Lama VII, 1708-1757

    [Blo sbyoṅ daṅ 'brel ba'i gdams pa daṅ sñan mgur gyi rim pa phyogs gcig tu bkod pa don ldan tshaṅs pa'i sgra bdyaṅs. English]

    Meditations to transform the mind/the Seventh Dalai Lama; translated, edited, and introduced by Glenn H. Mullin.

    p.   cm.

    Includes bibliographical references.

    ISBN 1-55939-125-1

    1. Spiritual life—Dge-lugs-pa (Sect) 2. Buddhist meditations. I. Mullin, Glenn H. II. Title.

BQ7935.B753E5   1999

294.3'444—dc21   99-16633
                                                                            CIP

Contents

Dedicated to
Allan, Joan, and Tina Mullin

Preface

This extraordinary body of writings by the Seventh Dalai Lama is my personal favorite of all the Dalai Lama literature. Known in Tibetan as *Songs and Advice for Spiritual Change,* most of the entries in the collection were written by the Seventh for various of his disciples, although several are spontaneous compositions. The works were compiled and published shortly after his death in 1757. Since then, the volume has stood as a classic of Asian literature and is an enduring favorite with Tibetans.

I first encountered these mystical verse works when the present Dalai Lama read several of them following a teaching he gave in 1975. The next year, one of my gurus, His Eminence Ven. Doboom Tulku, presented me with a copy of the entire collection and suggested that I translate it into English. I quickly took up the effort, working with numerous Tibetan monks and lamas. Lobsang Norbu of the Central Institute of Higher Tibetan Studies, Varanasi, was with me on the project from beginning to end, helping not only with my first reading of the text but also with the commentaries I received from various lamas. Geshey Lobsang Tenpa of Ganden Shartsey provided explanations of the entire work, and later I reread "Song of the Immaculate Path" with Geshey Sonam Rinchen of Sera Monastery and "Meditations on the Ways of Impermanence" with Chomdzey Tashi Wangyal of Drepung Loseling. Also, I had the privilege of checking all difficult passages with Kyabjey Ling Rinpochey, the late senior tutor to H.H. the Dalai Lama; Kyabjey Rinpochey also provided me with a foreword.

The Seventh Dalai Lama was an amazingly prolific writer. In addition to extensive commentaries on various tantric practices, his collected works contain several thousand verse compositions, gathered under numerous categories. Many of these are prayers to various great gurus and tantric mandala deities; others are hymns to the buddhas and bodhisattvas. His works contain dozens of long-life prayers for the great gurus of his time, written at the request of their disciples. There are also many prayers for the quick return of recently deceased lamas, which he wrote at the request of the monks in charge of the search for their reincarnations. In addition, an entire volume in his collected works is dedicated to verses that he wrote on the backs of religious scroll paintings that had been brought to him for consecration, or that had been written on paper to be placed inside statues or stupas. Looking at his collected works one can almost see him sitting in his reception room receiving pilgrims from far and wide, spontaneously dictating verses for them, copied by his secretary/scribe and given to his guests as momentos of their visit and as symbols of their spiritual connection. All of these bear evidence to his love of poetry and his enthusiasm for composing in verse. *Songs and Advice for Spiritual Change* is special among his works, for in these poems he writes his innermost spiritual thoughts and feelings, and gives his disciples his most heartfelt spiritual advice.

In this translation I have omitted the last entry of the Tibetan collection and replaced it with a hymn that the Seventh Dalai Lama wrote to the eleventh-century Tibetan yogi Milarepa. I did this for two reasons. Firstly, the piece that I have omitted would best be treated separately, partially due to its length and also because it incorporates a vast array of Buddhist ideas. Secondly, I wanted to include the Seventh Dalai Lama's hymn to Milarepa, the forefather of the Kargyu School of Tibetan Buddhism, because the Lam Rim and Lojong traditions that form the basis of *Songs and Advice for Spiritual Change,* and which are major lineages in the Gelukpa School into which the Seventh received his monastic ordination, are equally important in the Kargyu. One of the alternative names of the Kargyu School in earlier times translates as "The Lineage Combining Two Rivers," the two rivers being the Mahamudra teaching from Tilopa and Naropa on the one hand, and the Lam Rim and Lojong doctrines from Atisha on the other. Moreover, the Gelukpa fuses elements from a number of Tibetan Buddhist schools, the Kadampa lineages from Atisha and the

Kargyupa lineages from Marpa and Milarepa being the two most important. The writings of all the Dalai Lamas are laced with quotes from Milarepa and anecdotes from his life; "A Hymn to Milarepa" fits well with this collection, for it incorporates many of the Lam Rim and Lojong ideas.

Songs and Advice for Spiritual Change is the the seventeenth item in the fifth ("CA") volume of the 1945 Drebung redaction of the *Seventh Dalai Lama's Collected Works*. It is the sixth item in the first volume of the 1975 (Gangtok: Dodrup Sangye) edition (pp. 397-502). My translation is based upon an undated woodblock print. I checked this against a text found in the *Seventh Dalai Lama's Collected Works*, which the Library of Tibetan Works and Archives in Dharamsala, India, had borrowed from the Hermitage in St. Petersburg, Russia, and also against a modern photo-offset edition belonging to Tibet House, New Delhi.

I originally had some difficulty in deciding how to approach the actual work of translating the collection. The structure of Tibetan verse is quite different from its English counterpart: the grammar is back to front, and the use of meter is thoroughly different from ours. The Seventh Dalai Lama generally kept to a very terse style, and because his subjects are always technical and mystical, poetic license in translating is somewhat dangerous (although I have taken it from time to time). The Tibetan verses are usually four lines in length, although some are six, but the number of syllables in each line varies from as few as six to as many as twenty-two. Line-length presents no problem in Tibetan, as an entire poem is written from beginning to end in continuous, unparagraphed lines. As many as four or five lines of verse, each separated by a stroke, may appear on a single line of the page. I have tried to keep to a four-line system in the translation, but in a few poems found five and even six to be more workable.

My treatment of technical terms has not been completely consistent. Because the individual works are in verse form, are cryptic, and employ some Buddhist jargon, I have found it necessary to do a certain amount of literary juggling to facilitate the accessibility of the end result. Every Buddhist technical term has a number of synonyms, and should a term used in a particular passage in Tibetan be cumbersome to translate literally, I have resorted to translating it via a synonym. For example, *tong-pa-nyi* (Tib. *stong-pa-nyid*) may be translated as "emptiness," "voidness," "the void," "nothingness," "the way-of-things," "ultimate truth," and so forth. *Gewa* (Tib. *dge-ba*) is alternatively rendered as "goodness," "virtue," "positive karma," "wholesome action," "creative deed," and so forth, depending on the particular meter, sentence structure, imagery, and tone of its context. This is the case with many of the technical terms.

Transliterating Tibetan names is also problematic. For example, "mKhas-grub-rje" is simply pronounced as "Khedrup Jey." With all historical figures I have written these as they sound, and not as they are formally spelled. The problem comes with the names of present-day lamas who live in India or China. I have given their names with the spelling that they themselves use. Thus instead of Khetsun Zangpo I follow his own Khetsun Sangpo. Most Tibetans living in exile in India received the Western spellings of their names from an Indian official posted at the border. The Tibetan refugee would state his name, and the official would write it in English in his book in whatever form he felt was closest to what he had heard. Based on this, the Tibetan then received a refugee identity card, and the spelling thereafter followed him through the Indian bureaucracy. As a result, some of the names of Tibetans living in India have some rather wild spellings. This situation, however, isn't as bad as it currently is in Tibet, where the Chinese first render names into a phonetic Chinese, and from that version transliterate them into English. The end result is usually unrecognizable.

Instead of footnotes, which generally tend to distract more than to inform, at least in works of a poetic nature, I have appended a glossary of technical terms to the text. Buddhist literature abounds with categories and lists of things—the four noble truths, the five wisdoms, the three poisons—and these can be found there.

I have tried not to clutter my commentary with many technical terms. With the few I do introduce, I have used a dual system, one for pronunciation and one for the formal spelling, e.g., Lojong (Tib. *blo-sbyong*). The written form of Tibetan terms and names is given only in the introduction and in the glossary. Important Tibetan or Sanskrit terms used in the songs themselves can also be found in the glossary.

Most works in this collection begin with one or more verses of homage and conclude with a verse of benediction or a short prayer that is followed by a colophon by the Seventh Dalai Lama himself or sometimes by the compiler. This structure is not unique to the writings of the Seventh Dalai Lama, but is common to all Tibetan literature of a spiritual nature. In *Songs and Advice for Spiritual Change* the homage is usually made to Buddha, Atisha, Lama Drom Tonpa, Lama Tsongkhapa, or the Seventh Dalai Lama's personal root guru, Panchen Lobzang Yeshey, all of whom are important in the Lojong line of transmission. On a few occasions, homage is made to Buddha Vajradhara, indicating that what follows is largely tantric in nature. As for the colophons, although in the Tibetan these are found at the end of each item, I have moved them up into my commentaries, because they help in contextualizing the pieces, and thus in introducing the reader to a mental space from which to undertake the reading.

Although there are thousands of works written by the early Dalai Lamas, the number of English translations is rather small. It is hoped that this rendition of a small but important collection by the Seventh Dalai Lama may open at least a crack in the window looking into this fabulous body of sacred knowledge.

In conclusion, my undying appreciation goes out to my old friend Sidney Piburn, editor-in-chief at Snow Lion Publications, for his role in bringing the works of the Dalai Lamas to an English-reading public. I first met him in 1979, when he came to Dharamsala to attend a public discourse being given by the present Dalai Lama. At that time Snow Lion was a new company. Sidney had heard of my work with Tibetan literature and visited me at my home. Since then I have written nine books for Snow Lion, a small part of the several hundred titles that they have brought out. Indeed, they have become a major player in the effort to make available to an international audience the ancient wisdom embodied in the great Tibetan literary classics. Jeff Cox at Snow Lion has also been a constant source of encouragement and support in my various writing projects, as well as remaining a very dear friend over the years. Without these two champions, Tibetan studies, as well as popular awareness of all things Tibetan, would still be back in the stone age in North America. They, more than any other individuals I know, have brought knowledge of Tibet to the forefront. Following the example of the great bodhisattvas of the past, they have worked tirelessly and often thanklessly to keep Snow Lion not only alive and well, but vibrantly thriving and on the cutting edge of the Buddhist publishing world. They both deserve a medal.

Of all the books I have produced over the past two decades, *Songs and Advice for Spiritual Change*, published in its first edition as *Songs of Spiritual Change* by Snow Lion, remains my personal favorite. In addition, judging from feedback, no other work that I have done has had as profound an impact upon my readers. On my lecture, reading, and workshop tours around the world, I continually meet people who come up to me and thank me for translating it, stating that it transformed their lives more than anything else they ever encountered, and that, for them, it more than lived up to its title. For me, even though the Seventh Dalai Lama passed away in 1757, in many ways he still lives on, embodied in his many sublime works. Of all of these, none are more exemplary of his gentle spirit and pressing wit than his collection of mystical poems *Songs and Advice for Spiritual Change*.

Foreword

by Kyabjey Ling Rinpochey, The Ninety-Seventh Ganden Tripa
and Senior Tutor to H.H. the Fourteenth Dalai Lama

The Lotus Holder Gyalwa Kalzang Gyatso, the Seventh Dalai Lama, Omniscient Lord of all Buddhas, wrote an ocean of texts on the various practices of the sutra and tantra paths. Among them is included his *Songs and Advice for Spiritual Change*, a collection of thirty-eight songs and poems rich in oral-transmission teachings most helpful for taming and developing the mind.

It gives me great pleasure that Glenn H. Mullin has, out of devotion to and love for the Buddhadharma, been inspired by the auspicious thought to render this precious and delightful collection into English. I offer my prayers that his efforts and those of his mentors, the spiritual master Geshey Lobzang Tenpa and Lobzang N. Tsonawa, bring endless waves of joy and spiritual benefit to countless sentient beings.

Foreword

by Professor Nathan Katz

When I first met His Holiness the Dalai Lama back in 1973, I was nervous, to say the least. Walking down the expansive corridors of New Delhi's Ashoka Hotel clutching a white offering scarf, I anticipated a rather frightening encounter. How delighted I was to meet a man with a radiant smile and a warm handshake. My fears vanished as if miraculously, and we engaged in an uplifting and friendly conversation punctuated by laughter.

Since then, I have come to learn that this ability to set others so much at ease is a characteristic of the actualization of non-ego, and is a quality to be found in truly great religious teachers. So many times I have read interviews with His Holiness which comment on this uncanny skill, one which combines warmth, humor, and a very down-to-earth approach to life that exemplifies the sanctity of the everyday.

It is somewhat disappointing that this aspect of the Dharma is so often lost in translations of the scholarly writings of the Dalai Lamas. Even so charismatic a figure as Tsongkhapa often reads in translations as dry and almost lifeless. Pedagogic skill (*upaya kaushalya*), the ability to meet others on their own ground, is one of Buddhism's greatest contributions to humanity's common religious history, but much of this immediacy does not shine through the density of classical Tibetan scholastic writings. How fortunate we are that The Seventh Dalai Lama wrote these enormously accessible *Songs and Advice for Spiritual Change,* and that Glenn has directed his skilled translator's eye toward them!

Part of this problem lies in the way we Westerners read religious texts as compared with how they are read in traditional contexts. The seemingly lifeless philosophic treatises known as *siddhanta* (Tib. *grub-mtha'*), for example, come to life when accompanied by the oral commentary of a great lama. Reading a text as an isolated scholar and hearing a master teach it, replete with anecdote, humor, and personality, are as different as looking at a photograph of the Himalayas and actually trekking in them. The former is just no substitute for the latter.

There are a few notable exceptions to this rule in Tibetan literature. Perhaps the best known are the poems of Milarepa, the beauty and profound spiritual teachings of which transcend time and place and are not limited in access to a scholarly elite. They are, justly, enormously popular among Tibetans and non-Tibetans alike. Another is this collection of mystical poems by Gyalwa Kalzang Gyatso, the Seventh Dalai Lama. These are expressions of "the people's Dharma," unencumbered by abstruse references and scholastic form. As such, they reflect an aspect of Tibetan Buddhism we too often miss: its closeness to the everyman. Equally inspirational for the advanced adept as for the worldling, these poems are destined to assume a place among the classics of world religious literature by virtue of the author's consummate pedagogic skill and flesh-and-blood approach to spiritual transformation. Tibetan Buddhism never was the exclusive domain of a monastic elite; it is the very soul of the Tibetan people. One finds this to be the case in the spiritual mystical poetry of the Seventh Dalai Lama just as readily as one sees it during a visit to a Tibetan community.

While not as well known as the Great Fifth or the contemporary Great Fourteenth of the Dalai Lama lineage, Gyalwa Kalzang Gyatso was a vastly popular teacher not only in Tibet, but even among the Muslims to the west and the Chinese to the east. His ability to reach out so eloquently to others, his erudition and his saintliness, still evoke reverence from Tibetans. Similarly, the universality of these poems promises to evoke deep admiration from all who are fortunate enough to happen across this volume.

Many of these teachings, as the colophons show, were addressed to practitioners spread far and wide in remote regions of Tibet, ones who did not reside at the great monastic centers and were cut off from the oral instructions which enlivened more scholastic teachings. Their situation, then, is not unlike that of a modern Western practitioner, for whom routine access to the guru is impossible, facts which underscore the appropriateness of these verse works for far-flung students today.

If one reads enough of the Buddha's teachings, especially as pre-served in the early Pali texts, an image of humanity's greatest teacher emerges as one who was unfettered by abstraction, who spoke directly, compassionately, and understandingly with those he encountered. The Buddha rejected formalism and elitism both in the community he established and in the language he imparted. He spoke from the heart. After the Buddha's *parinirvana*, disciples sought to clarify the significance and implication of his teachings by analyses which become more and more precise and scholastic, Yet, from time to time during Buddhism's history, other masters—Shantideva, Saraha, and Milarepa, to mention a few—recaptured the pedagogic style of the Buddha by teaching great truths in this down-to-earth manner. It is within this latter stream of gurus that the Seventh Dalai Lama should be understood. He spoke the *subhasitam* (good speech) of the sutras more than the *vibhasa* (analysis) of the shastras.

Glenn Mullin's translation captures the earthy yet sublime flavor of these songs and homilies. A longtime student of the Dharma, resident of Dharamsala, and friend to the Tibetan people, he is a worthy conduit for these inspirational teachings. As the *prajnaparamita* would put it, he has accumulated a great store of merit in presenting these teachings. Nevertheless, as the Bodhisattvayana teaches, he undoubtedly will transfer that merit to his readers.

May all beings be happy! Sarvamangalam.

Translator's Introduction

The title "Dalai Lama" originated in the mid-sixteenth century, when an army of Timut Mongolians on a pillaging campaign in Eastern Tibet encountered a wandering mendicant of the Yellow Hat Sect. Greatly impressed by his spiritual presence, they sent an invitation to his teacher, Sonam Gyatso (1543-1588), to come to Mongolia. At first Sonam Gyatso did not accept, but after the request had been repeatedly pressed upon him, he was forced to acquiesce. He so moved the Mongolian court with his knowledge, wisdom, and power that the king, Altan Khan, ordered his nation to assemble and witness for themselves the greatness of this man. Under the guidance of Sonam Gyatso, the Timut Mongolians embraced Buddhism and pledged themselves to the path of peace. In tribute to the occasion, Altan Khan proclaimed him "the Dalai Lama," or "Teacher (Great As) the Ocean." Sometimes we see it said that this was a title bestowed upon him by the Khan. In fact, "Dalai" is a direct Mongolian translation of the second part of his name, "Gyatso." Altan Khan offered himself to the Dalai Lama as a lifelong patron and disciple. Since then, Mongolia has regarded the Dalai Lama as its foremost spiritual guide.

Yet this was not the beginning of the spiritual career of the Dalai Lama, for from the age of three Sonam Gyatso had been recognized as a reincarnation of the monk Gendun Gyatso (1475-1542), who had combined the teachings of the Geluk Yellow Hats with those of the Nyingma Red Hats, and had built the Ganden Potrang of Drepung Monastery, which was to remain the seat of the Dalai Lamas until the Potala of Lhasa was constructed by the Fifth Dalai Lama in the late seventeenth century. Moreover, Gendun Gyatso had from the age of two been known to be a reincarnation of Gendun Drup (1391-1475), founder of the renowned Tashi Lhunpo Monastery and a direct disciple of Lama Tsongkhapa, father of the Yellow Hat Order. Thus Gendun Drup and Gendun Gyatso posthumously became known as the First and Second Dalai Lamas, with Sonam Gyatso as the Third. Interestingly enough, the epithet was not applied to any of the earlier incarnations of Sonam Gyatso, even though the First Dalai Lama clearly spoke of his previous life as the Nepali master Pema Vajra, and the Third personally told Altan Khan that he himself was a reincarnation of Sakya Pakpa, who had traveled to Mongolia some two centuries earlier.

Moreover, it was stated in many prophecies of the *Kadam Lekbam* (Tib. *bKa'-gdams-glegs-bam*), or *Book of the Kadampa Masters*, that Lama Drom Tonpa, the eleventh-century disciple of the great Indian master Atisha, would some centuries later incarnate as the line of Dalai Lamas. Looking at this prophecy in reverse, we can say that the renowned Lama Drom was a previous incarnation of the Dalai Lamas. This same text also states that Lama Drom had previously taken birth as the eighth century Dharma-king Trisong Deutsen, who had brought the Buddhist tantric master Padma Sambhava to Tibet and had arranged the construction of Samyey, the first Tibetan monastery. Furthermore, King Trisong Deutsen was said to be a reincarnation of the seventh century King Songtsen Gampo, the first Tibetan king to offer royal patronage to the Buddhist movement in Central Tibet, and who ordered the formulation of a Tibetan script suitable for the translation of Buddhist Sanskrit scriptures. Thus all of these figures could be called "early Dalai Lama incarnations," but the title was only extended to Gendun Drup and Gendun Gyatso. Thus Sonam Gyatso, the first to use the name "Dalai Lama" during his lifetime, became the "Third" Dalai Lama.

From the point of view of the work herein translated, the most significant of the earlier "unofficial" incarnations is Lama Drom Tonpa, the eleventh-century disciple of Atisha, for it is Atisha who first brought to Tibet the spiritual traditions upon which the Seventh Dalai Lama's mystical songs are based. The full title of the Seventh Dalai Lama's collection is *A Well-Arranged Collection of Songs and Verses of Spiritual Advice Connected with the Lojong Tradition, Including "Song of the Immaculate Path."* Here the term "Lojong" refers to various lineages of Buddhist practice disseminated in Tibet by Atisha, and passed to his disciple Lama Drom. The last part of the title, *Song of the Immaculate Path*, is the name of the first poem in the collection.

Lama Drom Tonpa's work with the lineages of Atisha lead to the vast popularity that these achieved throughout Central Asia, and laid the foundations upon which the Atisha transmissions endured over the centuries to follow. He thus stands as one of the most important historical figures in the line of reincarnations of the soul that was to become the lineage of Dalai Lamas.

♦ ♦ ♦

In the early eleventh century, Buddhism in Tibet was undergoing great changes, and the Tibetan leaders, wanting to insure the purity of these developments, wished to bring in an authoritative Indian master to supervise the process. After much consideration, it was decided that Atisha, one of India's foremost teachers, was the most appropriate, and invitations were sent to his monastery in India.

The story of Atisha's coming is as beautiful as it is poignant. Many Tibetans made great personal sacrifices to bring him, traveling back and forth over the Himalayas and down to the hot plains of India with requests to his monastery. Tibetans love to tell the story of how Yeshey Od, the king of Western Tibet, willingly sacrificed his life in the effort to bring the great master to Tibet. It is said that at one point the process of negotiating with Atisha's monastery had come to a standstill; the elders had declined the invitation on the grounds that Atisha was too valuable a teacher for them to allow him to leave India on such a long and perilous journey. Shortly thereafter, it happened that Yeshey Od was captured and held for ransom by an enemy king. Yeshey Od's nephew came with the ransom amount in gold, but when he spoke to his uncle, the king said to him, "I am an old man, and my life is not worth that amount. Instead, send it to Atisha's monastery in India and tell them that our request for the master comes not only with this material offering, but also with the offering of the life of a king. Tell them the story of my dedication, and perhaps then they will acquiesce." Thus the king remained in prison, where he died at the hands of his captors, and the ransom money was sent to India. The monastery's elders were deeply moved, and gave their permission for Atisha to leave. He arrived in Tibet in 1042 A.D.

Though Atisha had many Indian disciples, most of whom were monks, it was prophesied that his great successor would be a Tibetan layman. One morning after he had been in Tibet for some months, Atisha packed a small lunch and carried it with him as he performed his daily tasks. When questioned on this, he stated that someone very special was about to come to him. Near midday the Nyingma adept Lama Drom Tonpa arrived in search of him. The two met by chance on the street. Without exchanging a word, Atisha pulled forth the lunch that he had been carrying and, before Drom had the opportunity to introduce himself or to state his purpose, Atisha said, "Here is nourishment. I have been waiting for you for a long time." Atisha taught in Tibet for seventeen years and thousands of disciples came to him, but none were to equal the great layman Drom Tonpa. Thus when Atisha died in 1059 (some sources say 1055, thus making his time in Tibet thirteen years instead of seventeen), it was to Lama Drom that he entrusted his lineages.

Atisha's work in Tibet was both vast and profound, and more than two hundred texts written or translated by him have come down to us in the corpus of Tibetan literature. His teachings became so popular that they are now used as major foundations for all extant Tibetan sects. However, two of his quintessential transmissions—the Lam Rim and the Lojong—outshone all others, and became profoundly popular in all schools of Tibetan Buddhism. The two are connected, with the latter being the practical essence of the former. As indicated by the full title of the Seventh Dalai Lama's *Songs and Advice for Spiritual Change*, i.e., *A Well-Arranged Collection of Songs and Verses of Spiritual Advice Connected with the Lojong Tradition, Including "Song of the Immaculate Path,"* the compiler of this volume of the Seventh's poems has rummaged through the many hundreds of verse works penned by the Seventh Dalai Lama and gathered together those that take the structure, linguistic format, and spiritual sentiment of the Lojong transmissions from Atisha. Many of them also follow the approach of the Lam Rim traditions, including *"Song of the Immaculate Path,"* the first piece in the collection. In the colophon to this entry the Seventh Dalai Lama states, "Pa Sonam Dargye requested me to compose a song on spiritual training, so I wrote this dry log of a thing. Not only do I expect not a single word of it to be of practical value to anyone—I myself am not really able to practice much of it—it is an embarrassment even to scholars.... However, I thought that perhaps some people would be interested in my views on how most people of this degenerate age seem to practice Dharma, and on how Buddha himself actually practiced.... It is based upon the general themes of *Song of the Stages in Spiritual Practice* by Lama Tsongkhapa, Manjushri Incarnate, the great reviver of Buddhism in Tibet, a peerless exponent and clarifier of the teachings of Shakyamuni Buddha."

Song of the Stages in Spiritual Practice is the shortest of three texts composed by the great Lama Tsongkhapa, in which Tsongkhapa presents the essence of the Lam Rim transmissions descending from Atisha. The colophons to several other items in the Seventh's collection also reveal that their source of inspiration is the Lam Rim tradition.

Thus the Seventh Dalai Lama's *Songs and Advice for Spiritual Change* is a collection of mystical verse works inspired by the Lojong lineages from Atisha and his disciple Lama Drom Tonpa, and also inspired by Atisha's Lam Rim transmission, the more panoramic source of the Lojong teachings.

This being the case, it would be useful here to say something on the nature of the Lam Rim and Lojong legacies.

◆ ◆ ◆

Three years after he arrived in Tibet, Atisha was requested to compose a text that would present the enlightenment teachings of the Buddha in a format most appropriate to the Tibetans. He proceeded to write *A Lamp for the Path to Enlightenment* (Skt. *Bodhipathapradipa*), together with a commentary to it, which is simply known as *An Autocommentary to A Lamp for the Path to Enlightenment*. These two texts achieved instant popularity with the Tibetans. Atisha himself stated that the text combined three of the most important lineages that he had received in India: the Profound Wisdom Lineage, which had been passed through the Indian teachers Manjushri, Nagarjuna, Aryadeva, Chandrakirti, and so forth; the Vast Activities Lineage, which had been passed through Maitreya, Asanga, Vasubandhu, Vimuktisena, and so forth; and the Tantric Practice Lineage, which had been passed from Vajradhara through the eighty-four mahasiddhas. In addition to uniting these three lineages, Atisha brought into his presentation of them the profound insights that he had achieved through twelve years of intensive meditative training under the Indonesian master Dharmakirti, known to the Tibetans as Serlingpa.

The spiritual legacy embodied in Atisha's *A Lamp for the Path to Enlightenment* became known as the Lam Rim Tradition, a condensation of the longer, more technical name "Jang Chub Lam Rim," meaning "Stages on the Path to Enlightenment." Atisha's two works on the subject instantly became fundamental reading to all schools of Tibetan Buddhism, each of which wrote numerous commentaries incorporating his transmission into their own linguistic formats and training regimes. This is evident from such Tibetan classics as *The Jewel Orna-ment of Liberation* (Tib. *Lam-rim-thar-rgyan*) of the Kargyupa School; *Separation from the Four Attachments* (Tib. *Zhen-la-bzhi-'brel*) of the Sakyapas; *The Great Stages of the Path to Enlightenment* (Tib. *Byang-chub-lam-rim-chen-mo*) by Lama Tsongkhapa, founder of the Gelukpa Or-der; and *The Words of My Perfect Teacher* (Tib. *Kun-bzang-bla-ma'i-zhal-lung*) of the Nyingma Order. Therefore the present Dalai Lama once stated that if anything could be held forth as the common denomina-tor of all schools of Tibetan Buddhism, it would be the Lam Rim tradi-tion imported into Tibet by Atisha.

The second lineage mentioned above is that of Lojong. Lojong is a special formulation of the practical essence of the Lam Rim teaching. Atisha embodied the pith of the Lojong teachings in his *Lojong Tsa-tsig* (Tib. *bLo-sbyong-rtsa-tshigs*), but did not write in detail on the tradi-tion, nor did any of the early masters. The lineage was at first passed by word of mouth, and was not written out until several generations of lineage gurus had passed. Many of Atisha's own Lojong teachings come to us only through passages found in the *Book of the Kadampa Masters*, a collection of early Kadampa teachings compiled by later disciples. The two texts on Lojong most studied today in all schools of Tibetan Buddhism are Geshey Chekawa's *Seven Points for Training the Mind* (Tib. *bLo-sbyong-don-bdun-ma*), and Geshey Langri Tangpa's *Eight Verses for Training the Mind* (Tib. *bLo-sbyong-tshigs-brgyad-ma*). Both of these were written in the twelfth century, and both are very short— the latter being only eight four-line verses and the former but a few pages in length—yet over the centuries they have come to be ranked among the most valuable works on the subject. More than a dozen commentaries have been written on each of them by masters of all the different schools of Tibetan Buddhism.

As said above, the Lojong transmission essentially is a condensa-tion and unique practical application of the Lam Rim teachings. One studies the Lam Rim to gain a panoramic understanding of the gen-eral teachings of the Buddha, and then receives the Lojong teachings in order to establish a quintessential regime of daily practice. This has generally been the case over the centuries. For this reason the Lam Rim transmission is usually given to large audiences, whereas the Lojong teaching is given to small, intimate groups. Many of the texts on the Lam Rim tradition are quite long. For example, Lama Tsongkhapa's *Lam Rim Chenmo* is over five hundred folios, or one thousand pages in length. On the other hand, the Lojong commentaries tend to be much shorter, usually just a few dozen folios, with much of the elaboration being given in the oral teachings that accompany the transmission.

◆ ◆ ◆

The Lam Rim tradition is also known as "the path arousing three stages of spiritual perspective" (Tib. *skyes-bu-gsum-gyi-lam*), because it is divided into three levels of training: initial, in which the mind is turned away from ordinary concerns and inspired to turn to the spiritual path; intermediate, in which it is caused to turn from the pleasures of spirituality and meditation, and instead inspired to seek true freedom; and, thirdly, advanced, where it is inspired to turn from the delights of personal freedom and inner peace to the greater goal of universal consciousness.

There are a number of traditions that speak of these three stages of spiritual development as being comprised of twenty-one meditations. There are variations in the list of twenty-one, but the most common form is as follows:

(1) Contemplating the importance of cultivating an effective working relationship with a spiritual master
(2) Contemplating the freedoms and opportunities of the precious human incarnation
(3) Contemplating impermanence and death
(4) Contemplating the nature of karma and its fruit, as well as the four noble truths: suffering, its causes, liberation, and its causes
(5) Contemplating the miseries experienced in the lower realms of samsara
(6) Contemplating the Three Jewels: Buddha, Dharma, and Sangha, the objects of Buddhist spiritual refuge
(7) Contemplating the unsatisfactory nature of even the higher realms of rebirth, and cultivating the three higher trainings: self-discipline, meditative focus, and higher awareness
(8) Generating the mind of equanimity toward friends, enemies, and strangers
(9) Generating the mind that sees all living beings as a child sees his mother
(10) Generating awareness of the kindness of all mother sentient beings

(11) Generating the attitude determined to repay that kindness by always being only beneficial to others
(12) Generating the mind of love for all living beings
(13) Generating the mind of compassion for all living beings
(14) Generating the mind of universal responsibility
(15) Generating *bodhichitta*, or "bodhimind," the aspiration to achieve enlightenment as the best means of fulfilling love and compassion
(16) Cultivating the perfection of the spirit of generosity
(17) Cultivating the perfection of the self-discipline of a universal hero
(18) Cultivating the perfection of gentleness, forgiveness, and tolerance
(19) Cultivating the perfection of joyous energy and effort
(20) Cultivating the perfection of meditative absorption
(21) Cultivating the perfection of highest awareness, or wisdom consciousness

When the Lam Rim is presented in this manner, the first six contemplations constitute the initial level of training, the seventh step constitutes the intermediate level of the training, and the remaining fourteen steps constitute the advanced stage of training.

All three levels of the path arousing the three spiritual perspectives, and thus all twenty-one stages, belong to the general teachings of the Buddha, commonly referred to as the Sutrayana, or "Way of the Sutras," and thus are methods of preparing the mind for tantric practice—the Vajrayana, or "Diamond Way." In many of his poems, the Seventh Dalai Lama dedicates verses to various of these twenty-one themes, and concludes with several verses on tantric practice. The twenty-one points are not limiting factors in his expression, but rather are launching points for his insights and realizations.

♦ ♦ ♦

The term "Lojong" literally means mental, or spiritual, transformation. *Lo* means mind, and refers to both primary mind (Tib. *sems*), and secondary mind (Tib. *sems-byung*), the mental events that arise within the stream of consciousness as responses to primary perceptions. *Jong* means to train, to discipline, to transform, or to change. The implication is that Lojong is a tradition directly aimed at transforming the patterns fusing within the spirit; its function as an enlightenment path is to change the flow of our mental continuum from negative to positive, from confused and distorted to clear and wise.

Generally speaking, the uplifting and improving of the mind is the aim of any spiritual practice. What is unique about the Lojong tradition is its approach. Lojong reduces the targets of practice to two specific areas: self-cherishing (Tib. *gces-'dzin*), and the belief in an inherently existent self (Tib. *bdag-'dzin*). The practices that aim directly at the destruction of these two are the immediate substance of Lojong.

Another unique characteristic of the Lojong tradition is that although it utilizes meditation, it does not rely exclusively upon it. Meditation is likened to the sharpening of the knife, but the bulk of the cutting is carried out while one goes about the daily tasks that constitute the greater part of life: eating, sleeping, working, walking, sitting, talking, and so forth. Of course, meditation is both valuable and indispensable, but it is not an end in itself. And most of us spend much more of our time away from our meditation cushions than we spend on them.

The essence of the Lojong tradition is expressed in Geshey Rujepa's commentary on Chekawa's *Seven Points for Training the Mind:*

> "Buddha turned the Wheel of Dharma three times [i.e., gave three types of teachings] and, after he had passed away, many Indian masters wrote commentaries to structure and elucidate his various discourses. Thus by both his own teachings and the works of later followers, the doctrine was spread throughout the world. However, all the various Buddhist teachings come under two categories—those of the Hinayana, or Way of Simplicity, and those of the Mahayana, or Great Way, which includes both the exoteric Perfection Vehicle and the esoteric Tantric Vehicle. Yet although the teachings of these different categories of Buddha's doctrines are tremendously numerous, all of them either directly or indirectly have two themes as their essence: firstly, replacing the tendency of self-cherishing with a sense of true love for others; and, secondly, totally eliminating the habit of grasping at an inherently existent self. No matter what tradition of Dharma we follow, if it is Buddhist, its aim is to work toward these two goals. If we keep this constantly in mind, our practice will never become fruitless and will always remain within the scope of Buddha's intent. The three lineages of Atisha—the Profound Wisdom, Vast Activities, and Tantric Practice Lineages—aim solely at these two goals. And it is the treasuring of these as the essence of one's own spiritual path that makes one a practitioner of Lojong."

◆ ◆ ◆

In order to give a better understanding of the general structure and tone of the Lojong teachings, it would perhaps be useful to present a brief outline of Geshey Chekawa's *Seven Points for Training the Mind*, as this is considered to be the most central of all the Lojong transmissions.

The first of Chekawa's seven points is called "the preliminary meditations." These meditations are the same as the first seven of the twenty-one listed above in the Lam Rim tradition, although here they are streamlined and taught as daily contemplative practices rather than as doctrinal materials. In other words, they involve the first two of the three stages of the Lam Rim, namely, the trainings for arousing the initial and intermediate stages of spiritual perspective. The remaining six of Chekawa's seven points are all a special formulation of the Lam Rim advanced training.

Thus the meditations that are here subsumed under the first point are as follows: meditation on establishing a link with the spiritual master; meditation on the freedoms and opportunities of the precious human incarnation; meditation on impermanence and death; meditation on the nature of karma and its fruit, as well as on the four noble truths; meditation on the miseries experienced in the lower realms of samsara; meditation on the Three Jewels of spiritual refuge; meditation on the unsatisfactory nature of even the higher realms of rebirth; and, finally, cultivating the three higher trainings: self-discipline, meditative focus, and higher awareness.

Many of the poems in this collection, such as "Meditation on the Ways of Impermanence" and "Song to Build a Link with the Lama," deal exclusively with these preliminaries, but almost every poem touches upon them in one way or another.

The themes are similar: the tremendous joyfulness of life, the reality of death, the infallible laws of karma, the nature of samsaric existence, the necessity of learning to work with a qualified guru, and so forth. However, they are always presented from an original perspective and with the inventive genius and stark immediacy of the Seventh Dalai Lama's personal experience. Familiar images are repeatedly constructed and unfolded before our eyes, yet like a clever magician's card tricks, they have discernible patterns but are never predictable, and are always loaded with elements of delight and surprise.

For example, in "Preparing the Mind for Death" we read,

> When comes the time to carry
> The load of life through death's door,
> One can take neither relatives, friends,
> Servants, nor possessions.
> Attached mind is instinctual mind:
> Abandon attachment.

The same idea appears in "Advice to a Throne Holder," but with an interesting variation:

> Friends, wealth, relatives, and admirers
> Usually just push one further from peace
> And bind one in chains of anxiety.
> Look upon your attachments as enemies.

Or, concerning the tragedy of human life, in "Song Rapidly Invoking Power":

> Precious humanity, the chance to be a buddha—
> But instead we create only misery with it
> And throw away all hope of ever
> Benefiting either ourselves or others.

A similar thought is presented with a movingly different style in "A Song of Erroneous Ways":

> This precious life now in hand
> Easily becomes a slave to the eight worldly concerns,
> Then every day works against truth.
> Look at the fools carried away in nonsense.

The second point in Geshey Chekawa's *Seven Points for Training the Mind* is the actual practice, which in the Lojong tradition refers to meditation upon the conventional and ultimate bodhiminds. Here the conventional bodhimind refers to what in the Lam Rim is called the bodhichitta, or "mind of enlightenment," and thus comprises much of points eight to twenty of the Lam Rim structure. The ultimate bodhimind refers to the wisdom of emptiness, the non-inherent nature of things, and thus is similar to point twenty-one of the Lam Rim structure. Thus the first two points in Geshey Chekawa's *Seven Points for Training the Mind* cover in quintessential form the entire Lam Rim teaching. His remaining five points are special applications of the advanced stage of the Lam Rim teaching.

Which of the two bodhimind trainings, conventional or ultimate, is given first to a trainee is decided by the master. A short Lojong commentary written by the First Dalai Lama states that if the disciple is of highest caliber, then the meditations to arouse the ultimate bodhimind, the wisdom of emptiness, should be taught first, and that only when this wisdom has been established should the meditations to arouse the conventional bodhimind be taken up. Alternatively, if he or she is only of initial or intermediate caliber, then the conventional bodhimind meditations should be presented first, and only after these have been stabilized should the trainee take up meditation on the ultimate bodhimind.

As said above, the ultimate bodhimind refers to the wisdom of *shunyata*, or emptiness, the manner in which both persons and objects lack any inherent "self." The training of the ultimate bodhimind therefore involves meditation upon emptiness. A number of the poems in this collection, such as "Meditations to Sever the Ego" and "Song of the Direct View," concentrate solely upon this topic. As well, the idea of emptiness appears to some degree in almost all the poems. For instance, in "Song of the Tantric Path":

> The manifold things we perceive
> Are deceptive projections of deluded thought.
> When we search for their ultimate essence,
> Emptiness free of an essence appears.
>
> The things that manifest also fade
> And only footprints of names remain;
> The other side of this is called dependent arising.
> What else need be known?

And the second verse of "Emptiness, Meditation, and Action":

> An image of a kingly eagle gliding high in space:
> Were one's mind to glide without grasping
> In the space of truth itself, clear and void,
> How excellent.

Emptiness, however, is said to be the most profound and difficult subject to understand, and it is perhaps a sign of the genius of the Seventh Dalai Lama that he makes it seem so simple for us. In "Song of Easy Joy" he writes:

> I perceived the deluded workings of mind
> That sees all things as standing alone.
> Vision fathoming the illusory drama of
> Manifestation and the void arose.

Now freed from the cliffs of "is" and "is not,"
By the king of views open as the sky,
My mind is filled with eternal delight.

In fact, he seems to consider it to be so simple that in "Meditations to Sever the Ego" he laughs at those who cannot see it:

Joy and misery are dances within a dream;
Forms and sights are a town projected by a magician;
Sounds are like one's own voice echoed in a cave;
Those who grasp at them are mindless children.

The conventional bodhimind takes several qualities as its basis: equanimity between friends, enemies, and strangers alike; recognition that all beings have been one's mother in countless previous lives; the wish to repay the kindness of these infinite mother sentient beings; compassion that wishes to see them have happiness and the causes of happiness; and the extraordinary attitude that takes the responsibility of trying to fulfill love and compassion. Then, because only an enlightened being can really benefit others on anything but superficial levels, the attitude of universal responsibility blossoms into the conventional bodhimind, which entails both the profound aspiration to personally achieve enlightenment in order to best be able to benefit the infinitely numerous sentient beings, and the determination to train in the ways of a bodhisattva, a lifestyle incorporating the practice of the six perfections.

In terms of the meditation practices of Lojong, the conventional bodhimind is achieved by what is called "exchanging self for others," a phrase that refers to the process of transforming the cherishing love that one usually feels for oneself into a cherishing of others. That the Seventh Dalai Lama returns to this theme again and again in his aphorisms is an indication of its importance. A number of his poems, such as "The Excellence of Meditation upon the Bodhimind," focus on it alone. Hundreds of verses scattered throughout the collection are dedicated to it. Perhaps the most beautiful are the third and fourth stanzas of "An Autumn Day":

The sky of unstained space,
I thought to blend my mind with it;
The center of fresh, hanging clouds,
I thought to touch their softness.

Like mist in the wind,
This mind yearns to drift;
Before the sun turns red and sets,
I would leave behind all squalor.

Chekawa's third point—turning negative conditions and hardships into aids on the path—is largely accomplished by changing one's attitude toward the negativities. For example, harms and difficulties that come to us are to be seen as the ripening of our own negative karma created earlier in this or in previous lives. We should understand that if we face them calmly rather than reacting with anger or frustration, we maintain a greater level of happiness even while experiencing these hardships. Furthermore, by taking this approach we burn off negative karma, and also create no more seeds of negativity for future difficulties. The Lojong tradition gives this spiritual application a special name: transforming hardships into friends.

On the other hand, if instead of facing hardships with patience and forgiveness we react with anger, we only add mental pain to that being inflicted upon us, and create more causes of future sorrow. By practicing patience and compassion, the previous negative karmic seeds that produced this misery are devoured and cleansed from our continuum. In addition, the result of our exercise in peaceful restraint causes our spiritual strength to increase. When thus correctly used, the difficult conditions actually become helpful here and hereafter. For this reason the present Dalai Lama has frequently said that we should see those who challenge or harm us as being as kind as our gurus, for they bring us the benefit of a useful spiritual exercise.

Another example of this style of reasoning is the idea that if others gain at our expense, all we need to do is to see things from their point of view. Then, not only do we overcome envy and jealousy, but we also further the practice of exchanging self-cherishing for the cherishing of others.

Our attitudes toward illness, scorn by others, disturbances by evil spirits, lack of food, and all forms of external hardship are to be similarly transformed if we are to make full use of the Lojong teachings.

This idea of transforming hardships into spiritual assets is woven into a short prayer concluding the poem "Melancholy Visions":

> When body and mind throb with aches beyond conception,
> May we make a profound effort to visualize them
> As friends who share our ripening black karma;
> And thus may our thoughts abide in unmoving joy.

> In brief, whenever any harm befalls us,
> May we see our pain as the product of negative mind;
> May we meditate on taking the world's misery upon ourself,
> For thus are negative conditions turned into aids on the path.

> Looking inside, one's own body and mind don't exist
>   to be harmed;
> Looking out, harmful agents are like a rope mistakenly
>   seen as a snake.
> Therefore may we understand suffering as the creation
>   of a mind
> That sees as true that which is mere mental fabrication.

The fourth point in the Lojong teaching is called "condensing all the practices of a lifetime into the five powers," which benefit us both during life and at the time of death. The five are: (1) the power of the determination constantly to practice the teachings on the bodhimind; (2) the power of familiarization through daily meditation upon the bodhimind; (3) the power of the white seed, or the force of goodness actualized in body, speech, and mind, which disperses the darkness of evil; (4) the power of disgust with self-cherishing and ego-grasping; and (5) the power of aspiration to highest enlightenment, which turns all actions into spiritually significant exercises. The Seventh Dalai Lama refers several times to these five, both by name and by allusion.

The fifth subject in *Seven Points for Training the Mind* is the measure of one's spiritual progress. Many outer indications, such as dreams and omens, may manifest as signs of progress, but most important are the inner signs. These are known only to the aspirant and his or her teachers, but in general it can be said that if one's anger, aversion, attachment, pride, and ego-grasping are weakening, and if love, compassion, discipline, humility, and wisdom are growing, one's practice is developing well. In stricter terms, if self-cherishing is being replaced by the cherishing of others, the spirit of Lojong is making itself known. Therefore in "A Song of Erroneous Ways" the Seventh Dalai Lama writes:

> One may generate a little compassion in meditation,
> Yet if waves of anger creep up from within
> When one meets with the aggression of cruel beings,
> The seed of the Great Way is thus lost.

And in "A Precept for Yeshey Gyaltsen":

> Although you strive with utmost energy
> Day and night to accomplish true virtue,
> When this is not done from a universal perspective,
> It lacks bodhimind and is not the Great Way.

The sixth point given by Geshey Chekawa concerns the commitments entailed by the Lojong training, or the "do's and don'ts" of the discipline; the seventh point concerns general advice or guidelines, which are less binding than, but in the same vein as, the commitments. The main principles of both these points are skillfully worked into the patterns of the *Songs and Advice for Spiritual Change*, and many may find these passages to be among the most useful for their spiritual practice. "A Song of Erroneous Ways," the seventeenth work in this collection, beautifully exemplifies these two points.

Interpreted in this manner, *Seven Points for Training the Mind* is a combination of only the Wisdom and Method Lineages and does not include, but rather acts as a foundation for, the Tantric Practice Lineage. Generally, however, the tantric teachings are blended in with the standard Lojong methods. This is done directly, master to student, at the time of the transmission.

◆ ◆ ◆

Atisha also arranged the Lojong teachings under seven headings, but his seven, concerning themselves more with the daily meditation practice of Lojong than with the tradition as an overall system, differ somewhat from those of Chekawa. Atisha's seven points are: (1) prayers to the lineage gurus; (2) meditation upon guru yoga, or spiritual union with one's personal teacher; (3) meditation upon love for all sentient beings; (4) meditation upon compassion; (5) cultivation of the wishing and actual bodhiminds within one's continuum; (6) transformation of negative conditions into aids on the path; and (7) meditation upon the illusory, void nature of things. Here, the first two points are used as preliminaries; points three, four, and five are the conventional bodhimind; and point seven is the ultimate bodhimind. In other words, these six headings are subsumed under the first two of Chekawa's system, and Atisha's sixth point is identical to Chekawa's third.

Of particular interest to us in Atisha's structure of Lojong is his emphasis upon the practice of guru yoga—an emphasis shared by the Seventh Dalai Lama throughout *Songs and Advice for Spiritual Change*. Of the several dozen songs in his collection, nine are poems in praise of, or are prayers to, the guru. Three of these focus on Lama Tsongkhapa, the root guru of the First Dalai Lama. Tsongkhapa is particularly important in the Lojong lineage because he reunited the various lines of transmission that had become splintered following the demise of Lama Drom Tonpa. The songs to him in this collection may be regarded as belonging to the first of Atisha's categories—prayers to the lineage

gurus. Also belonging under this heading is "To Shower Sublime Goodness," a prayer to all the main figures in the Lojong lineage. The remaining five poems of this nature are expressions of the standard
themes of guru yoga, common to all sects of Tibetan Buddhism, and
provide excellent examples of the ideal attitude to be held toward one's
spiritual teacher. Most noteworthy among them is "Guru Inseparable,"
which is as beautiful as it is powerful. Although this poem almost
serves as an encyclopedia of all the traditional images and metaphors
found in hundreds of Tibetan scriptures on the subject, the information is presented in a warm and immediate manner due to the excellence of the poet.

♦ ♦ ♦

Many people consider the Seventh Dalai Lama to be the greatest in
the line of Dalai Lamas. But the choice is a difficult one.

The First Dalai Lama, Gyalwa Gendun Drup, was born in Southwestern Tibet in 1391 and entered Nartang Monastery at the age of
seven. By his early twenties he had studied with teachers from all
schools of Tibetan Buddhism and had become a very great scholar
and meditator. His works on the most complex issues of perception
(Skt. *pramana*), metaphysics (Skt. *abhidharma*), and discipline (Skt.
vinaya) are standard textbooks in many monastic universities even
today. Tashi Lhunpo, the monastery that he established in Shigatsey,
soon became one of Tibet's four greatest monastic institutions. When
the time for his death arrived, he summoned his followers into the
main assembly hall of his monastery, gave them a final teaching, and
then sat in meditation. Before the eyes of his hundreds of followers,
his body emanated rainbows and slowly transformed from that of an
eighty-three year old man into that of a sixteen year old boy. He remained in the meditation posture for thirty days thereafter without
manifesting any of the signs of decomposition, even though his heart
had stopped beating and his breathing had ceased.

The Second Dalai Lama, Gendun Gyatso, was born in 1475 as the
son of a great yogi who combined the teachings of the Nyingma and
Shangpa Kargyu Schools. At the age of two he asked to be taken to
visit Tashi Lhunpo Monastery, and when he later entered its temple,
announced that he was a reincarnation of Gendun Drup. He was put
to many rigid tests by the proper authorities and dispelled all doubts

that in truth he was the great lama's reincarnation. Although he studied under many lamas during his life, he specialized in the Nyingma and Shangpa Kargyu teachings imparted to him by his father, and the Sarma, or New Sect lineages (Kargyu, Sakya, Kadam, and Geluk) as given to him by Khedrup Norzang Gyatso. He accomplished many great deeds, perhaps the most important being the consecration of the Oracle Lake southeast of Lhasa, together with the creation of Chokhor Gyal Monastery near it, and the building of the Ganden Potrang in Drepung Monastery. These three acts would strongly influence the destinies of all future Dalai Lama incarnations. The Ganden Potrang was to remain the seat of the Dalai Lamas until the Great Fifth was made the temporal and spiritual head of the entire Tibetan nation in 1642, at which time he moved to Lhasa's Red Fort, converting the structure into what became known as the Potala. The Ganden Potrang thereafter became the official name of the Dalai Lama's government. The manner of death of the Second Dalai Lama was as spectacular as that of the First, and left his followers with a strong faith in his level of attainment.

The Third Dalai Lama, Sonam Gyatso, was born in Tolung, a valley to the north of Lhasa, a year after the death of the Second, and was soon recognized as the reincarnation of the great Gendun Gyatso. He was entrusted to the renowned master Panchen Sonam Drakpa, quickly attained mastery, and became head of both Drepung and Sera Monasteries. During his lifetime, fighting broke out between the followers of the Kargyu and the Geluk sects and he was often called upon to mediate, for it was only to him that both sides were willing to listen. In 1578, at the request of Altan Khan, he traveled to Mongolia. When he met the Khan and was questioned as to the level of his power, he reached his arm into an enormous boulder lying near the Khan and from it extracted a huge conch shell, the matrix of which circled in reverse. He placed the conch to his lips and blew a sharp note, whereupon the earth shook. The Khan willingly listened to him, and became so moved by his teachings that he pledged his nation to Buddhism.

Thereafter Gyalwa Sonam Gyatso traveled widely throughout eastern Tibet and western China, establishing numerous monasteries as he went. His greatness forms the basis of many popular legends, for throughout his life he performed many miracles and gave numerous public teachings that attracted enormous crowds. He is most remembered for civilizing the Mongolians and for founding Kumbum Monastery in Amdo Province at the birthplace of Lama Tsongkhapa.

Kumbum rapidly became the largest monastery in eastern Tibet. Here he constructed a protective encasing to guard the "Tree of Mystic Letters" that had sprung from the earth above the place where Tsongkhapa's afterbirth had been buried. Every leaf of this sacred tree bore a mystic letter and each layer of its bark contained mantras, all of which were naturally formed. Furthermore, when viewed from different angles the tree resembled various bodhisattvas. Because of the protective wall constructed by the Third Dalai Lama, this holy phenomenon was protected over the centuries to follow, and many pilgrims have visited the sacred site.

The Fourth Dalai Lama, Gyalwa Yonten Gyatso, was the first Dalai Lama to incarnate in a high or aristocratic family. He was also the only Dalai Lama not of Tibetan stock. Born in 1589 as the great-grandson of Altan Khan, he was soon noticed to be of an unusual disposition. A delegation arriving from Lhasa determined that in fact he was the Dalai Lama and eventually placed him in Drepung for his education. In 1615 the Shen Tsung Emperor of China invited him to come and consecrate the Nanking temple and to teach the Ming Court. Gyalwa Yonten Gyatso declined to go to China but performed the consecration for the temple from Lhasa. As he concluded the ceremony, a rain of flowers is said to have fallen on the Nanking Temple.

By the time of the Fifth Dalai Lama, Gyalwa Lobzang Gyatso, the Geluk had become the largest sect in Tibet, and although they held no political power, the old rulers began to fear them. In 1618 several Geluk monasteries were attacked. An army of ten thousand Mongolian troops under the leadership of Aarsalan Khan was contracted by the king of Tsang, Southwest Tibet, to enter Central Tibet and destroy the Geluk monasteries. When Aarsalan Khan met the Dalai Lama, however, he was so impressed by his saintliness and splendor that he took ordination and became a Gelukpa monk under his tutorage. This greatly perturbed the king of Tsang, who proceeded to forge an alliance with the king of Beri, a kingdom in eastern Tibet, with the objective of invading Lhasa and eliminating the Gelukpas. However, Gushri Khan, the chief of the Qoshot Mongolians, a tribe with many of their children in the great monastic universities of the Lhasa area, heard of this conspiracy. He intercepted and defeated the Beri king and his armies, and then invaded Tsang and defeated its king. Tibet's civil war came to and end, and in 1642 the Dalai Lama emerged as the spiritual and temporal head of Tibet. The office of the Dalai Lama has maintained this function ever since.

Actually, the work of the Qoshot Mongolians in establishing the Dalai Lama as head of the Tibetan nation was anything but arbitrary. The present Dalai Lama has said that he felt that there was something of a master plan running through the lives and works of the early Dalai Lamas. The First had spread his teachings throughout western and southwestern Tibet; the Second had spread his message through central and southern Tibet; the Third had gone north and east. Thus by the end of the lifetime of the Third there was hardly a family anywhere in Tibet who had not developed spiritual links with the Dalai Lama lineage of incarnations. Moreover, not only were these three incarnations famed for their saintliness, but all three had on occasion coincidentally performed the role of peacemaker between feuding factions of Tibetan chieftains. When the Fourth Dalai Lama was born in Mongolia, this provided the final piece to the edifice. Thus when civil war erupted in Tibet, it was almost inevitable that the Fifth Dalai Lama would emerge as the leading candidate for spiritual and secular leadership of his people.

Moreover, in the fourteenth century national leadership had been provided by the Sakya lamas, beginning with Sakya Pakpa, a previous incarnation of the being who became the line of Dalai Lamas. The period of Sakyapa rule was viewed as one of peace. It was thus natural that the Tibetans would now look to a lama to put the country back together after the long and painful wars that had marked the period of aristocratic rule, and as the Dalai Lamas had become the most popular incarnate lama office in the land, his name was at the top of the list.

Another reason that the Fifth Dalai Lama was seen as the prime candidate for the position of leadership was that the school into which he had been ordained, the Gelukpa, was in fact a fusion of all the earlier schools. This made him unlike the Sakyapa or Kargyupa lamas, both of whom essentially practiced lineages of Buddhism coming directly (and independently of one another) from India. As a leading Gelukpa lama, the Dalai Lama held lineages from all the earlier sects, including both the Sakya and Kargyu schools. Also, having been born into the family of the renowned Nyingmapa lama Jigmey Lingpa, he was highly respected within that sect. Every day as part of his tantric practice he would read prayers to the masters of all the different lineages.

This affiliation with the lineage masters of the different schools meant not only that the great monasteries and spiritual heads of the various schools held him in high regard. More importantly, because of it, the lay people of the country perceived him as unbiased and non-affiliated, and thus in a position to equally serve the interests of all Tibetans.

The Mongolian role in originally lobbying his name for this position, of course, was important in the initial stages. Mongolia was the superpower of Central Asia at the time, and having a head of the nation who was held in high regard by the Mongols was imperative to regional peace. Not only could the Dalai Lama's relationship with Mongolia keep the Mongols out of Tibet, it could also help in influencing the Mongolians toward a generally more pacific approach to relations with its many neighbors. However, had the Tibetans not agreed, there is no way that the Dalai Lama office would have evolved into an institution that continued successfully into the present era. Had this not been the case, it is difficult to believe that even now, three and a half centuries later, the institution would be as strong and popular as ever.

The Fifth Dalai Lama studied under lamas of all Tibetan sects, though, as have most Dalai Lamas, he specialized in a combination of Nyingma and Geluk lineages. Following his ascension to power, his first official act was to pass laws legally prohibiting sectarian rivalry and intermonastic squabbling. He also established a basic form of national health care and greatly encouraged the monastic schools of all sects to offer free education to the young of all classes and segments of Tibetan society. He then set up a government structure in which he would have to participate only minimally, and withdrew to the religious life. Once, when criticized for his lack of political interest, he replied, "I am a lama, and my first duty is to study Dharma, to meditate, and to teach. So this is the best course for me to follow while I am young." However, he did not ignore the interests of his people, but carefully monitored events from a distance, actively intervening to guide and assist only when things were not proceeding well. He is most loved and revered by the Tibetans for his wise and just rule, his excellent teachings, and his work in creating the Potala, an eternal monument to the sublime in man. He is also regarded as one of the greatest philosophers, writers, and poets of Tibet's long history, and in fact wrote as much as all other Dalai Lamas combined.

The Sixth Dalai lama, Tsangyang Gyatso, was more radical than any of his predecessors. Born into a Nyingma family, at the age of twenty-one he renounced the monkhood, refused to accept political power, and took to living the simple life of a layman. He spent his days talking to people and his nights in taverns or with girlfriends. To the Tibetans his behavior in no way contradicted the view that he was the sixth incarnation of the Dalai Lama; rather, they tended to see it as a special teaching.

The Mongolians, however, had no such faith, and felt that a mistake had been made in the choice of the incarnation. They invaded Tibet and attempted to seize the young tulku. Thousands of Tibetans surrounded him to prevent his abduction, but in order to avoid bloodshed he begged them to let him go with the Mongols. The people consented only when he had given them three promises: he would not leave Tibet, he would not permit the Mongols to harm him, and he would return to them unharmed. As he left Lhasa with the Mongol army a child ran up to him. The child had the same name as he, Tsangyang Gyatso, and the mother called out to the boy, "Tsangyang, come back." The Sixth Dalai Lama, always quick to break into verse, replied with a poem that was to become famous,

> O white crane, fear not,
> I go not far.
> Lend me white wings
> And from Litang shall I return.

He left with the Mongol army, but one night a few weeks later, as they neared the Tibet-Mongol border, he dressed in his tantric cloak, sat in meditation and mysteriously passed away.

Shortly thereafter a boy was born in Litang who showed signs of being the reincarnation of the Dalai Lama. His body bore all of the correct signs and he successfully chose from amongst imitations all the possessions of the previous Dalai Lamas that were placed before him. The boy was given to the Panchen to be educated and quickly manifested realization. This was the child destined to become the Seventh Dalai Lama.

♦ ♦ ♦

The Seventh Dalai Lama, Gyalwa Kalzang Gyatso, was a simple, unassuming man and an exemplary monk, perhaps in order to set a contrast with the flamboyant image created by his predecessor. He rarely slept more than three hours a night, and passed all his time in study, meditation, teaching, and writing. He showed little interest in politics and preferred to leave them to those who had the inclination. Often he would slip out of his residence for weeks at a time and travel incognito through the mountains, coming to the people as a simple traveler or beggar, teaching them not through formal gatherings but by means of everyday life situations. It is this characteristic simplicity that most strongly marks his writings, which are straightforward, earthy, and alive with a natural and disarming imagery.

The popular stories of the Seventh Dalai Lama's impromptu excursions are many and varied, but always filled with fun and magic. Once, it is said, he disguised himself as a professional prayer reader, the lowest class of the monkhood, and traveled through the villages of Kham province offering his services door-to-door. Whenever he performed rituals, the family that had hosted him instantly met with unexpected good fortune and prosperity. All were deeply moved by the simplicity and gentleness of this quiet monk.

Khenpo Konchok Gyaltsen once told me a popular story associated with the Seventh Dalai Lama. The Seventh was wandering in Eastern Tibet in the guise of a professional ritualist, offering his services in the villages through which he passed. A peasant in Litang village commissioned him to do a ritual in his house for a day, but in the evening was so impressed by him that he begged him to stay for yet another day. This continued for a second and then a third time, until in the end Kalzang Gyatso had remained with him for several weeks, constantly reading prayers and performing rituals. Finally the monk begged his leave, stating that he simply could not remain any longer, as he had other commitments to keep. On the day of his departure the patron offered him a small plate of pure gold, but Kalzang Gyatso, not wishing to accept it and also hoping to avoid insulting his patron, hid it behind the paraphernalia on the man's altar. As he left he told him, "If you come to Lhasa, please come and stay with me. Just ask around for the professional ritualist Kalzang Gyatso."

A few days later, while cleaning his altar, the patron was surprised to discover the presence of the small golden plate that he had offered to the lama. Distressed that his offering had not been taken, and not wishing to take back an object that he already had offered to one of the monkhood, he whispered a short prayer and tossed the plate into the air. The plate instantly vanished.

The following year the villager made a pilgrimage to the sacred city of Lhasa. While there he asked throughout the city for the professional ritualist Kalzang Gyatso, but none were familiar with the name, and his search met with no success. However, some attendants of the Dalai Lama happened to hear of this and mentioned it to their master.

The Dalai Lama immediately sent for the man. Thus it came to pass that the farmer from Litang unexpectedly spent a week in the Potala with his friend, the professional ritualist Kalzang Gyatso. To end the tale, upon the Dalai Lama's altar he beheld the small golden plate that a year ago he had tossed into the air.

Most Tibetan biographies of the Seventh Dalai Lama deal only with the spiritual side of his life, and don't delve into the complicated political maze of the times in which he lived. This is partly because his biographers were monks, and thus neither took interest in nor pretended to understand the political events of the times. Their primarily interests lay in the Seventh's roles as teacher, spiritual leader, and lineage holder, and therefore it is these that they documented.

The Seventh Dalai Lama certainly lived in an extremely tumultuous time. Mongolia's power in Central Asia was waning, and Manchuria was the new rising star. The Manchus had recently invaded and captured China and had allied themselves with various Mongol tribes as a means of dividing and thus weakening the Mongol power structures. It was a time of dramatic change and of the formation of new alliances. The different factions of Tibet's power brokers were split on the issue of with whom to ally the nation. The Seventh Dalai Lama, as Tibet's figurehead spiritual and temporal leader, was caught in the middle of it all. In all probability several of the longer teaching tours that he undertook during the middle period of his life were in fact unofficially forced upon him by the Lhasa power brokers as a means of keeping him away from the heat of their intrigues. One period—and it lasted for several years—could even be said to be an unofficially forced exile. Tsechok Ling, one of his biographers, simply wrote: "Not long after His Holiness had completed his *abhidharma* studies, political problems developed between powerful aristocratic factions in Central Tibet. Taking his tutor, the Throne Holder Palden Drakpa, with him, he left for the place of his birth in the east." This is similar to a passage in the biography of the Second Dalai Lama, wherein we read, "At that time some skirmishes broke out between the various factions of chieftains, and the master entered into a retreat in the Olkha mountains to avoid them."

Throughout all the maneuverings of Tibet's chieftains, however, the Seventh himself remained deeply loved by all, and every effort was made to keep him safely away from the conflicts. Nonetheless he was very much aware of them. We see these events subtly referred to in his poems, although he uses them as material for his Buddhist meditations. For example, in "Meditations on the Ways of Impermanence" we read:

> Spirits were high with expectations this morning
> As the men discussed subduing enemies and protecting the land.
> Now, with night's coming, birds and dogs chew their corpses.
> Who believed that they themselves would die today?

> If you look closely at and contemplate deeply
> The people and things that appear around you,
> You can see that all are in constant flux.
> Everything becomes the teacher of impermanence.

The Seventh Dalai Lama is lovingly remembered for many of his deeds, but especially for the excellent corpus of tantric literature that he left behind, much of which is widely studied even today. His written works, which are collected into eight thick volumes, comprise several hundred titles. Most of these are tantric in nature. Perhaps the most famous is *The Sacred Word of Vajrasattva Revealing the Meaning of Clear Light and Appearance*, which is a 417 folio (834 page) commentary on the initiatory processes of the Marpa lineage of the tantric deity Guhyasamaja. His commentaries on the meditative processes and yogic methods of the tantras of Kalachakra, Yamantaka, Vajrasattva, Vajrapani, and Avalokiteshvara are of almost equal renown.

There are numerous biographies of the Seventh Dalai Lama in Tibetan. The most extensive is the official account of his life written by his chief spiritual heir, Changkya Rolpai Dorjey. Another popular account is that by Tsechok Ling Kachen Yeshey Gyaltsen. I occasionally quote from these in my commentaries to the individual poems, because they frequently refer to *Songs and Advice for Spiritual Change*. In fact, the most strongly tantric work in the collection, "Song of the Tantric Path," was written at Changkya's request.

In the next section of this volume I include a translation of a modern Tibetan summary of Tsechok Ling's account.

A Biography of the Seventh Dalai Lama

The following account of the life of the Seventh Dalai Lama is translated from Khetsun Sangpo's six-volume work *A Biographical Dictionary of Indian and Tibetan Saints*, which he compiled in India during
the late 1960s and early 1970s. An anthology of life stories from the
great Buddhist masters of India, as well as the masters of all Tibetan
schools of Buddhism, it contains short biographies of hundreds of
Buddhist masters. Naturally the Dalai Lamas, being important historical figures, receive more attention than do most other lineage lamas in Khetsun Sangpo's collection.

For his life of the Seventh Dalai Lama, Khetsun Sangpo draws from,
or rather, edits down, a biography that appears in an eighteenth-century
Tibetan work called *Lives of the Lam Rim Preceptors*. This important text
was written by the First Tsechok Ling (1713-1793), also known as Kachen
Yeshey Gyaltsen and as Yongdzin Yeshey Gyaltsen. "Yongdzin" means
"tutor," for he was the tutor to the young Eighth Dalai Lama.

Tsechok Ling was one of Tibet's greatest writers, and his *Lives of the
Lam Rim Preceptors* is his magnum opus. In two thick volumes, it presents accounts of the lives and deeds of all the great lineage masters in
the Lam Rim transmission. It begins with the Buddha, proceeds with
the early Indian masters through whom the lineage descended, eventually comes to Atisha, and then deals with the great Tibetan masters,
beginning with Lama Drom Tonpa, and culminating in the Seventh
Dalai Lama, who was the primary lineage holder when Tsechok Ling
was still a child. The First, Second, Third, Fifth, and Seventh Dalai
Lamas are listed as important lineage gurus, and thus their biographies receive treatments by him.

Tsechok Ling's account is especially relevant to the present collection of poems, as it emphasizes the aspects of the master's life that are connected to his role in the Lam Rim and Lojong transmissions. In addition, Tsechok Ling quotes in full some half-dozen of the poems from *Songs and Advice for Spiritual Change,* to present the essence of the Seventh's spiritual teachings and also to demonstrate the Seventh's character as a Buddhist monk, two points always important in Tibetan biographical literature. Khetsun Sangpo omits these in his condensation for reasons of space.

In accordance with Tibetan literary tradition, Tsechok Ling's account begins with a verse of homage and makes a brief mention of the Seventh's ancestry. It then proceeds to relate the highlights of his discovery as a Dalai Lama incarnation, his enthronement, his monastic ordination, the various teachings he received during his training, his role as a teacher, and finally his death. In accordance with the Kadampa legacy of humility and secrecy, the list of the various meditation retreats he undertook is not provided, for these are considered to be too personal for open publication.

Of special note is the Seventh Dalai Lama's relationship as a young man with the elderly Second Panchen Lama, who was one of his most important gurus; later in the Seventh's life he served as a teacher to the young Third Panchen Lama. The Tibetans call these two lamas "Yab Sey," meaning "Father-Son." Throughout the early histories of these two lamas, whoever of the two was the elder would serve as the guru, or spiritual father, to the younger. The two were also instrumental in the process of tracing down and enthroning one another's reincarnations, as well as in participating in their monastic ordination ceremonies. This continued over the centuries until the modern era. In time, these two incarnation lineages came to be recognized as Tibet's two foremost tulku offices, and thus "Father-Son" came to mean the role that the two played as leaders in keeping the Tibetan people spiritually on track.

This is significant in the face of recent developments in Tibet. In 1995 the present Dalai Lama recognized a young boy as the reincarnation of the recently deceased Panchen Lama. The Chinese Communist government proceeded immediately to deny that he was the right incarnation, and then arrested and imprisoned the child, his parents, and the forty-eight monks of Tashi Lhunpo Monastery who were in charge of the search. They then declared another child to be the "true reincarnation," and enthroned him as such. All of this from Chinese Communists, who claim not to believe in the theory of reincarnation. Presently, in Tibet all monks and nuns are forced by China to sign a document declaring the "Dalai Lama's Panchen" to be the wrong incarnation, and the "Chinese-selected Panchen" to be the authentic incarnation. I mention this, because the relationship between the Seventh Dalai Lama and the Second and Third Panchen Lamas reveals the profound link between these two incarnation offices. Amnesty International has registered today's Panchen Lama as the world's youngest political prisoner.

Another interesting point in the biography is the relationship that the Seventh established with several other lamas. His tutor Ngawang Chokden, from whom he received the lineage of the Six Yogas of Naropa as well as Kalachakra, was in future lives to become an important tulku lineage. His reincarnations came to be popularly known by the name of the monastery in which Ngawang Chokden lived: Radeng (sometimes transliterated as Reting). Two future Radeng Rinpocheys were to serve as regents during the minority of future Dalai Lamas. In recent times, the previous Radeng became regent after the Thirteen Dalai Lama passed away in 1933, and oversaw the search for and enthronement of the present Dalai Lama. He died in the late 1940s. Another lama mentioned in Tsechok Ling's biography is the Demo Tulku incarnation, whose training the Seventh personally oversees with care. The names of future incarnations of this lama were also to appear on the short list of lamas competent to serve as regent of Tibet in the Dalai Lama's minority.

As stated in the Seventh's biography, his early years were spent in Kham and Amdo on the borders of Tibet and China, and he was not brought to Central Tibet until 1720. This was because civil wars in Mongolia had spread over into Tibet and were the cause of major disruption to Lhasa life. The Manchus, a Tartar race that had recently invaded and taken over the rule of China, became staunch followers of Tibetan Buddhism and adopted the stance of the Seventh's protector and bodyguard during his early years. Mongol armies at the time roved everywhere, pillaging and killing as they went, and the Manchus did not want the lama whom they held in the highest regard to be inadvertently harmed. Several texts in the Seventh Dalai Lama's collected works were written at the request of his Manchu disciples. The Manchu Emperor even had at least one son living in Tibet as a Buddhist monk under the spiritual guidance of the Seventh. A Yamantaka *sadhana*, or meditation practice, was written by the Seventh at his request and for his personal daily practice, an indication of the princely monk's spiritual dedication.

The Seventh Dalai Lama's audience room in the Potala Palace today still bears witness to the Manchu Emperor's devotion. Prominently placed on display (by the Chinese Communist government) is a text, hand-copied in ink made from gold dust, and adorned with pearls and precious stones, that had been given to the Seventh by the Emperor. It is but one in a three hundred volume set of scriptures created by the Emperor and sent to the Seventh as a gift. The Manchu emperor also sponsored a complete translation of the Tibetan canons into the Manchu language, both the Kangyur, or "Translations of Buddha's Words," and Tengyur, or "Translations of Works by the Indian Masters," a total of almost 5,000 texts. Over a hundred monks worked continuously on the project for over a decade.

The friendly and mutually beneficial relationship between Tibet and the Manchu Empire, known to the Tibetans as *cho yon*, or "teacher/ patron," was established during the life of the Seventh Dalai Lama and continued until the fall of the Manchu Empire in 1911. This was essentially a spiritual bond, with the Tibetan lamas providing priestly and educational duties for the Manchus, and the Manchus materially supporting and protecting Tibet from the Mongols and the Han Chinese. Many Tibetan monasteries had departments that accepted Manchu children as students, and many Tibetan lamas lived in China, in temples and monasteries built for them by the Manchus.

The marriage was one made in heaven. The Dalai Lamas had always been regarded as incarnations of Avalokiteshvara, the Bodhisattva of Compassion, while the Manchu Emperor was regarded as an incarnation of Manjushri, the Bodhisattva of Wisdom. In that compassion and wisdom are the two qualities to be brought to perfection in order for enlightenment to arise, and more conventionally, for peace and prosperity to prevail, the theory was that the two working together would bring about great benefits to the world.

Indeed, there is no doubt that the arrangement worked very well for over a century. Tibet's spiritual and cultural life prospered under Manchu patronage, and the Manchus became sophisticated and wise under Tibetan Buddhist spiritual tutorage. Tibet retained its political independence and cultural integrity, while sharing in the stability established by fostering this unique relationship with an Asian superpower.

Unfortunately, during the last half of the nineteenth century the Manchus went adrift, unable to navigate the treacherous waters of the European age of colonization. Russia brought instability and violence overland from the north, and Britain did the same with their navy from the oceans of the south and east (as well as flooding the country with opium). The last years of Manchu rule in China were characterized by confusion, violence, and turmoil.

In the end Manchuria, after ruling Han China for some two hundred years (the so-called Ching Dynasty), eventually came to be ruled by the Hans. When the Manchus succumbed to revolution in 1911, Manchuria became part of China. The wheel of karma had turned full circle upon them. Reinterpreting the Manchu/Tibetan friendship to suit an expansionist vision, the new China laid claim to Tibet. The result is the uncomfortable situation that exists between Tibet and China today.

It is unfortunate that modern Han China has used the close ties that existed between the Tibetan and Manchu peoples as an excuse to invade and occupy Tibet, claiming Tibet as "a sacred and inalienable part of China since the time of the Seventh Dalai Lama." In the process they have transformed the relationship from teacher/patron into occupied/occupier.

The roots of this important and unfortunate historical development lie in the life and times of the Seventh Dalai Lama. But that is another story, perhaps for another book. Let's leave it for the moment, and go to Khetsun Sangpo's account of the Seventh Dalai Lama's life and deeds.

A Biography of the Seventh Dalai Lama

Homage to the supreme teacher Lobzang Kalzang Gyatso,
A peerless buddha who, with the laughing power
Of compassion, placed countless living beings
Within the radiant sphere of truth
By revealing the sublime path to illumination.

To fulfill an ancient pledge to benefit the people of the Northern Lands of Snow, and to act as a light of the Buddhadharma during this coarse age, the Seventh Dalai Lama took birth in Litang, Amdo, East Tibet, near the Tubchen Jampa Ling Monastery on the nineteenth day of the seventh Tibetan month of the Earth Mouse Year [1708]. Sonam Dargyey was his father's name, and Sonam Chotso his mother's. His birth was accompanied by wondrous signs beyond comprehension. His head was shaped like an umbrella, his forehead enormous, and his eyes wide and smooth. As had been prophesied, shortly thereafter he was given the name Kalzang Gyatso by a master interpreter of omens who was blessed by the buddhas and the bodhisattvas.

The intensity of the young boy's spiritual growth was like the growth of a water lotus. At the age of four he received a vision of Buddha Shakyamuni and the Sixteen Arhats, thus gaining their blessings. When he was only five years old he received a vision of Lama Tsongkhapa, who advised him to quickly go to the Dharmic fields of Central Tibet. These and many other auspicious events occurred.

Even when still a delicate child, Gyalwa Kalzang Gyatso poured forth the ambrosial nectars of Dharma in accordance with the specific karmic dispositions of those to be trained who came to him with faith. Once the Amdo Lama Chuzang Nomonhan came to him for blessings, made a symbolic offering of the universe to him, and asked him to bestow ambrosial Dharma; the Dalai Lama spontaneously composed and sang the following verse. At the time he was five years old.

> O Tsongkhapa, a lord of Dharma,
> Whose body supports the robes of a monk, victory banners
> of the Buddhadharma,
> Whose speech resounds with the 84,000 sections of the
> teachings,
> And whose mind never stirs from the sphere of *dharmadhatu*,
> O master of truth, send forth your blessings.

At the age of six the boy was given Tsagan Nomonhan Ngawang Lobzang Tenpa as his tutor and gradually received a steady stream of initiations, scriptural transmissions, and oral teachings from him. Thus even at an early age he became a treasury of the doctrine. Once, after being requested many times, he himself gave an initiation into the mandala of Mahakaruna Avalokiteshvara, together with the scriptural transmissions.

During his eighth year, he made a pilgrimage to all the great spiritual centers of the Kham and Amdo provinces, including Dergey. In each place he also gave blessings and teachings. On one occasion during this journey, he gave the initiation into the mandala of Mahakaruna Avalokiteshvara, together with an extensive discourse on all the meditative disciplines that are preliminaries to that tantric system. All who attended were awed by the brilliance and depth of the child's words and were placed in the sphere of immutable faith.

In the Fire Monkey Year [1716] he was requested by the Manchu Emperor, an incarnation of Manjushri, to visit the great Kumbum Monastery that had been built by the Third Dalai Lama on the birthplace of the mighty Tsongkhapa. There, he sat upon the Dharma throne that had been constructed by the Third Dalai Lama and gave an extensive discourse upon Ashvaghosha's *Previous Lives of the Buddha* (Skt. *Jatakamala*) to several thousand monks, thus fulfilling the purpose of the Doctrine and of living beings.

On the twentieth day of the tenth month of this same year, the young Dalai Lama cut his long hair and, taking the eight vows under Tsagan Nomonhan and Chuzang Nomonhan, put on the maroon robes of a monk. His ordination name became Ngawang Chodak Tubten Gyaltsen Palzangpo, "Master of Wisdom Speech, He Famed in Truth, A Victory Banner of the Buddhadharma, A Glorious and Sublime One."

Thereafter, the boy expressed his wish to study the great scriptures of India and Tibet. Taking Chuzang Nomonhan as his tutor he entered into a study of fundamental logic and debate, which is the door to the five great themes of Buddha: *pramana*, or valid thought and perception, as compiled by Dharmakirti; *prajnaparamita*, or the "perfection of Wisdom," as compiled by Maitreya / Asanga; *Madhyamaka*, or the theory of emptiness, as elucidated by Nagarjuna and his disciples Aryadeva, Chandrakirti, and Buddhapalita; *abhidharma*, or the encyclopedic categorization of metaphysics, as compiled by Vasubandhu; and *vinaya*, or ethics and self-discipline, as compiled by Gunaprabha.

On the full moon of the ninth month of the Iron Mouse Year [1720] Gyalwa Kalzang Gyatso arrived at the Jokhang, the Great Temple of Lhasa, and gave a religious discourse to many thousands of monks and lay people. Thus the Tibetans gained a breath of fresh air and experienced profound serenity. After the discourse, the youth went to the Potala and for the first time met with the omniscient Second Panchen Lama, Jetsun Lobzang Yeshey, an emanation of Buddha Amitabha manifest in the form of an ordinary monk, the very crown ornament of the Bodhisattva of Compassion. On the fifth day of the following month he received the ordination of a novice monk from the Panchen Lama, assisted by the Ganden Throne Holder Gendun Puntsok. The name Lobzang was suffixed to his childhood name, resulting in the title by which he came to be known: Lobzang Kalzang Gyatso.

Now a young novice, Kalzang Gyatso began a course of study under the Panchen Rinpochey. Beginning with the *Great Stages of the Path to Enlightenment* [Tsongkhapa's *Lam-rim-chen-mo*], he listened to a steady stream of Dharma. In particular, he received the four complete initiations into the Vajrabhairava tantra system, together with detailed teachings on this highest yoga tantra path.

Kalzang Gyatso then took up residence in Drepung Monastery in order to study under the Ganden Throne Holder Lobzang Dargye. First he repeated the study of fundamental logic that he had made some years before when in Litang Monastery, but as he had already mastered the subject, he finished the several year program in a few months, and then went on to study Dharmakirti's *Seven Treatises on Pramana.* From the Throne Holder Palden Drakpa he also received two daily sessions of instruction on the emptiness doctrines, beginning with the basic texts of Nagarjuna and his main successors. Under his tutor's supervision he also read Tsongkhapa's great commentaries to Nagarjuna's and Chandrakirti's fundamental treatises, as well as Tsongkhapa's *Essence of Good Explanations* (Tib. *Legs-bshad-snying-po*) that reveals which teachings are figurative and which direct. He also read Tsongkhapa's great and medium length expositions on insight meditation upon emptiness (Tib. *Lhag-mthong-che-chung*). Studying all of these works very deeply and with tremendous enthusiasm, before long he had attained mastery of the Madhyamaka system.

On the full moon of the fourth month of the Fire Horse Year, Kalzang Gyatso received the full ordination of a Buddhist monk. The ceremony took place in the Great Temple of Lhasa before the sacred image of Buddha Shakyamuni, with the Panchen Lama as the ordaining abbot, the Throne Holder Palden Drakpa as the *acharya,* the highly learned and realized Gyumey tantric abbot Ngawang Chokden as the consulting ordination master, and the great master Kachen Lobzang Monlam as the timekeeper. In all, thirty-one of Tibet's foremost monks were present at the ceremony, including Gyalsey Tulku Jigmey Yeshey Drakpa. Thus Kalzang Gyatso was empowered to become a regent of the Buddha himself.

Thereafter Bhikshu Kalzang Gyatso requested Panchen Rinpochey to teach him the most vast and profound points of the sutra and tantra paths. The two retreated into the Tushita Chamber of the Potala, and Panchen Rinpochey gave him all four initiations into the Guhyasamaja Tantra. He also gave the young student the empowerments associated with the "Hundred Lineages of Bari Lotsawa," together with a transmission of all the related sadhana practices. Panchen Rinpochey also taught him Chandrakirti's commentary to the *Guhyasamaja Tantra,* together with three important works by Lama Tsongkhapa: *Supplement to the Guhyasamaja Tantra* (Tib. *Shan-'grel*), *Summary of the Essential Meaning of Guhyasamaja* (Tib. *bsDus-don*), and *Establishing the Frontiers of the Guhyasamaja Teaching* (Tib. *mTha-gCod*).

Having completed these studies, the boy then requested Panchen Rinpochey to initiate him into the Heruka Chakrasamvara mandala, foremost among the Mother Tantra systems, in accordance with the lineage of the Indian mahasiddha Luipa. Again the teacher and his student retreated into the Tushita Chamber, and the secret initiations and examinations were performed.

The following year, Kalzang Gyatso asked to be taught the abhidharma system of metaphysics, and as a preliminary memorized both Vasubandhu's *Treasury of Abhidharma* (Skt. *Abhidharma-kosha*) and Asanga's *Compendium of Abhidharma* (Skt. *Abhidharma-samucchaya*). Studying these together with all the principal Indian and Tibetan commentaries, he quickly gained knowledge and insight into the essential meaning of Buddha's teachings on abhidharma.

Not long after His Holiness had completed his abhidharma studies, political problems developed between powerful aristocratic factions in Central Tibet. Taking his tutor, the Throne Holder Palden Drakpa, with him, as well as numerous lamas and gesheys from Ganden, Drepung, and Sera monasteries, who would help him in his studies, he left for the place of his birth in the east. His tutor died shortly after their arrival in Do-kham, and so His Holiness, determined to complete his studies without interruption, requested the master Ngawang Chokden to serve as his tutor. Treating this teacher with a respect equal to that which he had shown to his deceased tutor, and devoting himself both in attitude and conduct as described in the scriptures, he studied the Fifth Dalai Lama's *Sacred Word of Manjushri* (Tib. *'Jam-dbyangs-zhal-lung*), which is the practical essence of all the oral teachings of Lama Tsongkhapa, a second Buddha. Studying and meditating upon this holy text in great detail for many months directly in accordance with Ngawang Chokden's personal experience, and repeatedly questioning his teacher on all points of doubt, he quickly gained the certainty of insight.

Thereafter he left Gartar for Central Tibet. Countless monks and lay people gathered along the road as he passed, hoping to gain his direct blessings in their spiritual quests for high rebirth and nirvana itself. As he traveled he had to continually stop in order to give discourses, initiations, and hand empowerments, but eventually arrived at Lhasa and the Potala.

Ten years had now passed since his full monastic ordination, and when the new incarnation of Demo Tulku repeatedly requested him to bestow the primary vows of a monk on him, His Holiness accepted. The event, which was his first ceremony of this nature, was performed on the full moon of the auspicious fourth month. He was in his twenty-eighth year. From this time onward, he uninterruptedly bestowed monastic ordination upon the spiritual aspirants who requested him with sincerity.

Just as the layman Lama Drom Tonpa had devoted himself to his preceptor Atisha, Gyalwa Kalzang Gyatso devoted himself intensely to his teachers. Immediately upon returning to Lhasa he invited the omniscient Panchen Lama Lobzang Yeshey to come to the Potala and transmit the Dharma to him. However, the Lama was now very old and his health too delicate to make the journey. Consequently, in the Dragon Year, Gyalwa Kalzang Gyatso left for Tsang Province to meet his aged master in his residence at Tashi Lhunpo Monastery, Shi-gatsey. Here the two reunited and spent many hours each day engaged in discussions on the various points of Dharma that were still unclear to Kalzang Gyatso. Living in Tosamling, His Holiness visited his teacher's residence daily to receive teachings on the Second Panchen Lama's text *The Direct Path to Enlightenment* (Tib. *Lam-rim-myur-lam*), as well as White Tara initiations and teachings, the linked Amitayus/Hayagriva system of tantric meditation, and many more profound transmissions. While at Tashi Lhunpo, Gyalwa Kalzang Gyatso himself gave teachings in the Great Assembly Hall on the stages of the path to enlightenment, using Tsongkhapa's *Essential Meaning of the Stages of the Path* (Tib. *Lam-rim-bsdus-don*) as the basis of his discourse.

Throughout his stay at Tashi Lhunpo, His Holiness was inseparable from the Panchen Lama and was always seen deeply engaged in conversation with him. The more time they spent together, the deeper became the love and respect that His Holiness held for this aged master, and the more profound became their daily discussions.

While at Tashi Lhunpo, His Holiness also received a complete transmission of all doctrines of the ancient Kadampa Tradition, such as Geshey Potawa's *Cloud of Precious Similes on Dharma* (Tib. *dPe-chos-rinchen-spung-pa*), from his tutor the Gyumey Abbot Ngawang Chokden.

At the request of the Drepung tantric master Lobzang Chopel, His Holiness then gave a detailed teaching to 330 monks on the generation-stage mandala meditations of the Luipa Tradition of the Heruka

Chakrasamvara Tantra, combining the waters of both the Sre-gyu Tradition and the ear-whispered Wensapa Tradition. Giving the discourse not from scriptures but purely from his own experience, he satiated many spiritual aspirants with the ambrosial waters of highest yoga tantra.

He also taught both the eight great treatises of the Me-gyu Tradition and the six great treatises of the Sre-gyu Tradition. Throughout this period he himself continued his own tantric studies under his tutor Ngawang Chokden, who now had become the Ganden Throne Holder. From him His Holiness received the Thirteen Golden Dharmas of the Sakyapa Sect, initiations into the mandala of the Four Great Meditation Deities of the Kadampa sect, and empowerments into the practices of various Dharma protectors such as Six-armed Mahakala. At the request of Tatsak Tulku, he himself gave all four initiations into the five-deity mandala of Heruka Chakrasamvara as passed through the Indian mahasiddha Tilbupa [Gantapada].

The tantric colleges of both Drepung and Sera then requested him to give an initiation into the thirteen-deity mandala of Vajrabhairava, an event that was attended by some 1,280 monks, including the entirety of the Drepung and Sera tantric colleges. Many incarnate lamas, such as the young Demo Tulku, and many accomplished scholars and yogis also requested permission to attend.

His Holiness then went to the tantric college at Sera and gave a tantric initiation into the Vajrabhairava mandala to the monks there, and at the request of Dayab Tulku gave an extensive discourse upon Tsongkhapa's *Great Stages of the Path to Enlightenment* to more than a thousand monks. To a select few from amongst these he gave an initiation into the Padma Tradition of the thousand-armed Mahakaruna Avalokiteshvara mandala. During this time he himself received teachings from the Throne Holder Ngawang Chokden on the tantric technique known as "the mother and son sunlight accomplishing magical activity," which is found in the cycle of Vajrabhairava activities providing emanation power over the three worlds. His Holiness quickly mastered this technique. Ngawang Chokden also gave him the lineage of the Six Yogas of Naropa, which had come to him in an unbroken line from the yogi Milarepa, as well as the profound doctrine of Ganden Mahamudra and the six-branched yoga of the Kalachakra Tantra's completion stage.

At the request of Angkar Zhabdrung, His Holiness himself gave a discourse upon the First Panchen Lama's *The Easy Path to Enlightenment* (Tib. *Lam-rim-bde-lam*), with special instructions on the section describing the rites for developing the bodhimind. His Holiness also listened to Ngawang Chokden give a transmission of all the works written by Gyaltsep Dharma Rinchen, Tsongkhapa's main successor.

At this time His Holiness strongly requested his tutor Ngawang Chokden to collect together and master all the lineages of the Kalachakra Tantra that had been gathered and propagated by Lama Tsongkhapa and his disciples, as these had become in danger of extinction. Although very old, out of respect for His Holiness and in order to preserve the full doctrine of Lama Tsongkhapa, the aged Throne Holder collected the various fragmented traditions with great difficulty to himself, accomplished the practice through intensive retreat, and then passed the endangered lineages on to His Holiness Kalzang Gyatso. His Holiness in turn made the appropriate retreats and accomplished the practices, thus becoming fearless in giving initiations into and teachings upon the Kalachakra Tantra.

In the Wood Ox Year, at the request of many lineage holders, His Holiness gave the four complete initiations into the Vajrabhairava Tantra to more than a thousand devoted trainees. During the day of the actual initiations, the sky became utterly clear and released a flower rain. When His Holiness invoked the wisdom emanations, several tantric yogis and knowledge holders who were present directly perceived the appearance of these mystical forces. All attained unshakable faith. At the request of Manjushri, he also taught the *Root Tantra of Heruka Chakrasamvara*, chief of the Mother Tantras, together with Tsongkhapa's commentary to it, *Totally Elucidating All Hidden Meanings* (Tib. *sBa-don-kun-gsal*).

Thus teaching the fundamental Indian scriptures in conjunction with Lama Tsongkhapa's commentaries, His Holiness greatly restored the essence of Buddhism in general and, in particular, restored the quintessential teachings of Lama Tsongkhapa. His kindness in this regard can never be repaid.

In the Water Dog Year, His Holiness traveled to Ganden Monastery, which had been built by Lama Tsongkhapa. Thoughts of Tsongkhapa's life and his kindness to Tibet welled up within him, and he wrote many prayers and songs to Jey Rinpochey at that time. At the request of Lhatsun Toyon Dargyey, His Holiness gave an initiation into the Jina Samudra system of the Mahakaruna Avalokiteshvara mandala to fifteen hundred monks. At the request of Tatsak Jey-drung he also gave transmissions of the complete works of Tsongkhapa, the Thirteen Golden Dharmas of the Sakya Sect, and many other profound subjects. At the request of Chuzang Tulku he gave an initiation into the nine-deity Mandala of Amitayus to some three hundred monks and, to a select few from amongst them, an initiation into the Vajrabhairava Tantra.

While he was at Ganden Monastery, many meditators from Jungkar came to him for blessings. Their abbot, the Throne Holder Gendun Drakpa, requested His Holiness to give them a transmission of the essence of Lama Tsongkhapa's teachings. His Holiness complied and also wrote several mystical poems on the main points of practice for them.

Shortly thereafter, the newly discovered reincarnation of the Panchen Lama came to Central Tibet and requested His Holiness to bestow the ordination of a novice monk upon him. His Holiness agreed to the request and, returning to Lhasa, performed the ceremony on the full moon of the auspicious fourth month in front of the sacred buddha image at the Jowo Temple, with the prerequisite number of monks in attendance. His Holiness himself acted as both abbot and acharya during the ceremony.

The Panchen Lama listened to many teachings from him on the sutras and tantras at this time. After having gained competence in the fundamental doctrines, he requested His Holiness to give him special oral transmission teachings. His Holiness was pleased with the young lama's progress and consented to do so. At that time he gave the Panchen Lama the following advice, "Listen to and study the vast corpus of scriptures, just as did the incomparable master Lama Tsongkhapa, until you gain a profound understanding of the visions of the buddhas. Then you should listen well to the special oral transmission teachings on the sutras and tantras, and draw a direct experience of them into your heart. Finally, you should generate the thought of turning the wheel of Dharma for the benefit of living beings near and far."

The young Panchen Lama took this advice of His Holiness to heart and lived up to it. He studied extensively with His Holiness and always lived within the teachings given to him. He completed his scriptural training very quickly and then requested His Holiness to give the oral transmission teachings.

When Ngawang Chokden, the tutor of His Holiness, reached his seventy-fifth year, his body became very heavy and he even had difficulty in rising from his seat unassisted. His Holiness went to the lama's residence, offered him the symbolic mandala of the universe as well as symbols of the body, speech, and mind of the Buddha, and many wondrous material gifts, and requested him to use his powers to extend his life span.

The elderly guru replied, "From childhood I have lived as a Buddhist monk and have had the fortune to meet with the teachings of Lama Tsongkhapa. Moreover, I have had the excellent fortune to study, contemplate, and meditate upon the Dharma to my utter satisfaction, and to have served as a tutor to Your Holiness, the protector of the Tibetan people. It has been a great joy to me to have been able to transmit to you many lineages of the sutra and tantra branches of the Buddhist path, as well as the exclusive oral transmission teachings from the meditative experiences of Lama Tsongkhapa. Now my mind is ready to meet death. This body of mine is worn out. All this old man wants now is to be in solitude at Radeng Monastery when the time of his death falls."

His Holiness visited his guru's room again and again, and engaged in many profound conversations with him. He repeatedly requested his teacher to remain with him in the Potala and not to leave for Radeng, but the old lama politely declined. On the morning of the departure His Holiness went to the great guru and spoke at length to him of spiritual matters. As his teacher was about to leave, His Holiness placed the crown of his head against the old guru's chest for several moments and, shedding tears, sent forth many prayers and auspicious thoughts. The lama himself asked His Holiness for his blessings and made prayers to meet with and be cared for by His Holiness in all his future incarnations.

After Ngawang Chokden had left, His Holiness offered tea ceremonies at the three great monasteries of the Lhasa area—Sera, Drepung, and Ganden—with prayers that the old lama would live sufficiently long to complete his journey to Radeng without any obstacles. His Holiness himself performed many rituals for this purpose.

Ngawang Chokden eventually reached Radeng Monastery and passed away peacefully not long thereafter. His attendants sent His Holiness many offerings, together with the lama's relics. His Holiness retreated into an upper chamber of the Potala to offer prayers and to meditate. He also offered extensive rites before the sacred Buddha image in the Central Temple of Lhasa and commissioned smaller prayer ceremonies at all the major monasteries in Tibet, including Ganden, Sera, and Drepung. He sent offerings to all the great incarnate lamas of the land, requesting them to make prayers. He then took his teacher's relics and retreated into his private chamber, where he entered into prayer and meditation. He continued his retreat throughout the period in which the silver urn in which the remains of the cremation would be placed was being made. Later, His Holiness placed his teacher's relics in the urn and performed all the appropriate rites himself.

His Holiness Gyalwa Kalzang Gyatso was famed throughout Tibet as being a true incarnation of Avalokiteshvara, the Bodhisattva of Compassion and protector of the Land of Snows, and thus himself was an object worthy of the devotion of men and gods alike. In less mystical terms, even on the conventional level there was no scholar or meditator in the entirety of Tibet to match his fame in learning or realization. Moreover, at an early age he had been enthroned as the supreme spiritual and temporal authority in the nation. Nonetheless throughout his life His Holiness never showed the slightest trace of pride or arrogance. This fact is clearly evidenced by the respect and open devotion that he demonstrated toward his spiritual preceptors, as reflected in his conduct during the passing of the great guru Ngawang Chokden. Just as the layman Lama Drom Tonpa had opened his heart totally to his preceptor Atisha, similarly His Holiness the Seventh Dalai Lama demonstrated all the correct attitudes and activities in his training under his spiritual masters, leaving for future generations an inspiring example of what can be accomplished by working correctly under a spiritual master who can open up the pathways of realization within the mindstreams of those to be trained. Thus his life truly was an unprecedented saga of liberation.

Shortly after his guru's death, His Holiness gave the great initiation into the Kalachakra mandala to more than 1,300 monks at the request of Angkar Shabdrung. He next went to the Gyumey Tantric College and gave initiations into the Luipa lineage of Heruka Chakrasamvara to some 1,800 monks.

The most extensive transmission to be given by His Holiness occurred the following year at the behest of the young Panchen Rinpochey, who requested to be given a panoramic transmission of Dharma. His Holiness was pleased with the request. He accepted, and embarked upon a festival of initiations and teachings that was to continue every day for more than six months. The following list is of only a few of the lineages transmitted at that time: the forty-two mandalas of the Vajramala Tradition, together with the three mandalas of auspicious activities; the hundred traditions of the thirteen-deity Vajrabhairava mandala; the complete initiations of the body, speech, and mind mandalas of Kalachakra, which were performed on the basis of a colored sand mandala; the thousand-armed form of Mahakaruna; the extraordinary Siddharani method of practice for longevity; the sadhanas in the collection of the Indian mahasiddhi Abhayakara; the hundred sadhanas in the lineage of Bari Lotsawa; the hundred sadhanas of Narthang Monastery; the seventeen-deity mandala of Vajrasattva; the mandala of Solitary Yamantaka; the Eight Medicine Buddhas; the Lion-headed Dakini; the thirteen Mahakalas; the mandala of four-armed Avalokiteshvara; Palden Lhamo; Jambala; an explanation of certain tantric practices in the Ganden Lhagya Tradition, and of the genera-tion and completion stage practices of the Siddharani Tradition of the Amitayus mandala; the works of the previous Changkya Tulku, supplemented with scriptures from the works of Ney Nyingpa to en-compass all the lineages transmitted by the omniscient Changkya; the *Ocean of Sadhanas* (as found in the Tengyur); and a hundred assorted Indian transmissions.

Privately he gave the Panchen Rinpochey the initiations of the six Chakravartins and a special Kalachakra initiation. During this last empowerment, which was given with a painted watercolor mandala, he had the Panchen Lama sit upon a lion throne, dress in the full Kalachakra costume, hold all the implements of a Buddha Vajradhara, and had countless offerings of victory banners and so forth made to him. His Holiness entered into the subtle yoga of a mandala lord and summoned forth the cycles of peaceful and wrathful deities until the skies were filled. He then transmitted the water initiations of the vic-torious vase, the lord of all mandalas initiation, the teacher of all mandalas initiation, and the initiation of a tantric overlord.

At the request of Jamyang Shepa Tulku, His Holiness then visited Drepung Monastery. Here, in the Great Assembly Hall, he gave a twenty-day discourse on the ear-whispered lineage of Gyalwa Wensapa as embodied in the First Panchen Lama's *The Easy Path to Enlighten-ment* to more than 5,000 monks. To the 1,500 monks from amongst the gathering who held an initiation into highest yoga tantra, he gave an extensive Vajrayana discourse interweaving the essence of four dif-ferent commentaries.

In the Fire Mouse Year, His Holiness expressed the wish to visit Chokhor Gyal Monastery, which had been established by the Second Dalai Lama near the Oracle Lake. On the way he visited Sera Monas-tery and at the request of the abbot Paljor Drakpa performed the ini-tiation of Manjushri Arapatsana for 1,300 monks. At the request of Jey Ngawang Jampa [Purchokpa] he also gave the empowerment of the Sixteen Arhats.

Continuing his journey to Chokhor Gyal, His Holiness visited Ganden Monastery, where he sat upon the Golden Throne and gave hand empowerments to countless monks and lay people, and also poured forth a discourse of ambrosial Dharma. At the request of Lama Sangyey Chopel he taught the yogas for the three essential moments—death, the intermediate state, and the moment of rebirth—to more than a thousand monks.

When His Holiness arrived at Chokhor Gyal he was met by a sangha from Nga, Dvak, and Gyal monasteries. During his sojourn at Chokhor Gyal he gave a discourse on the Ganden Lhagyama practice and performed many rites before the sacred statue of Palden Lhamo there, requesting protective activity for the strength of the Buddhadharma.

On each of the three occasions that His Holiness visited Chokhor Gyal, he also made pilgrimages to Dvakpo and Olkha, two retreat sites in which Lama Tsongkhapa had spent many years in meditation and had gained realization. Deeply moved by thoughts of the life and liberation of Lama Tsongkhapa, His Holiness composed many prayers and poems to him during these visits. On this particular occasion, His Holiness reflected on how Lama Tsongkhapa had traveled throughout Tibet collecting all the lineages of the Buddhist sutra and tantra paths that he could find, and how without the reviving impact that his work had had upon the Buddhadharma in Tibet there was little possibility that Buddhism in all its completeness of Sutrayana and Vajrayana lineages would have survived intact. Intense respect arose within him and he was inspired to compose his renowned prayer to the three principal lineages of transmission, "A Rainfall of Siddhis."

In general, throughout his life, His Holiness continually gave ambrosial advice on the spiritual path, in accordance with the capacity, needs, and predispositions of all who came to him for guidance. In particular, from the age of twenty-eight until he reached the age of forty-nine, he transmitted the various levels of monastic ordination upon thousands of spiritual aspirants who came to him with a pure heart and a clear mind. Indeed, disciples flocked to him from as far west as Kashmir and as far east as the great ocean. A glance at his many accomplishments bestows full confidence in the truth of the popular belief that he was in reality a true incarnation of Avalokiteshvara, the Bodhisattva of Compassion and patron saint of Tibet.

Perhaps the greatest work of Gyalwa Kalzang Gyatso was his effort in preserving and transmitting the Dharma. As has been said,

Of all activities, the supreme
Is that of transmitting Dharma;
For when thoughtful people hear Dharma
Their minds turn toward enlightenment.

His Holiness the Seventh Dalai Lama wrote many texts elucidating the various teachings of the Buddha. Collected together, these constitute eight bundles, and cover all the major topics of both the Sutrayana and Vajrayana paths.

He worked in this way for forty-nine years for the benefit of the enlightenment tradition and for living beings. Then, on the third day of the second moon of the Fire Ox Year [the spring of 1757], Gyalwa Kalzang Gyatso understood that his work for those to be trained was complete.

In order to demonstrate the laws of impermanence to those of his disciples who still clung to the idea of permanence, and to give inspiration in Dharma practice, His Holiness sat in meditation, absorbed his mind into the clear light of death and then, arising from the clear light, transmigrated to the Tushita Pure Land and into the presence of Maitreya Buddha.

A year later, a child was born in Tsangto who showed all the signs of being a high incarnation. Many miracles occurred in the vicinity of the birth, and the house was clothed in rainbows for several days. Eventually a delegation came from Lhasa and examined the boy. All tests confirmed that indeed he was the reincarnation of the Seventh Dalai Lama.

SONGS AND ADVICE FOR SPIRITUAL CHANGE

by The Seventh Dalai Lama

Song of the Immaculate Path

In the colophon to this poem the Seventh Dalai Lama writes, "I myself don't have much experience in the spiritual matters on which I speak, therefore do not expect my words to be of any great benefit to anyone. Moreover, my lack of literary skills probably even renders my work an embarrassment to scholars. Nonetheless, Pa Sonam Dargyey requested me to compose a song on spiritual training, so I wrote this dry log of a thing. I thought that perhaps some people would be interested in my views on how most people of this dark age seem to practice Dharma, and on how Buddha himself actually practiced. It is inspired by *Song of the Stages in Spiritual Practice* that was composed by Lama Tsongkhapa, the great reviver of Buddhism in Tibet, a peerless exponent and clarifier of the teachings of Shakyamuni Buddha, and an incarnation of Manjushri, the Bodhisattva of Wisdom. It was transcribed by the secretary Ngawang Yonten Jungney."

The literal translation of the title of this piece is "Song of Brahma." However, here the name Brahma is not used to denote the Indian god of this name, believed by Hindus to be the creator of the universe and also a rather good singer and poet, but rather Brahma as *brahmacharya*, a path or way characterized by purity and leading to the purified state of enlightenment. Hence my rendition as "Song of the Immaculate Path."

As the Seventh states, in composing the poem he drew inspiration from Lama Tsongkhapa's *Song of the Stages in Spiritual Practice*. This is the shortest of Tsongkhapa's three Lam Rim texts, and is itself a verse work of only a few pages in length. Here the Seventh Dalai Lama writes a versified reinterpretation of Tsongkhapa's classic poem. In fact it is only so in a very general sense, and does not, at least in terms of its poetry, resemble Tsongkhapa's work in any direct way.

As a lead-in to this work, the Seventh wrote, "A poem to transform the mind written with references to a few drops from the ocean of tales on how Buddha practiced the six perfections in his previous lives." Here he indicates that his work refers to the *Jataka* tales, the stories of the previous lives of the Buddha, which illustrate how he cultivated the six perfections while still a bodhisattva in training. The twelfth century Kadampa masters had considered the *Rosary of Jataka Stories* by the Indian master Aryasura to be one of the six essential texts to be studied by all Kadampa monks, and in 1410 Lama Tsongkhapa instituted the tradition of having a senior monk read from this text to the crowd at the full moon ceremony of the Monlam Chenmo Festival. This was thereafter celebrated in monasteries throughout Central Asia, and soon, at least for lay people, became the highlight of the two-week Monlam festival. From the time of the Second Dalai Lama, the reading in Lhasa's sacred Jokhang Temple was usually performed by the Dalai Lama incarnation, or in his minority by his regent. The Seventh Dalai Lama did this reading for the first time when he visited Kumbum Monastery in 1716, when he was a mere eight years old. From this time on he continued to perform this function annually, and when he moved to Lhasa in 1720 he did so in the Jokhang Temple whenever he was in town during the new year season. The reading of the *Rosary of Jataka Stories* is always accompanied by a sermon, which in Lhasa usually concludes with what could perhaps be considered a spiritual state-of-the-union address by the Dalai Lama. The present Dalai Lama continues this tradition, and gives a public sermon every full moon of the new year, using the *Rosary of Jataka Stories* as the centerpiece of his sermon. Because this is the most important religious festival of the year, seeing and hearing the Dalai Lama on this day has always been regarded as an auspicious omen for the months to come. The Seventh Dalai Lama, by giving Jataka references in his poem, is invoking the power of this centuries-old tradition.

The Seventh begins his poem with a verse of homage to Atisha, who in 1042 brought the Lam Rim tradition to Tibet. He follows this with a verse to Lama Drom, Atisha's chief disciple, and then one to Lama Tsongkhapa, whose *Song of the Stages in Spiritual Practice* embodies the quintessence of Atisha's Lam Rim teaching.

After this he dedicates several verses to speaking about the unsatisfactory nature of unenlightened life. He points out the unique opportunities afforded by a human incarnation, and then commences with a series of very cynical verses on how many of those around him seem to misuse the enlightenment legacy that they claim to uphold. As he states in the colophon, "I thought that perhaps some people would be interested in my views on how most people of this degenerate age seem to practice Dharma, and on how Buddha himself actually practiced." He obviously is not very impressed by how the Tibetans of his day used Buddhism, and he styles his poem as a vehicle to point out what he feels is the pure way taught and exemplified by the Buddha.

Indeed, the Seventh Dalai Lama dedicated much of his life to the task of simplifying and clarifying the essence of the enlightenment tradition, and until his death remained a strong critic of spiritual vanity and ostentation. This poem, perhaps better than any other, illustrates his sentiment in this regard. He had come from a humble background, and the instability of his times kept him in strong contact with his roots.

The person at whose request the poem was written, Pa Sonam Dargyey, is none other than the Seventh Dalai Lama's father. The Seventh seems to have remained quite close to him throughout his life. Sonam Dargyey was a farmer from the borderlands of Tibet and China, but the recognition of one of his children as the reincarnation of the Dalai Lama quickly changed his lifestyle. He came to Central Tibet with his family when the Seventh was brought to the Potala in 1720, and instantly threw himself into Lhasa life with a fury. However, his provincial upbringing hardly prepared him for the shifting sands of Lhasa's political intrigues, and eventually he was forcibly exiled from the city for some years. The Seventh himself conveniently left at that time on a teaching tour of the eastern provinces.

It seems that the Seventh sympathized with his father, rather than blaming him for the inconvenience. In the fine Buddhist tradition of always showing respect to one's parents for their kindness in bringing one into the world, he always treated him with respect and affection. Nonetheless, perhaps his father's penchant for trouble is one of the reasons the poem has something of a biting edge to it, yet with the critical blade always turned to a constructive end.

◆ *Song of the Immaculate Path*

Namo Shri Mangura Ye!
Homage to the feet of Atisha Dipamkara, the sole
Refuge, the peerless navigator,
Who, abiding in the blissful dharmadhatu,
The spontaneously born and deathless abode,
Frees countless beings from the limitations of samsara and nirvana.

Drawing from Atisha's vast treasury of perfect teachings,
The disciple Drom took the gem of the sublimely blissful path
To fill the vaselike minds of beings.
O source of countless buddhas, pray,
Bestow upon us your transforming powers.

And homage to the omniscient Tsongkhapa, an all-kind lord of truth
Who, although attained to mastery of both the world and beyond,
Abandoned not the thought to benefit living beings
But from love entered into the scorching pits of samsara.

For many lifetimes we have amassed spiritual energy
Through generosity, discipline, and pure aspiration.
Thus has been won this precious human life,
This ground from which ultimate goodness can be grown.

More rare is human rebirth than for a blind turtle
To put its head through a yoke floating on the ocean,
Than for a handful of dried peas tossed in the air
To stick to a stone wall—
So taught the masters of old.

Most wondrous is this opportunity found but once,
This vessel of eight freedoms and ten endowments,
Yet impermanent, like a rainbow.
For who can be certain that even today
Consciousness will not leave the body?
We die, young and old alike, and, in the end,
Who meets not with death?

Even in the blissful abodes of the desire gods,
Where incautious minds by attachment are bound,
Descent follows unbearable suffering
When signs of death appear.

And the gods of the heavens of form and formlessness
Nowhere approach the path of liberation.
The effects of their *samadhi* and virtue deplete
And again they wander through death's gates.

In the lesser heavens, fighting gods chop at one another's limbs;
In the hot hells, denizens boil, burn, and are pierced with weapons,
And in the cold hells their bodies
Crack with pus and explode.

From hunger, thirst, fatigue, and terror, ghosts continually suffer;
Animals eat one another, are worked, beaten, slaughtered, and,
Not knowing spiritual methods,
Live with the continual threat of misery.

Bad karma and delusion—
Evil spirits riding upon the horse of mind,
Shaking the very thread of life.
Thus helplessly directed, this life is made short,
And the next, destitute.
In this degenerate age, light is shrouded in darkness.

With back turned toward the guru and Three Jewels
And lifestyle conflicting with the laws of karma,
The land fills with the habits of barbarians,
And superstitions just wax and grow.

Practice of the ten virtues is like sandalwood,
Yet these days the people burn black coals of vulgarity.
By meaningless transient diversions are the masses deceived,
Their faces turned from things of lasting joy.

Struck by the cold touch of attachment, hostility, and confusion,
The lotus garden of spirituality each day withers more.
Watching this everywhere happen,
Who with sense is not saddened?

On the seas of existence one rises
And falls on waves of suffering.
Even the worldly pleasures we taste
Are like food mixed with poison,
Destroying the very life of goodness and joy.

"That suffering is the very method by which liberation is
    attained," they say,
And they take to the robes and talk religion,
But even while they preach, five poisons rule their minds.
Qualities they feign and faults they hide.
Corruption can thrive anywhere, it would seem.

"We understand impermanence and suffering," they state,
But, "Today we will do this and tomorrow that,"
Comes out on their very next breath.
O you who grasp for permanence, lost in an endless cycle
    of planning,
How will your time to pass beyond imperfection ever come?

At present they cannot endure even the slightest pain,
Yet it could come to pass that, living in unconscious abandon,
They will end up in hell.
Blind action: the rope which binds them to the hollows of the world.

"I've opened the wisdom eye,"
Or, "I love others more than myself," they claim,
But when they see others' happiness, the snake's tongue
    of jealousy darts.
Trying to save another, they sink the two.
I call them butchers dressed like men of peace!

"Whatever I see is seen in the light
Of the emptiness wisdom," they announce,
Yet they cannot bear even slight upsets
And become lost like owls
In inner fires of explosive frustration.
Theirs is not the path to freedom.

"I'm a tantric master," they proudly boast,
Yet I see them kill the root of tantric practice,
The vows and sacred pledges of the Tantric Way.
They adorn their bodies with the costume of a yogi,
But their hearts are sterile, like a fruitless tree.

Therefore the root of all attainments
Depends on correctly following a spiritual friend, a master.

But rely upon a qualified guru,
One with control, peace of mind: every excellence.
Able even to die for him,
Be constantly aware of his kindness
And make him the offering of practicing just as taught.
With the certainty that any faults that appear
Are reflections of your own negativity,
Practice with unshakable confidence.

A wind blowing over a sandalwood garden indeed smells sweet;
Blowing over shit, it smells foul.
Likewise, be one's friends high or be they low,
One's life is affected accordingly.
Choose wisely.

Even the great creator-god Brahma,
Himself bound in chains of obscuration,
Is hardly a worthy object of refuge.
But worthy are the buddhas,
Who have generated all excellences
And transcended all flaws.

And worthy is the Dharma taught by them, as well as
The realized Sangha following in their wake.
But rely upon them wholeheartedly
And not on empty words alone.
Live in accord with the teachings.

Having raised the mind's eye to enlightenment
In the presence of these three precious jewels,
Uncover all karmic residue left from previous negativity
    and failings.
Engage the four opponent forces,
That uproot the tree of darkness.

Look at the shortcomings of samsaric existence
And of delusion and compulsive karma,
The sources of all suffering.
The mind is staggered!
Develop confidence in practice
And strive in the ways bringing freedom.

In countless previous lives all living beings
Have again and again been our parents and have shown us
     great kindness.
Take upon your shoulders the load of repaying them
And think only of what brings good to others.

Subdue attachment and aversion, and instead dwell within
An attitude moist with the love that looks on all living beings
     with pleasure,
In compassion that wishes to see all beings freed from misery,
And in the mind of universal responsibility
That carries the weight of the welfare of the world.

Break off from the mentality that holds self above others.
Generate bodhimind, which yearns
For enlightenment for the sake of all,
And have a firm will to train in the ways of the mighty bodhisattvas.

With the key of generosity bold and pure,
Spring the lock most difficult to open—the tightness of the heart.
Train in detachment,
Which gives whatever is needed.

The benefits of the generous mind
Excel rebirth as the God of Wealth,
For they never end.
Develop fearless inner strength,
Able to give even flesh, bones, and marrow to anyone.

Think, "May I perfect generosity,
Just as did Buddha in past lives
As Palgyi Dey, Jampai Tob, Tsugnor,
Dawai Od, and various animal incarnations,
When he cultivated the bodhisattva ways by dedicating
Wealth, body, and even his very life
To the well-being of the world."

Work day and night on the elephant of the unaware mind.
Strike it with sharp hooks of attentive mindfulness
And the thought of transcending negativity.
Guard self-discipline as you would the pupils of your eyes.

Self-discipline is the chief of causes
Of both high rebirth and enlightenment.
Therefore spiritual seekers always practice it,
As related in the biographies of past bodhisattvas.

Think, "May I perfect self-control
Just as did Buddha in his previous lives
As Loma Katupchen and Gelong Mitrupa,
Never staining personal integrity
With imperfect actions."

When others spitefully abuse you
And when physical and mental trials rain down,
Know that it is only your own ripening karma,
And stand firm in unmoving patience.

Put on the best of armors, patience strong and steady.
Harmful weapons of torment no longer can touch you
And you gain rebirth with a beautiful form.
Teach yourself to be patient.

Think, "May I attain perfect patience,
The most sublime asceticism,
The capacity to endure challenges to body and even life,
Just as did Buddha in previous lives
As Zopa Mawa, Gyalbu Gedon, and Dzawoi Bumo."

Take up joyous perseverance,
Which when engaged in meditation
Or when working for the good of the world,
Knows untiring joy alone, even should the body fall to dust.

All spiritual realizations lie in the palm of the hand,
And with joyous effort are easily attained.
One literally glows with pure energy, and
All works quickly reach completion.
Constantly hold joyous effort.

Think, "May I strive in the trainings
Just as did Buddha Shakyamuni
When previously as a bodhisattva

He practiced joyous effort with vigor,
Once as Donkun Drup even emptying a great ocean
With a tiny turtle shell."

Arrest the five rivers obstructing meditation
With the dam of the eight antidotes,
And accomplish *shamatha*, yogic quietude,
The power to dwell unwaveringly upon any object of
    contemplation.

This, the power of meditation, penetrates to the heart of practice.
It brings the joy of mental and physical control,
And bestows the six miraculous powers and five eyes of knowledge.
Strive therefore to perfect meditation.

Think, "May I practice just as did Buddha in previous lives.
He practiced intensely on the mountain near Jewel Island,
Without attachment to the false comforts and securities of
    the world—
Like yesterday's spit, and also like his life as Buram Shingpa,
Who meditated in a valley for years to attain samadhi."

And endow yourself with the bonds of wisdom's spiked wheel,
Which slashes through the darkness
Obscuring conventional and ultimate realities,
Like the tenth incarnation of Vishnu slings
His deadly wheel through Rahula's head.

Only wisdom brings sure liberation
From the manacles of ego's steely prisons.
Through it, buddhas past, present, and future find enlightenment.
Strive therefore to perfect wisdom.

Think, "May I strive just like Buddha in his pervious lives
As Donkun Drubpa, who cultivated wisdom clear, quick, vast,
    and profound;
And Sadak Melong Dong, who engaged in marvelous ways
During the course of his training."

For long has the mind dwelled under the iron rule
    of ego's malicious army,
Destroyer of all joy and happiness.

Strike it with the spur of mystic vision, *vipashyana*,
And leave behind even the word ego.

An image reflected in a mirror, a rainbow in the sky,
    and a painted image
Make their impressions upon the mind,
But in true nature are other than what they seem.
Look deeply at this world, and see
An illusion, a hallucination, a magician's creation.

In these ways train the mind in the general paths, foundation
    to the Secret Way.
Then seek initiation into the esoteric tantras.
Generate the vision of the world as mandala,
And realize the significance of Vajrayana's two stages.
Look to the words of the masters; pluck the fruit of buddhahood.

Think, "Now that I have a human body and mind,
Have tasted the unsullied Dharma,
And am embraced by the fatherly compassion of
    a spiritual guide,
May I practice well and generate never-ending
Joy within my mindstream."

The master Tsongkhapa, a Dharma lord
Who directly perceived thatness, the-way-things-are,
Mapped out a path perfectly bridging the traditions
Of both the sutra and tantra teachings of the Buddha,
Synthesizing the thought of masters past, present, and future.
His teachings are not a toy for blowing words and bubbles
    from the mouth,
But are a golden nugget for practice.
May we use them only to pass beyond the devils of inner
    and outer faults,
And to tame the stream of our mind.

By amassing the radiance of goodness done and to be done,
He eliminated all veils hiding the deepest nature of being.
Now he dwells in Tushita as Jampal Nyingpo,
And, dancing an illusive dance, fills the universe with emanations.
May you be moved by his teachings as are gods by a goddess queen.

Grasping at duality, fearing birth, illness, age, and death,
Travelers adrift on the waters of life are slashed
By the merciless fangs of horrendous sea monsters.
Blow the conch shell of Dharma, which drowns all sorrow,
And soar to the jewel isle of enlightenment.

By any merits this work may yield,
May all spiritual practitioners quickly attain their goals.
May they live in accord with Refuge and karmic law,
And may there be a universal feast of goodness and joy.

A Sun to Lift Sleep from the Weary

The colophon to this poem reads, "As the saying goes, 'Loudly shouting the teachings at others when your own practice is poor only belittles the authentic spiritual tradition.' However, my spiritual friend Ngawang Jampa from Purpuchok said that he needed a song that would inspire him both to develop inner freedom and to practice Dharma well, so I took the risk and wrote this, 'A Sun to Lift Sleep from the Weary.' It was transcribed by the secretary Ngawang Yonten Jungney." A lead-in to the poem reads, "Advice to give inspiration in the practice of Dharma."

The person at whose behest the Seventh Dalai Lama wrote this song is the First Purchokpa Rinpochey, who was born in 1682 in Kham, Eastern Tibet, in the town of Chamdo. Though he was twenty-six years older than the Seventh Dalai Lama, he became one of his important disciples and also outlived him.

This extraordinary lama joined a local monastery at the age of thirteen. His brilliance was quickly recognized, and two years later he was sent to Sera Jey Monastery of Central Tibet for higher training. He completed this and moved to Tashi Lhunpo Monastery of Shigatsey in order to train under the Second Panchen Lama. Eventually he established a residence at the Purpuchok Hermitage and became known as Purchokpa Rinpochey. He made long meditation retreats at the hermitage, and after his death his ashes were placed in a reliquary there; consequently his future incarnations also became linked to the place. Slightly more than a century later the Purchokpa incarnation was to serve as a guru to the Thirteenth Dalai Lama. Moreover, the reincarnation of that Purchokpa became an important disciple of the Thirteenth, and later, after the Thirteenth's passing, also his biographer.

In all probability it was Purchokpa Ngawang Jampa's connection with the Second Panchen Lama that brought him into such close contact with the Seventh Dalai Lama, for they both shared a common guru. In addition, Purchokpa attended numerous teachings and initiations given by the much younger Seventh Dalai Lama, thus becoming his disciple as well as his friend.

The Seventh obviously was not intimidated by the age difference, and the poem of spiritual advice that he writes to Purchokpa bubbles over with confidence and authority.

Most of what he says should be clear enough to the general reader. One passage perhaps deserves an added comment: "With this kind of reasoning, heart of the Middle View,/ The Madhyamika masters eliminate ego-grasping." The words "Madhyamika masters" refer to lineage holders in the line of transmission coming from Indian teachers such as Nagarjuna, Aryadeva, and Chandrakirti. The Gelukpa school of Tibetan Buddhism places great emphasis upon this lineage. The word "Madhyamaka" (spelled with an *a*) means "Middle View," and refers to the philosophical and spiritual stance that these masters adopted; "Madhyamika" (with an *i*) refers to a proponent of this approach. It is called the Middle View because it avoids the two extremes of eternalism (or reification) and nihilism (or denial) by holding to a central position between the two. It avoids the former by appreciating how ultimately nothing has true, inherent, or separate existence, and therefore is empty of true existence; it avoids the latter by appreciating how on the conventional level all things nonetheless operate on the basis of causes, conditions, and mental labeling.

Two poems later in this collection ("Song of the Direct View" and "Meditations to Sever the Ego") focus exclusively on this topic, which so often in Tibetan literature is referred to as "the essence of wisdom."

◆ *A Sun to Lift Sleep from the Weary*

Namo guru bhyeh.
Honor to Jey Tsongkhapa, most renowned of ascetics,
Manjushri incarnate as an ordinary being,
Who with perfect meditation understands
All teachings of the mighty Buddha
And everything to be known.

In the muddy waters of this, my mind
Are found no sweet teachings to point the way.
Yet listen to this song
Which echoes the words of the wise.

Whether you win happiness or misery
With human life fragile and rare,
And whether you gain confusion or peace,
Lies entirely in your own hands.
If you don't practice the essence—
Abandoning negativity and cultivating the good—
What benefit is there even in living in meditation
On the peak of the most remote mountain?

Taking upon yourself the commitment
Of training in the bodhisattva ways
But then not striving to produce the causes
Of enlightenment, or at least of higher rebirth,
Are you not one to be scorned by the masters?

One may shave one's head and wear
A hundred sets of beautiful robes,
Yet still one is swept into misery
If one lives unwisely and is overpowered by attachment.
O you lazy mind, why won't you get the message?

This life, slipping like a mountain stream,
Pauses not for a moment;
Within a century it ends, and mind leaves body.
Will the devil of death not come to you too?

Lead by death, only karmic memories follow.
Look now to what you will do, alone and friendless,
Wandering through the great path of the *bardo*,
That long, narrow, treacherous pass.

Lost in fantasies about the material world,
Thrown adrift by the winds of the eight worldly concerns,
Clinging to things of superficial satisfaction alone,
At death one is weighed down
With the pain of an empty soul.

Although one's body or that of another
May seem attractive if one looks not deeply,
In reality it is oozing with germs, blood, and pus,
Like a crystal pot filled with shit.
How naive the mind that takes pride in it!

If when you meet someone who challenges you
Flames of anger rise up from within,
All your previous good karma is consumed.
This was taught by the sages of old.
Do you get their message?

Fruitless as the water tree are samsaric indulgences,
And like mead that intoxicates.
Turn your back on deluding objects
And strive solely to practice Dharma.

Do not deceive yourself for a moment
With the laziness that thinks to act later,
Or you will die praying for help.
Quickly, quickly, help yourself
And seize the essence of truth.

A living being who has never been your parent
Cannot be found by even an omniscient mind.
All have cared for you just as has
Your kind mother of this very life.
Meditate on beings as having once been your mother,
And meditate on their infinite kindness.

Knowing that all creatures have been so close,
In whom but the fool does the altruistic
Aspiration to enlightenment not arise?
Therefore develop the attitude that appreciates their kindness,
And meditate on love for friends and enemies alike.

Should your mother of this life fall into a pit of fire,
You would not even be able to watch.
Meditate on great compassion that cannot bear
The sufferings of the endless beings
Languishing in the blazing pits of the world,
And arouse a sense of universal responsibility
That carries the thought to benefit them all.

However, only a fully enlightened being
Can be of ultimate benefit to anyone.
Therefore develop the wishing bodhimind,
That yearns for enlightenment for other's sake,
And within your continuum generate actual bodhimind
That trains in the mighty bodhisattva ways.

The bodhisattva ways, the six perfections,
Move in the expanse of bodhimind made firm,
Like clouds gliding in the vastness of space,
Releasing a steady rain of goodness and joy.
Work with the methods that spontaneously unfold
The flower petals of this joyous tale.

Walk up the nine steps to samadhi,
The stages of profound meditative absorption,
And actualize shamatha, yogic quietude that can abide
Joyfully, lightly, and thoroughly on any object.
Then turn awareness to the void, to pure distinguishing awareness,
To the intuitive perception of emptiness.

Just as the sky knows neither birth nor death,
All things are free of an ultimate beginning or end.
Were things to have a findable essence,
Would it not be absurd to say they are named
According to parts, causes, or conditions?

With this kind of reasoning, heart of the Middle View,
The Madhyamika masters eliminate ego-grasping.
Strive to understand their point—
That the dreamlike, rainbowlike,
Miragelike world that appears
Is completely and utterly empty and void.

Having been asked to compose a song,
The stick of affection beat on the drum of my mind,
And seven melodic tones burst forth.
May its meritorious energy spontaneously help
All mother sentient beings quickly to attain
That sublime state called "thus gone."

The Excellence of
Meditation on the Bodhimind

The colophon to this piece reads, "A brief poem on a few of the benefi-
cial effects of meditation upon the bodhimind, the entrance to the Great
Way, written at the repeated requests from afar of Lobzang Dargyey
and Lobzang Tashi, two retreaters from Tsawa Zhau, by Gyalwa
Kalzang Gyatso while he was residing on Mt. Potala. The secretary
Ngawang Yonten Jungney transcribed it."

The Seventh Dalai Lama wrote this poem while in residence in the
Potala Palace, the great building constructed by the Fifth Dalai Lama
on the hill at the center of Lhasa, previously known as Red Mountain.
The words "requested from afar" indicate the two monks who asked
for the poem of spiritual advice had done so by letter from their mon-
astery in Eastern Tibet. In all probability they had known the Seventh
Dalai Lama in his youth while he had been in residence in Litang or
Kumbum.

The Sanskrit term "bodhichitta," (Tib. *byang-chub-kyi-sems*), literally means "mind of enlightenment." I have rendered it as "bodhimind,"
following Geshey Wangyal's lead in his *The Door of Liberation*. "Bodhi"
means enlightenment. The term is borrowed from the enlightenment
experience; that is, a buddha has it in all its completeness. However, it
does not mean that someone cultivating the bodhimind is fully enlightened, just that they have entered the path leading to enlightenment.

Various texts use the term in different ways. The Tibetans adopted
the usage of Indian masters such as Nagarjuna and Asanga, wherein
it refers to a heightened sense of universal love and compassion. In

brief, it is the universal love and compassion with the aspiration to attain full enlightenment as the best means of benefiting the world. This is sometimes called "the aspirational bodhimind," which is to be distinguished from "the engaged bodhimind." The latter is the inner state of universal love and compassion coupled with the aspiration to enlightenment, but brought to a degree of engaged maturity, in which one always practices the ways of the bodhisattva, i.e., the six perfections: generosity, self-discipline, patience, joyous energy, stabilized meditation, and wisdom.

Another way of speaking about the bodhimind, and we see this in some of the Lojong literature, is by the twofold division of conventional and ultimate. When this is done, what was said in the previous paragraph refers solely to the conventional bodhimind; the ultimate bodhimind is the mind of a bodhisattva focussed in meditation on emptiness, or the ultimate nature of being. In this poem the Seventh Dalai Lama is using the term in the conventional sense, referring to the consciousness pervaded by universal love and compassion that sees the attainment of enlightenment as the best means of universal fulfillment.

This unique consciousness is also called *sem-kyey* (Tib. *sems-skyes*) in Tibetan, meaning "expanded awareness," for it has taken the ordinary self-cherishing mind, which loves only oneself and those who are good to one, such as family and friends, and expanded it into universal love for all living beings, including those who bring harm. As the First Panchen Lama once put it, "Ordinary beings care only about themselves and those who are good to them. The buddhas care equally for all living beings. Look at the difference between the two! Ordinary beings vacillate between happiness and suffering, whereas the buddhas dwell in constant joy."

In the Tibetan tradition, a daily seven-round meditation is used to arouse and sustain this unique consciousness. The first step is reflecting on how, because we all have had countless previous lifetimes, everyone must have been a mother to us in some past life or another. Next, one contemplates the many ways in which the mother is beneficial to her children, firstly giving them life itself, and then feeding, protecting and caring for them. The third step is reflecting on how an old debt is no different from a recent one, and that therefore the kindness of one's mothers should be repaid by being kind and helpful to others. Fourthly, one rests the mind in the thought of universal love, the aspiration that others only have happiness and its causes. One next rests in the mind of universal compassion, the aspiration that others be free from suffering and its causes. Sixthly, the mind is rested in the thought of universal responsibility, asking the question, "If I don't take responsibility for others, who will?" Finally one contemplates how only a fully enlightened being is able to truly be of benefit in all situations, and thus one arouses the aspiration to attain full enlightenment as a means of being of ultimate benefit.

When this meditation has transformed the mind to the degree that it spontaneously cares for others as much as it cares for self, the first stage of the bodhimind has been aroused. Tibetans, basing themselves on the writings of the Indian master Asanga, speak of it as then developing through twenty-two stages of increasing maturity and depth, until it achieves its final flowering in the enlightenment experience.

In his colophon the Seventh Dalai Lama refers to the bodhimind as "the entrance to the Great Way." In other words, it is the key to the bodhisattva path. As Lama Tsongkhapa, founder of the Gelukpa School, once wrote, "Whether or not one has the bodhimind as an inner experience determines whether or not one is a practitioner of the Great Way. If one has it only as a belief or as a commitment, then one's Great Way is only in one's mouth." The bodhimind is a state of actual consciousness and not a theological position.

Although the Seventh Dalai Lama does not state the fact, his poem is inspired by the first chapter of Shantideva's *A Guide to the Bodhisattva Ways*, a great Indian classic that is studied by all Tibetan sects. He did not have to state this in his colophon, for he knew that anyone reading the piece would immediately recognize the connection. Shantideva's text was one of the six Indian works listed as mandatory reading in the old Kadampa School. Its popularity continues today, and the present Dalai Lama has used it as the basis for dozens of public discourses both in Asia and the West.

◆ *The Excellence of Meditation on the Bodhimind*

Homage to Buddha, a supreme sage,
A cosmic overlord who awakened
Living beings from drunken ignorance
By manifesting the hundredfold light
Of truth's brilliant portal.

Even should the earth be covered with a layer of lesser jewels,
Their radiance would be far surpassed
By one fragment of a sparkling diamond—
Similarly does one with bodhimind outshine followers of lesser paths.

Of this thing called bodhimind,
Source of all spiritual qualities,
The supremely significant,
The psyche of a High One,
The force producing all buddhas,
I now sing this praise.

The expanded mind which thinks
Only of that which benefits others
Is a tree of endless fruit;
One touch of its divine sap
Quells even the word suffering.

Merely looking at hunger and deprivation
Turns one's stomach with horror;
Bodhimind is the only medicine able to cure all forms of need,
Just as a naga-king's jewel
Fulfills the wants of even hungry ghosts.

Instinctive passion which clouds the mind,
Instinctive stupidity blind to spiritual potential:
The one sun to dispel them
Is bodhimind, torch of infinite rays.

For destitute beggars at the door
Of the treasury of higher delights,
Bodhimind is the gatekeeper,
And it fulfills all mundane needs as well.

Only bodhimind, the aspiration to become a buddha,
Totally purges the heaviest of karmas—
Negativity that results in suffering
A fraction of which would break a man.
It is a magic thing
To destroy misery now and forever,
A fabled potion able to open
The passage of a mother in labor.

The sole thought on everyone's side,
The precious mind aiming at enlightenment as a way
      to further the world,
Was seen by Buddha to be
The highest of spiritual means.

For the sake of both yourself and others,
Plant the fertile seed of bodhimind,
Which quickly produces the state of a buddha,
Freedom from every limitation;
Make it firm as a mountain.

The Buddha said, "By cultivating the seeds of bodhimind
All spiritual qualities are born."
Those who have developed it
He called kings of doctors.

It can be read in both the sutras and shastras
That the bodhimind is the door to the Great Way,
And that the supreme practitioner who arouses it
Becomes a bodhisattva, a child of the buddhas.

Whether or not one is a bodhisattva
Is determined by whether or not one has bodhimind;
Those anointed with its sandalwood fragrance
Are adorned by the richest of good qualities.

Even the eagle, king of birds, cannot fly if he is missing a wing.
Many find the wing "perception of emptiness,"
But only those also with the wing of bodhimind
Fly to the omniscient state of buddhahood.

Were the advantages of bodhimind to take form,
The universe could not contain them.
Generating it but for a moment produces more goodness
Than offering a world filled with the seven jewels
To the buddhas of the ten directions.

This is but a drop from the ocean
Of the beneficial effects of the bodhimind,
All of which even a buddha could not describe.
Therefore wrap closely around your shoulders
The cloak of admiration and joy
For this one path all buddhas have trod,
And become living legends, having attained
The states of inner freedom and knowledge.

By virtue of this song
On the magic potion which transforms ironlike beings
Into beautiful, golden buddhas,
May all living beings expand their vision
And embrace the universal love of the bodhimind.

Alphabetical Song I

This is a type of poem unique to Tibetan literature, in which each line begins with a successive letter of the alphabet. Hence the style is known as *ka kha tsigchey*, or "A-B-C verse." Two poems of this nature are included in this collection, the other being located toward the end of the volume.

The Seventh Dalai Lama does not give a colophon, so there is no way to know the situation under which the composition took place. Presumably it was a spontaneous piece, as otherwise the person who requested it would be mentioned.

The closing verses, however, do give us a clue to its context:

> In this age of tension and conflict,
> When beings are weakened by misery
> And are blind to Dharma's significance,
> Even the buddhas and bodhisattvas
> Can do little to benefit the world.
>
> So what can this simple man
> Called Kalzang Gyatso do?
> For I have no white feathers
> Of super-compassion to flash,
> Being but a crow amongst crows,
> Taking joy only in the impure,
> Collecting karmas only for hell,
> Cawing only ugly sounds based upon ego.

Here we see the author contemplating the nature of his life, and how even in his role as a Dalai Lama it was not easy for him to solve the problems with which he was confronted. However, rather than be depressed at the situation, he finds humor in it, seeing himself as a crow amongst crows, devoid of white feathers of "super-compassion," the "super" referring to a magical power able to instantly dispel the world's ills. A Dalai Lama, like anyone else, has his limitations.

♦ Alphabetical Song I

Ka: A haunting song
to spread the tune
of the garland of letters (*ka-treng*),

Kha: Some precepts
not merely from the mouth (*kha*)
but from the heart;

Ga: Still, the age being so degenerate,
there are always faults,
no matter from where (*ga*) we speak,

Nga: For we give voice
largely to thoughts
based on pride (*nga-gyal*),

Ca: To little else
but false concepts and
meaningless babble (*ca-co*).

Cha: Our minds are not one
with even a single (*cha-shey*)
word of the Awakened Ones;

Ja: We are satisfied
merely to eat food
and drink tea (*ja*).

Nya: We have studied
as many teachings as a
fish (*nya*) has seen water

Ta: And thus have the imprints
of having heard the advice
of the Thus Gone Ones (Tathagata),

Tha: Yet still we
        pass our time
        in mere intellectualization (*tha-nye*).

Da: Beginning right now (*da*),
        practice purely from within
        and extract life's essence.

Na: It is a joy to overcome
        physical diseases (*na*)
        and mental afflictions;

Pa: Therefore, as is pointed out
        in the words of the scriptures
        clear as the planet Venus (*Pa-sang*),

Pha: Learn to enjoy harms done to you
        by others (*pha-rol*), for these can
        dry up the rivers of misery,

Ba: Just as the mists (*ba-mo*) of dawn
        refresh young flowers,
        This is the most practical attitude,

Ma: For it simply is not possible
        to separate all (*ma-lu*) living beings
        from their aggressive tendencies.

Tsa: Best just to take all upon yourself
        and to go to a cave surrounded
        by mountains and meadows (*tsa*),

Tsha: And, with mind concentrated,
        to brave the hardships
        of heat (*tsha*) and cold,

Dza: And thus gain control
        over the malevolent spirit (*dza-lang*)
        called ego

Wa: By generating transcendental wisdom
        through meditation on emptiness,
        the clear (*wa-ler*) middle vision.

Zha: Ah, we who follow the Yellow Hat Tradition (*zha-ser*)
that stainlessly preserves
all teachings of Buddha,

Za: And that works for the world's benefit
by giving food (*za-ma*) to the hungry,
educating the backward, and
protecting the oppressed:

A: Because of the ups and downs
in spiritual development and
the fluctuations (*a-aur*) in
goodness and joy,

Ya: Countless obstacles arise for us.
Many are the trials in completing
the wondrous (*ya-tsen*) path to liberation.

Ra: All sentient beings,
even goats (*ra*),
have been our parents;
in some past life

La: Not merely a few (*ta-la-tsam*)
have been kind to us, but all
have been our very mothers.

Sha: Therefore, we should not be
cruel to others,
like an evil ghost (*sha-za*),

Sa: But should meditate upon love
and compassion for all that lives
within the three worlds (*sa-sum*).

Ha: At present, in this era
covered by five thick (*ha-chang*)
layers of darkness,

Ha: The land is filled
with ignorance (*ha-ma-go*)
and wrong views;

Ya: My conclusion, in brief, is this:
Until all warped (*ya-yu*) karmic forces
have faded from within,

Ah: We should relentlessly pursue meditation
upon the mystic sound *AH*,
symbol of suchness.

In this age of tension and conflict,
When beings are weakened by misery
And are blind to Dharma's significance,
Even the buddhas and bodhisattvas
Can do little to benefit the world.

So what can this simple man
Called Kalzang Gyatso do?
For I have no white feathers
Of super-compassion to flash,
Being but a crow amongst crows,
Taking joy only in the impure,
Collecting karmas only for hell,
Cawing only ugly sounds based upon ego.

Preparing the Mind for Death

The colophon to this poem simply states, "Written at the request of Taktsang Lama Rabten of Domey, who said that he needed a short instruction to prepare his mind for death."

In this brief poem the Seventh Dalai Lama responds to a disciple, Taktsang Lama Rabten, on the question of how to live life in such a way as to best prepare the mind for death. The first of his names associates him with Taktsang Monastery, or "The Tiger's Nest." This is another monk (like Purpuchok Ngawang Jampa, at whose request the second poem in this collection was written) with whom the Seventh Dalai Lama established a friendship because of the two sharing a strong spiritual bond with the Second Panchen Lama. Rabten had been born in Domey of Eastern Tibet in 1676, and thus was twelve years older than the Seventh Dalai Lama. He had joined a local monastery at a young age, but then at seventeen had been sent to Drepung Gomang near Lhasa for higher education. When he was twenty-seven he received his full monastic ordination from the Second Panchen, and thereafter remained a close disciple. The Panchen eventually requested him to return to his homeland and build a meditation retreat. This became known as Taktsang Ritro, or "Tiger's Nest Hermitage." From that time on he was popularly known as Taktsang Lama. His ordination name from the Panchen Lama was Lobzang Rabten, so the Seventh Dalai Lama refers to him as Taktsang Lama Rabten. Presumably he is the first incarnation in the line of lamas known as the Taktsang Tulkus.

The Seventh begins his poem, as in all his works, with a verse of homage. Here this is dedicated to Lama Tsongkhapa, for in his next four verses he condenses the meaning of a short text by Tsongkhapa entitled *The Three Principal Paths*, in which Tsongkhapa points out that the three basic spiritual qualities one needs to extract from the general Buddhist teachings are (1) detachment from cyclic existence, (2) the universal bodhimind, and (3) the wisdom of emptiness. The Seventh Dalai Lama gives two verses to the first of these qualities: one for detachment from the ordinary things of life, and the second for detachment from higher spiritual pleasures. He then dedicates one verse to the cultivation of the bodhisattva mind, and one to wisdom.

We can also interpret these four verses in terms of the Lam Rim teaching of arousing three spiritual perspectives. When this is done, the first verse is related to arousing the initial spiritual perspective of turning the mind away from attachment to the ordinary things of this life, and the second is linked to the second level of training: arousing the spiritual perspective of detachment from higher samsaric pleasures. The remaining two verses, dedicated to bodhimind and the wisdom of emptiness, are of the third Lam Rim level of training: arousing the bodhisattva perspective.

From the point of view of the general Buddhist teaching, using our life to generate these qualities within the mind is the best way of preparing for the death experience.

The Seventh Dalai Lama then writes one verse to describe what should be done at the actual time of death from the viewpoint of the ordinary teaching. Here he suggests that we withdraw the mind from all negative states and keep it focused in the sphere of spiritual thoughts. The state of the mind at the moment of death is said to be an important factor in determining our evolution in the bardo, and thus our rebirth.

This is followed by a verse on the special tantric method of dying, in which the yogi applies the *kundalini* yogas at the moment of death. In this application, one synchronizes the yogic kundalini experience with the natural evolution of the dying process, so that at the precise moment that the clear light consciousness of death arises, the clear light consciousness induced by the tantric yogas also occurs. This process is known in tantric literature as "the yoga of attaining enlightenment at the moment of death," and also as "the bardo yoga." Another reference to it is as "the lazy person's method for enlightenment." It is found in numerous tantric teachings, and also is one of the Six Yogas of Naropa.

The Seventh Dalai Lama concludes his advice to Taktsang Lama Rabten with a verse in which he points out that we should begin the preparations for our death now, without procrastinating, and that the best preparation is the attainment of spiritual knowledge, both from the exoteric Sutrayana side and the esoteric Vajrayana side.

◆ *Preparing the Mind for Death*

O embodiment of all refuge objects,
Essence of the ocean of buddhas,
Lama Jey Tsongkhapa, Manjushri Incarnate,
Pray, sit forever in the drop at my heart.

When comes the time to carry
The load of life through death's door,
One can take neither relatives, friends,
Servants, nor possessions.
Attached mind is instinctual mind:
Abandon attachment.

No matter how intense the pleasure
One may gain on the peaks of samsara,
Again one shall fall to misery.
Spinning on the wheel of unknowing,
No shelter:
Abandon samsara.

The limitless beings around us,
Parents who have kindly nurtured us,
Are creatures seeking only happiness:
Cultivate the altruistic bodhimind.

All that appears to the senses
In ultimate nature is empty,
Yet in fallacious and illusory images
We continue to grasp for truth:
Abandon self-imprisonment.

When death's moment falls,
Withdraw the mind from distortion, craving, and superstition.
Avoid samsaric hopes and fears
And take refuge in your gurus and in the buddhas,
Offering them your heart.

After the essential bases and the gross and subtle energies
Of the body have gradually dissolved,
The subtle mind of death arises.
Transform it into the essence
Of the path of clear light,
And abide there unwaveringly.

Gain meditation experience now
In the practices of the exoteric path,
The door of all spiritual realizations.
The moment you accomplish that, apply yourself to the quick path,
Vajrayana, the way of secret methods.

Three Meditations

The colophon for this poem reads, "Written at the request of Ritropa Samdrub, an Amdo monk from Dechen Monastery, who begged for a short teaching."

The prefix "Ritropa" in the name of the monk who requested this piece of spiritual advice from the Seventh Dalai Lama literally means "mountain dweller" or "hermit." It refers to someone who has dedicated his life to living in meditation retreat. (The feminine equivalent is *ritroma*.) His monastery, Dechen, probably refers to Dechen Rabgyey Gonpa, a small monastic community located in Namling, not far from where the Central Tibetan airport stands today. This monastery was built by students of the Panchen Lama, once more meaning that the monk's connection with the Seventh Dalai Lama was established through their shared master-disciple relationship with the Panchen Lobzang Yeshey.

The Seventh Dalai Lama advises him to establish three central pillars in his spiritual practice: (1) a disciplined spiritual connection with his teacher; (2) awareness of the preciousness of life, and the uncertainty of the time of death; and (3) the mind of love and compassion for all living beings, coupled with the aspiration to enlightenment as the best means of fulfilling that love and compassion.

The first of these is also known as guru yoga, and all schools of Tibetan Buddhism place very strong emphasis on it. Most Tibetan meditators begin every session with a prayer to the guru and end with a similar dedication. Yoga here means union, or integration; one wants to unite with the stream of realization represented by the guru, or integrate into one's stream of being the spiritual qualities that he or she symbolizes.

Similarly, with the second theme, the early Kadampa masters had a saying: "If you don't meditate on death and impermanence when you wake up, the morning will be wasted. If you don't meditate on it at noon, the afternoon will be wasted. And if you don't meditate on it in the evening, the night will be wasted."

As for the third theme, the Seventh Dalai Lama dedicated an entire poem to it earlier, "The Excellence of Meditation upon the Bodhimind."

✦ *Three Meditations*

If one does not sow the seed
Of appreciation for a perfect guru,
The tree of spiritual power is not born.
With undivided mind entrust yourself.

Human life is rare and precious,
Yet if not inspired by thoughts of death,
One wastes it on materialism:
Be ready to die at any moment.

All living beings have been our mothers,
Three circles of suffering always binding them.
Ignoble it would be not to repay them,
Not to strive to attain enlightenment.

Song of the Direct View

The colophon to this piece states, "Once when in the mountains of Olkha Cholung, where Lama Tsongkhapa had made his long retreat, His Holiness Gyalwa Kalzang Gyatso lead a tantric feast dedicated to Heruka Chakrasamvara. After the ritual was over, a patron in the assembly requested him for a mystical song. His Holiness spontaneously composed and sang the above, hoping to lay an impression of the direct view of emptiness upon the minds of those present."

Olkha Cholung, located above Dvakpo, is a mountain region studded with caves. These have been used by the Tibetans for centuries as meditation dwellings. Lama Jey Tsongkhapa, the guru of the First Dalai Lama, had dedicated more than four years of his life to meditation there, and as a result it was especially popular with Gelukpa adherents as a place for making long retreats. Lama Norzang Gyatso, the guru of the Second Dalai Lama, meditated at Olkha Cholung for fourteen years. Moreover, the Second Dalai Lama had established Chokhor Gyal Monastery below the Oracle Lake not far from Olkha Cholung, and as a consequence most later Dalai Lamas used Olkha Cholung for meditation purposes, or at least went there on pilgrimage whenever they visited Chokhor Gyal. The Seventh Dalai Lama did so three times on his way through the region, his last visit being in 1756, the year before his passing.

This song is an excellent example of Buddhist ideas on emptiness, or shunyata, the infinity aspect of things, and embodies the quintessence of wisdom. In it the Seventh Dalai Lama celebrates his mystical experience of infinity, declaring himself "an unborn yogi of space." He borrows this expression from the Second Dalai Lama, who signed many of his mystical works as "the Space Yogi." The Seventh Dalai Lama is "unborn," for he realizes that the self does not exist as a separate, self-existent entity, and is empty of an independent nature; he is a yogi, for his mind is always united with the vision of ultimate reality; and this experience of voidness is like space, for it is not constricted by any limitations, and embraces all of reality.

He begins the piece with a verse of homage to Lama Tsongkhapa, for he has composed and is singing it in Tsongkhapa's retreat site, and also because Tsongkhapa is regarded as an incarnation of Manjushri, the bodhisattva symbolizing the wisdom of emptiness.

◆ *Song of the Direct View*

Inside the indestructible drop on the eight-petal lotus
At the center of the main energy channel,
The most precious root guru appears in the form
Of Jey Rinpochey, a most precious master,
And performs the dance of the vajra mind.
To him I bow down.

All things in samsara and nirvana are
Mere projections of one's own mind.
That mind too is beyond birth and death,
Abiding in the ultimate mode of Being.
Eh-ma-ho: How wondrous!

In the vision of my mind as being inseparably one with emptiness—
A cloud suspended in the autumn sky—
All mental entanglements subsided:
I, an unborn yogi of space.

Nothing truly existent, all things a great falsity:
Sights and sounds I now understand as scenes in a play.
Through experiencing this great union
Of appearance and emptiness, a union joyous to behold,
I gained knowledge of the infallible nature
Of the conventional level of existence.

Owing to the kindness of my perfect master
And to the excellent teachings of mighty Tsongkhapa—
He, One with Manjushri, the Treasury of Wisdom—
To this song of plain facts, I could not but give voice.

A Precept for Yeshey Gyaltsen

The colophon to this entry reads, "At the request of Yeshey Gyaltsen, this was composed by Lobzang Kalzang Gyatso, a Buddhist monk whose only concerns are eating, sleeping, and shitting."

The identity of Yeshey Gyaltsen remains uncertain. Perhaps he was the monk who became the guru of the Eighth Dalai Lama, and whose *Lives of the Lam Rim Preceptors* is the source of Khetsun Sangpo's biography of the Seventh, which is included in this volume. This seems possible, for the Seventh Dalai Lama and that Yeshey Gyaltsen shared many spiritual connections.

Yeshey Gyaltsen was born in 1713 in Kyirong of Tsang Province, near the Nepal-Tibet border. At the age of seven, he entered Tosamling, a local monastery, under the tutorage of a monk from Tashi Lhunpo. His genius was soon noticed, and three years later he was sent on to Tashi Lhunpo Monastery for higher Buddhist training. That same year he received his novice vows and the name Yeshey Gyaltsen from Lobzang Yeshey, the Second Panchen Lama. He completed the Tashi Lhunpo curriculum at the age of twenty-one, and then was sent to Central Tibet by Panchen Lobzang Yeshey to receive certain oral transmission teachings from Purchokpa Rinpochey, a disciple of both the Second Panchen Lama and the Seventh Dalai Lama. This is the same Purchokpa at whose behest the second poem in this collection was written. Yeshey Gyaltsen spent four years receiving tantric teachings in Central Tibet, after which he returned to Tingri, near his place of birth, and took up residence in a cave in which both Padampa Sengey and the great yogi Milarepa had practiced. After twelve years of solitary meditation, there he achieved realization.

After this, his fame spread throughout Tibet, and when he was sixty-two years old he was invited to come to Lhasa and serve as the tutor to the Eighth Dalai Lama. He spent the remainder of his life at the Eighth's side, and passed away at the age of eighty-one. The Eighth Dalai Lama was so enamored of this great guru that he personally wrote his biography, and also oversaw the search for his reincarnation. The monastery of Tsechok Ling became the seat of Yeshey Gyaltsen's future incarnations, and therefore he became posthumously known as the First Tsechok Ling.

As we can see from the lives of the Seventh Dalai Lama and those around him the eighteenth-century in Tibet was a spiritually vibrant period. For me it represents the highest flowering of Tibetan civilization, at least within the Gelukpa School. Many of Tibet's greatest incarnate lamas began their multi-lifetime careers during that era, and most of them were disciples of the Seventh Dalai Lama. Yeshey Gyaltsen is an excellent example of that dynamic era. Although born of humble stock in a remote region on the border of Tibet and Nepal, he rose to become one of the most highly revered figures in the land, surpassing many of the incarnate lamas of his time.

He also had a wicked sense of humor. During his many years as a student, and during his twelve years of meditation in the caves of Tingri, the people from his homeland showed no interest in him whatsoever. However, after he became guru to the Eighth Dalai Lama they all suddenly remembered him, and a delegation of them came to Lhasa to visit, claiming themselves to be his relatives. He had an elaborate table set forth for them, but when he came in and his own dish was served, the visitors were surprised to see that on it, instead of food, was gold and jewels. He then prostrated to the dish and said, "I bow to wealth and fame. Before I possessed these two things I had few countrymen, and no relatives. Wealth and fame has magically produced so many of both for me."

Although the poem of advice that the Seventh here writes to Yeshey Gyaltsen is not long, it contains all the essentials of the Lojong teaching. Yeshey Gyaltsen extracted maximum mileage out of it, and through twelve years of meditation became a living legacy of everything good in the Gelukpa tradition. Like Khedrup Jey, the First Dalai Lama, and Gyalwa Wensapa before him, he achieved enlightenment in one lifetime, and then went on to bring many disciples to that same exalted state. He was also one of the greatest writers in Gelukpa history, and the twenty-five volumes in his collected works preserve for posterity some of the loftiest thoughts emanating from Tibetan Buddhism.

♦ *A Precept for Yeshey Gyaltsen*

O Lord of the five wisdoms and three *kayas*,
Perfect embodiment of all buddhas,
All-kind guru inseparable from the *yidam*,
Pray, sit as an ornament on the crown of my head.

Although having wandered forever in samsara,
Only now has precious humanity been attained;
Guard well this jewel which fulfills all wishes
Against the thief of a life spent in vain.

When materialistic thinking is not transcended,
All works benefit this one life alone.
Then at death one stands as weak as a beggar.
How will happiness be experienced hereafter?

From birth until this very moment,
Life in useless plans has been spent.
Lost in preconceived works unending,
When death comes, you jump, but too late.

The most lethal assassin, the great Lord of Death,
Is blocking every direction and path.
His messengers even now are watching you;
Quickly your time to pass will fall.

You can live alone in a meditation hermitage,
But if then you generate no passion for truth,
The discipline and the environment are
Nothing but an empty pretense.

Most important for practice and insight
Is inspiring influence gained from the guru.
And this depends upon attitude and conviction,
So with mind single-pointed, approach him.

In the vast waters of painful existence,
Beings beyond number cry out and groan.
If, on hearing them, your hair stands not on end,
Surely your heart is other than human.

Although you strive with utmost energy
Day and night to accomplish the true virtue,
When this is not done from a universal perspective,
It lacks bodhimind and is not the Great Way.

Like pleasure and pain known in a dream,
That which appears in the circle of ignorance
Holds nothing at all to be grasped at as real.
Lose grasping to unaffected vision.

By the rhythm of this song,
A collection of essential precepts,
May all living beings join in the festival
Of temporary and lasting joy.

Meditations to Sever the Ego

The colophon to this poem reads, "Requested by Lama Tashi Delek from the Samten Dokor retreat quarters of Ganden Dondrup Ling Monastery, Pomtserak, who asked me many times from afar for a poem on the view, meditation, and action which cut out the roots of the belief in a final self. Written by the lazy Buddhist monk Lobzang Kalzang Gyatso, a Holder of the Yellow Hat."

Pomtserak is a mountain region located in Domey, Eastern Tibet, south of the headwaters of the Yellow River. The monk at whose behest this poem of spiritual advice was written lived in the retreat hermitage associated with Ganden Dondrup Ling, a small Gelukpa monastery that had been established there in the fifteenth century but that during the civil wars of the seventeenth century had been destroyed by the local Bonpo king. It was rebuilt after the king's head was cut off by the Mongolian chieftain Gushri Khan, who didn't take lightly to the warlord's murderous ways or anti-Gelukpa militancy. The monastery survived from then until the Chinese Communist takeover of the 1950s, when it was again destroyed. At present a miniature of it has been rebuilt.

That the piece was "requested from afar" suggests that Lama Tashi Delek was a monk with whom the Seventh Dalai Lama had connections since his early years in Kham, and that the request came in the form of a letter while the Seventh was living in Central Tibet.

In general, the Lojong transmission has two main facets to its teaching: the conventional practice, which involves cultivating universal love, compassion, and the bodhimind; and the ultimate practice, which involves cultivating the wisdom of emptiness, the non-duality of self and phenomena, the final nature of being. This poem is a superb example of the latter. Because for the Tibetans, Lama Tsongkhapa is an embodiment of that wisdom, it opens with a verse of homage to him.

♦ *Meditations to Sever the Ego*

Om swasti.
Homage to he beyond the gods, the all-kind master
Who is inseparably one with Manjushri Vajra,
Lama Tsongkhapa in tantric form, who nakedly showed
The nature of mind, pure since the beginning.

Dream objects in the mind of one drunk with sleep,
The horses and elephants conjured up by a magician:
Only appearances; on those foundations,
Nothing real; merely mental imputations.

Similarly, all things in the world and beyond
Are simply projections of names and thoughts.
Not even the tiniest atom exists by itself,
Independently and in its own right.

Yet anything perceived by an ordinary being,
Whose mind is clouded by the slumber of unknowing,
Is taken as something ultimately true.
Look at how the samsaric mind works!

That "I" seen by the deluded mind,
That way things seem to exist on their own,
Is known by realized beings not to be.
How important to check the mind that believes in it!

If that called "I" actually exists, and is not
Merely a label placed upon the body and mind,
"I" would not be related to "my" body and mind;
They would be like eastern and western mountains.

When one searches the "I" in terms of cause and effect,
And asks whether it is one with or other than the body and mind,
The wisdom of emptiness, void as the sky, arises
And melts the thought that grasps for ultimates.

That wisdom is the perfect view which, joined
With relentless mindfulness, the spy of alertness,
And firm samadhi, transports one to the peak
Of clear, blissful, non-conceptual meditation.

Mind thus poised and repeatedly searching,
One gains a diamond-hard understanding,
A weapon of one hundred unbreakable spikes
Which undoubtedly will destroy the mountain of ego.

During meditation, keep the mind unobstructed as space;
After meditation, regard the flow of events as a rainbow;
Thus the things which so allure the world
Are seen to be insubstantial hallucinations.

Joy and misery are dances within a dream;
Forms and sights are a town projected by a magician;
Sounds are like one's own voice echoed in a cave;
Those who grasp at them are mindless children.

Just as a reflected image distinctly appears
When a man holds his face to a mirror,
All things are both radiantly manifest and empty.
For that very reason is cause and effect unfailing.

Thus, by abandoning the negative and increasing the good,
By keeping one's mind tethered with the three bonds
And by following a lifestyle unstained by even minor faults,
Ultimate aims are quickly and easily attained.

This body is a pot filled with blood, pus, and excrement;
Possessions are like the honey collected by a bee;
Friends and relatives are like strangers met in the marketplace;
Prosperity and comfort are deceptive assassins.

This life races toward death
Like a river pouring over a cliff;
No one is sure to be alive even this evening
When the grinning sun drops behind the mountains.

Engrossed in the dance of the eight worldly dharmas,
Immature people lose sight of deeper values.
Watching them thus flounder in delusion and fiction,
The hearts of those like me retch and groan.

If you wish to attain supreme, perfect enlightenment,
Meditate day and night upon the bodhimind.
Merely engaging the body, speech, and mind in virtue
Will not bring your practice to the Great Way.

Develop ever greater waves of enlightened thought
And strive savagely to cross to the other shore
Of the infinite sea of bodhisattva deeds,
Just as taught in the sutras and tantras of Buddha.

May this song on meditation upon the perfect view
Be a dragon's roar to awaken living beings
From the beginningless sleep of ignorance;
May it help fulfill the endless needs of the world.

Song of Easy Joy

The colophon to this poem states, "Written by the Buddhist monk Kalzang Gyatso, most insignificant of tantric yogis." However, it would seem that at this point in his life his spiritual growth was anything but insignificant. In fact, perhaps this piece could best be regarded as the Seventh Dalai Lama's enlightenment testimony.

Although recognized at the age of four as the reincarnation of the Sixth Dalai lama, due to political unrest in Lhasa, the Seventh did not come to Central Tibet until 1720, when he was twelve years old. Nonetheless he had begun the spiritual training expected of a Dalai Lama while in the east, first in Litang and then in Kumbum. In Central Tibet he continued his studies under numerous gurus, most notably the Second Panchen Lama. However, when he was nineteenth years old, a conflict again arose between various political factions in Lhasa. He still had not completed his studies, and as a Dalai Lama the political disturbances could easily prove a distraction to him. His guardians decided that the best course would to take him to the monastery in Litang, his birthplace in Kham, Eastern Tibet, to continue his training there. That monastery had been built by the Third Dalai Lama a century and a half earlier, and thus was an appropriate residence for him. Consequently, he left for the east with his tutors and a large entourage of senior monks and lamas from Ganden, Drepung, and Sera monasteries, who would assist with his training. He was to remain in the east until he was twenty-seven years old.

However, shortly after the group arrived in Kham, his senior tutor, Tripa Palden Drakpa, passed away. Ngawang Chokden, a former abbot of the Gyumey Tantric College, was requested to be his new guru. The formula was perfect, and under this master the Seventh's spiritual life blossomed. Ngawang Chokden threw him into an intensive regime of tantric studies and transmissions. By the time they all returned to Lhasa eight years later he had become firmly established on the tantric path, and a master in his own right. From this time on he gave tantric teachings and initiations whenever requested.

Not long afterwards, Ngawang Chokden was appointed to the position of Ganden Tripa, the official head of the Gelukpa school. This role alternates between former abbots of the Gyuto and Gyumey tantric colleges, and the fact that he was the Seventh Dalai Lama's guru was not a factor in his nomination to the post. However, it meant that the Seventh's two main gurus—the Second Panchen Lama and Tripa Ngawang Chokden—were now the two most highly regarded lamas in the country.

In the Fire Dragon Year (1736) Ngawang Chokden took him to Tsang to receive several special lineages from the elderly Panchen Lama. When the transmissions had been completed, they returned to Lhasa, and the Seventh Dalai Lama entered retreat. In his meditations one day, he suddenly crossed the line between the ordinary and the extraordinary, and attained the fruit of tantric practice. As his biographer Tsechok Ling puts it, "At that time he experienced all the higher realizations exactly as described in the tantric scriptures. He composed the following song to celebrate his attainment." Tsechok Ling then quotes in full the mystical song that he wrote on that occasion.

♦ Song of Easy Joy

O most kind lama, lord of the four perfect kayas,
Master of the mandala of five wisdoms,
Who abides in the inconceivable mansion
Spontaneously produced from all precious things,
A mansion of wisdom bright as a rainbow,
In nature light, radiant and clear:
Pray, rest at the center of my heart.

I took advantage of this precious human incarnation,
    a product of infinite virtue,
By leaving behind unrewarding, fruitless worldly works,
And followed in the footsteps of the Buddha.
Now I can look back with a song of easy joy,
With a mind filled with eternal delight.

I turned the forces of selfishness
By trying to practice the sublime bodhimind,
Essence of the oral teachings of the perfect gurus,
The one practice all buddhas have followed,
The focal point of all Mahayana scriptures.
My mind is now filled with eternal delight.

I perceived the deluded workings of mind
That sees all things as standing alone.
Vision fathoming the illusory drama of
Manifestation and the void arose.
Now freed from the cliffs of "is" and "is not,"
By the king of views open as the sky,
My mind is filled with eternal delight.

I drew into the depths of my heart the waters
Of the four tantric empowerments
That have power to purify all faults and stains.
Then under the guidance of a qualified master
I entered into a perfect tantric path proved valid
    by living oral tradition
And thus filled my mind with eternal delight.

Wisdom-power sees the world as a mandala
And the dance of the beautiful consort flows.
The mind locks in samadhi focused
Upon youthful awareness of bliss and void,
And the delight which soars freely
In all situations is known.

Thus through the kindness of my root gurus
I found the unmistaken path to perfection
By which is perceived the sublime countenance

Of All-Pervading Heruka, the Self-Born One
Who abides in the dark recesses
Of the hollows of the heart;
And by the kindness of Lama Tsongkhapa,
Which is far beyond description.

In the house of contemplation divorced from mindlessness,
I turned my back on the eight worldly concerns
Which bind one to that which benefits only superficially;
I made an offering of meditation, to give each day increasing meaning,
And to ever please my gurus and the meditation deities:
To these two ends I direct my deepest prayers.

Meditations on
the Ways of Impermanence

The previous mystical song, penned by the Seventh Dalai Lama immediately after his tantric realization, is a celebration of the joys of the enlightenment experience. After quoting it, Tsechok Ling then says, "After this extraordinary mystical attainment, His Holiness requested an oral transmission of the complete works of the Great Master [Lama Tsongkhapa] so that he could uphold the unbroken living tradition. This took place over a period of many days. At that time, he wrote the following poem on the nature of death and impermanence." Tsechok Ling then goes on to quote the poem in full.

The colophon to the piece simply reads, "Verses for meditation on the ways of death and impermanence, written by the Dharma teacher Lobzang Kalzang Gyatso to inspire the minds of myself and others." Thus, he wrote it not at the request of any of his friends or disciples, as is the case with many of his writings, but rather it arose as a spontaneous composition. This is the first poem in the collection in which he signs himself as "the Dharma teacher Kalzang Gyatso," an indication of the confidence he had recently achieved through his mystical experience.

This poem perhaps more that any other in the collection gives us a taste of life in classical Tibet as seen through the eyes of a great lama. The metaphors and similes that the Seventh uses reveal his connectedness to the common experiences of life, and to the heart and soul of his people.

◆ *Meditations on the Ways of Impermanence*

To the Lama-lha, my refuge, my father,
The recollection of whom dispels all sadness,
I turn for spiritual guidance.
Bless my mind with your transforming powers,
That the thought of death may never evade me,
And that I may practice the holy Dharma perfectly.

On the golden mountains far in the distance,
Rings of mist hang like belts on the meadows.
Now seemingly solid, so soon they dissolve.
My mind turns to thoughts of my death.

In spring, the season of warmth and growth,
The stalks of the crops were turquoise green.
Now, autumn's end, the fields lie naked and parched.
My mind turns to thoughts of my death.

On each branch of the trees in my garden
Hang clusters of fruit, swelling and ripe.
In the end, not one piece will remain.
My mind turns to thoughts of my death.

From behind the peaks of Mount Potala
The sun rose like an umbrella in the sky.
Now it has gone, fallen behind the western ranges.
My mind turns to thoughts of my death.

They die old, they die young, day upon day.
I am asked to throw their souls to a pure land
Or to prophesy their conditions of rebirth.
My mind turns to thoughts of my death.

Gray clouds cover the sky, obscuring it;
The first drops of rain are about to fall,
To be scattered everywhere by the dark, red wind.
My mind turns to thoughts of my death.

In the belly of the vast plateau below me,
The campfires of visiting traders glow like stars;
But tomorrow they depart, leaving only refuse.
My mind turns to thoughts of my death.

Warm summer days, the earth thronging with life;
The minds of the people are lost in gaiety.
But soon the cold winter wind will crash.
My mind turns to thoughts of my death.

High above, turquoise dragons roared in harmony;
Around me, cuckoo birds chattered sweetly.
But times have changed; where are they now?
My mind turns to thoughts of my death.

Dharma, the precious teachings of the Awakened Ones,
Is a medicine supreme, curing all the mind's ills.
These days many saints of old look down from Pure Lands.
My mind turns to thoughts of my death.

Hard it is to leave the mother who carried us,
And hard to part from relatives and friends;
Yet as the years pass, our links with them corrode.
My mind turns to thoughts of my death.

A young man, with teeth for the future,
With plans for months and years ahead, died,
Leaving but scant traces. Where is he now? Passed away!
My mind turns to thoughts of my death.

Buddha attained the glorious, immortal vajra body,
Yet he still enacted a death scene.
This body of flesh, blood, and bone, covered in skin,
Like a bubble of water, is bound to perish.

From his very birth, a child sees his parents age,
Sees them each day come closer to the grave.
How can you say to me, "But I am still young?"
I warn you there is no hope of hiding from death.

Spirits were high with expectations this morning
As the men discussed subduing enemies and protecting the land.
Now, with night's coming, birds and dogs chew their corpses.
Who believed that they themselves would die today?

Look and ask among the people of your land
For anyone even a hundred years old.
You will be lucky to find even one!
Do you not think your own death certain?

If you look closely at and contemplate deeply
The people and things that appear around you,
You can see that all are in constant flux.
Everything becomes the teacher of impermanence.

I remember this body when it was a child's,
And as it gradually took the form of a youth.
Now its every limb is twisted and worn.
It is my own body, yet it delights not even my own eyes.

The mind itself is impermanent, constantly oscillating
Between feelings of pleasure, pain, and indifference,
The fruits of positive,
Negative, and neutral karmas.

Look where you will, at yourself or others,
Life passes like a flash of lightning.
When Yama's agents surround you, intent on murder,
What do you think will happen to you?

Relatives, friends, wealth, and property
Shine with splendor in the eyes of worldly people;
Thus they bind themselves in shackles of attachment.
This pathos—how will it end?

Body lying flat on a last bed,
Voice whispering a few last words,
Mind watching a final memory glide past:
When will that drama come for you?

If you create nothing but negative karma,
You will stand naked of instincts to benefit the hereafter.
Where will you go after death?
The mere thought of it makes you flinch.

Therefore I myself and beings like me
Should leave behind meaningless ways
And entrust ourselves to the gurus,
Mandala deities and dakinis,
Begging them to prepare us for death's road.

In order to die well, with the joy and confidence
Of being within the white rays of spiritual awareness,

It is essential to begin readying yourself now.
Familiarize yourself with the profundities of the sutras and tantras.

By this song may those like me,
Irreligious people, little better than savages,
Be caught in the flames of renunciation.
May they evolve in spirit
And may they attain liberation.

Inspiration for Meditation upon Death

In the colophon to this poem, the Seventh Dalai Lama writes, "The spiritual friend Rinchen Gyaltsen, a former acharya of Sera Mey Monastery, said that he was in need of a prayer requesting Jey Rinpochey for inspiration in meditation upon impermanence, and requested me to write one for him, in which I would express my inseparable links with Jey Rinpochey. Because of his persistent requests, this was written by Lobzang Kalzang Gyatso, a Buddhist monk whose only real concerns are eating, sleeping, and shitting."

Tsechok Ling's biography of the Seventh comments that at the time he wrote this piece, the Seventh Dalai Lama was in the middle of giving a discourse to three hundred monks on the Heruka Chakrasamvara tantric system. This had been requested by the former abbot of Drepung Tantric College. The former abbot had asked that the discourse be experiential, and that it combine the instructions from the traditional lineage of transmission with the special oral teachings coming from Gyalwa Wensapa, one of the greatest of the early Gelukpa lamas. An "experiential discourse" is one of the four ways of teaching, and is a mode of transmission based on one's own personal experiences in the system, as opposed to a general, literal, or academic presentation. According to Tsechok Ling, the lama who requested the poem, Acharya Rinchen Gyaltsen, was present at the teaching, and requested the Seventh Dalai Lama to write a prayer for him that would reveal the inseparable nature of Tsongkhapa, the Seventh Dalai Lama, and Heruka Chakrasamvara. For this reason in his verses the Seventh makes numerous references to both Heruka

Chakrasamvara and Lama Tsongkhapa. The latter had widely propagated the Heruka Chakrasamvara tantric system in Tibet, calling it "the greatest of all the female tantra systems," so for the Seventh Dalai Lama to link Tsongkhapa and Chakrasamvara in his work is not at all inappropriate.

It is obvious that Tsechok Ling especially likes the Seventh Dalai Lama's writings from this phase of his life, for again he quotes the piece in full in his biographical account.

The first verse in the composition is an adaptation of the first verse in a very famous prayer to Tsongkhapa known by heart to every Gelukpa monk, nun, and lay person in Central Asia. The prayer is known as *Ganden Lhagyama*, or *The Hundred Deities of Tushita*, for it begins with a line that says, "From the heart of the lord of the hundred deities of Tushita...." The reference is to Maitreya Buddha, who is prophesied to be the next universal teacher to descend to earth. Buddhists await him much in the same way that Christians await the second coming of Christ. It is said that Maitreya has already attained his enlightenment, and is presently dwelling in Tushita Pure Land, patiently awaiting the time of his prophesied incarnation.

The Gelukpa school of Tibetan Buddhism gets its name from Ganden, the monastery that had been established by Tsongkhapa in 1409. Ganden is the Tibetan translation of the Sanskrit name Tushita. In the early days the school was called Ganden Ringlug, meaning "The Primordial Legacy of Tushita." Eventually this was shortened to Geluk, meaning "Wholesome Way." The school has always held a fascination with the Maitreya legends, and it is said that after every Dalai Lama passes away, he travels to Tushita, where he discusses where and when next to incarnate in order to further prepare the world for Maitreya's eventual coming.

The *Ganden Lhagyama* prayer is used as the basis of Tibet's annual butterlamp festival, which is celebrated on the twenty-fifth day of the tenth month of each year, and honors Tsongkhapa's birth, enlightenment, and passing. By adapting it here for his first verse, the Seventh Dalai Lama hopes to invoke the emotional atmosphere of the butterlamp festival in the minds of his readers. This is one of Tibet's most exquisite festivals, and on that day every Tibetan temple, monastery, and stupa is ringed with hundreds of butterlamps. As night falls the festival builds in intensity. Lay people often set lines of butterlamps on their rooftops, and stay on the roof long into the night, singing and dancing to the sounds of *Ganden Lhagyama*.

The lama at whose behest the piece is written, Rinchen Gyaltsen, is a former teacher from Sera Mey Monastery. Drepung and Sera were the two very large monasteries in the Lhasa area, and both of them had two principal colleges, as well as a number of smaller ones. Sera Mey was one of Sera's two major colleges. It has over the centuries produced a large number of great lamas, and continues to do so today. Being called a "former acharya" means that Rinchen Gyaltsen is a retired teacher, probably a former abbot, and thus is of advancing years. No doubt he requested the piece from the Seventh Dalai Lama in order to use it as part of his daily prayers and meditations, in the hope that at the time of his death its blessing would guide him to a happy rebirth.

◆ *Inspiration for Meditation Upon Death*

Perfect master riding the peak of a white cloud that
Issues from the heart of the Lord of Tushita's hundred deities,
Jey Rinpochey, Lobzang Drakpa, all buddhas in one,
Pray, descend to the space before me.

One who sits on a lion throne, lotus and moon seats,
The thought of whom dispels samsara and nirvana,
Jey Rinpochey, lama inseparable from glorious Heruka,
Pray, descend to the space before me.

Infinite buddhas have infinite manifestations,
Yet a prayer to you is a prayer to them all.
Bless my mindstream with your transforming powers;
Pacify even violent mental distortions;
Blend my mind with the taste of truth.

This body produced by a hundred auspicious deeds,
More precious than Brahma's own crown-jewel,
And this human mind of unsurpassed potential,
Found now at last and so difficult to regain,

Directed to the things of this life alone,
Guided solely by crazy darkness and delusion,
Never once mixed with teachings or insight,
To the vacuum of fruitlessness forever are lost.

You who toss spiritual aims to the wind,
You crazed by evil spirits of greed,
Forget all tales of the glories of materialism
And begin now to prepare for death.

With nothing but shallow experiences of life,
How can your mind be beyond fear?
By years, months, and days, life slips away
As the powers of body and mind steadily fade.

That form of yours, once bubbling with youth,
Is being reduced to a senile and haggard frame.
Age: Is it an incurable disease?
Is it a curse thrown by a hateful devil?

No matter where you prepare your last bed,
No matter when the sword of death falls,
The terrifying messengers of death descend,
Horrid and giant, and glare with thirsty eyes.

Friends and family, weeping, surround you.
Eyeing your wealth and possessions,
They offer prayers and enshroud you.
Unprepared, you pass away, helpless and alone.

Certain it is that death will come,
And uncertain that the mind will not leave
This contaminated body before night falls.
Then it will enter the dark horizons of the bardo.

Wandering powerless and alone
Through frightful, wilderness regions,
We walk protectorless to the next world,
Leaving former companions far behind.

O Lama Jey Tsongkhapa, embodiment of all mystic forces,
I need rely upon none other than you.
Venerable One of perfected spirit,
Out of compassion grant me guidance.

Bestow upon me transforming powers
To practice Dharma in body, speech, and mind,

And successfully to pass my days and nights
Piercing my delusions with arrows of wisdom.

The precious beings in the ocean of becoming
Are now meeting with unbearable pain without end.
O Lama, bestow upon me waves of inspiration
To transform my energies into all-beneficial enlightenment.

And when this life one day ends,
May Jey Rinpochey take the form of Heruka
And come with his dakas and dakinis to receive me
And lead me to Vajrayogini's Pure Land.

From this very moment until the end
Of this life shaped by karma and delusion,
May we all be protected by a tantric master
And thus complete the sublime path which so matures
        and frees the mind.

In the Twelfth Month of the Water Dog Year

The colophon to the next poem identifies only the time at which it was composed. It reads, "Written by the lazy Buddhist monk Kalzang Gyatso at the end of a meditation session, during the twelfth month of the Water Dog Year." Thus it was composed in 1742, when he was thirty-four years old.

Tsechok Ling states that this was a very busy year for the Dalai Lama. His tutor Ngawang Chokden was in the process of transmitting a large number of tantric lineages to him in order to ensure their preservation. Included in these was the transmission of the six yogas of the Kalachakra completion stage, the practice of which had become increasingly rare in Tibet. Also included were numerous lineages of the Six Yogas of Naropa in the line coming from Lama Tsongkhapa, which also had become rare.

In fact, the Seventh Dalai Lama had asked his aged guru to gather together all the extant lineages of Kalachakra from the few masters who were still alive, in order to transmit these to him. The preservation of the esoteric Kalachakra doctrines is considered one of the great kindnesses of the Seventh, and several important treatises on the Kalachakra tantric system can be found in his collected works. It is said to be due to the Seventh Dalai Lama's efforts in this respect that the Kalachakra lineages survived and have come down to the present generation intact.

Tsechok Ling refers to this poem as being "reflections on the radiance of impermanence." It is a collection of insights into the positive messages that we should extract from the transformations we continually experience within the world around us.

The poem is written as ten pairs of verses, with the first half of each pair describing a natural situation in which the reality of impermanence is self-evident, and the second half describing the spiritual lesson to be learned from it. Each verse has six lines, each of six syllables in length. Tibetan is a monosyllabic language, and its terseness lends itself well to this structure. I managed to keep the number of lines in sync with the Tibetan, but we don't have enough one-syllable words in English to keep the length of each line to that degree of brevity. Nonetheless, I hope I have captured the essence of the charm that Seventh Dalai Lama brings to the piece.

♦ *In the Twelfth Month of the Water Dog Year*

The marigolds blooming in the gardens,
Embellishing the entire estate,
To dust are reduced
When come winter's piercing storms.
Now, while radiantly beautiful,
They should be offered to the objects of refuge.

> One may cherish property and wealth
> Gained by cunning means,
> But one day, all one's possessions
> Will fall to others' hands.
> Now, while you have power over them,
> Use them to benefit the world.

The fully grown turquoise dragon,
With three powers, roaring loudly,
Loses its strength to cry out
When summer comes to an end.
It flies through the heavens now;
It should beat its summer drum hard.

> Talking of worldly matters,
> One can easily speak for long,
> But soon will come the day
> When the path of breath must close.
> The tongue is flexible now;
> Use it to recite mystic mantras.

The billowing clouds of gray,
At present high in the sky,
To all directions are blown
When comes a gust of wind.
Now, while they have the chance,
They should pour down their essence.

>   We are much attracted to this body
>   Made from the sperm and egg of others,
>   But one day we must drop it
>   Like feces when we empty our bowels.
>   Now you have a form of infinite potential;
>   Make it a servant to spiritual practice.

The river so sparklingly clear
Meanders lazily over the plains;
One day it will disappear,
Leaving behind not a drop of water.
Now, while it flows with strength,
It should be used to irrigate the fields.

>   They work, the various magical crafts
>   For harming others and benefiting oneself,
>   But one day these methods are forgotten
>   And even their names are lost to darkness.
>   Now, while your mind burns clear and strong,
>   Meditate on the teachings vast and profound.

Merchants come from the north and south,
To gather in the trading center,
But after three days have passed,
Each goes his separate way.
Meeting for but a flash in time,
They should avoid fights and fancies.

>   Hooked by karma from previous lives,
>   Love and hatred run fierce,
>   But soon we all go our own ways
>   And each takes his suited rebirth.
>   Right now abandon interpersonal discrimination
>   Made on the basis of attachment and aversion.

The pale autumn moon
Hovers high above us in space,
Yet down here on the face of the earth
It cools scorching and tortured beings.
O source of physical and mental delight,
Forever send down refreshing white light.

> One's wish that others be happy
> Exists only in one's own mind,
> Yet it benefits other as well as oneself
> In all times, places, and situations.
> Therefore abandon faults of body and speech
> And conceive the sublimely altruistic thought.

The Naga King's all-powerful gem
Shows partiality to no man,
But he who propitiates the Naga King
With rituals and offerings
Has the objects of his yearnings
Fall into his very hands.

> The guru, lord of the three perfect kayas,
> Is above liking or disliking disciples,
> Yet whoever concentrates upon him
> With unfluctuating appreciation,
> Actualizes the happiness
> Of this and future lives.

Due to the effects of an eye disease,
The sky fills with kaleidoscopic fantasies,
But when medicine is applied
And the disease overcome,
The hallucinations of themselves disperse,
And clear space nakedly appears.

> When the ghost of "I"-holding haunts you,
> Countless illusions automatically appear.
> Stand in the mental posture
> That slashes through intellectual garbage,
> And watch the visions of ultimate truth
> Topple habitual thought patterns.

A thing shining from the face
Of the sky must be unreal.
Yet look at a marvel,
A rainbow hovering over a mountain,
Insubstantial yet manifest,
A relative thing of causes and conditions.

> If one really searches,
> Nothing substantial is found,
> Yet witness the apparitions around us
> Which perform so many functions—
> Mental imputations on the caused,
> The conditioned, and the composite.

Nothing real stands
Behind an echoed sound; still,
When one's voice unexpectedly echoes
In the stomach of a cave,
The mind jumps
With great strength.

> Similarly, this string of empty words
> Has no ultimate essence,
> No ultimate power or meaning,
> Yet maybe it will affect mankind,
> Whose nature also
> In illusion is bound.

Emptiness, Meditation, and Action

The following poem is one of the most exquisite in the Seventh Dalai Lama's collection. The colophon to it states, "Kalzang Gyatso is in one of his retreats, and has just arisen from his morning meditation session. It was the nineteenth day of the black month. He beheld a pair of eagles flying south, playing freely between fluffy white clouds sharply defined against a dazzlingly bright sky. He was immediately moved to compose this song."

Unlike earlier Dalai Lamas, most of whom made the traditional Gelukpa four-year retreat, the Seventh Dalai Lama preferred to make numerous short retreats, usually of a week to a month in length. He undertook dozens of these during his life. The colophon does not mention the year that this composition occurred, just the month and day, which he calls "the nineteenth day of the black month." The "black month" is the third lunar cycle of the Hor calendar. The nineteenth day of the month is associated with Yamantaka, the wrathful form of Manjushri, the bodhisattva of wisdom. I presume that he wrote it during a meditation retreat he made in the Water Dog Year (1742), for both the poem before and the one after it are both identified as being written during that year.

The subject of the poem is what Tibetan mystics refer to as *ta-cho-gom-sum*, or "view, action, and meditation." This threefold classification subsumes everything that we have to do to attain enlightenment. All teachings of the Buddha can be condensed into them.

He dedicates the first verse to action, or conduct. This should always be based on love and compassion for all living beings. When this is done, all vows and precepts are naturally fulfilled, and all activities become spiritual.

The second verse is dedicated to view, which means the vision of the wisdom of emptiness. Here he suggests that we always hold the mind in the state of inner freedom, like an eagle gliding in space. "Without grasping" means experiencing the objects of perception without falling into the extremes of holding them with the conceptualization of having a duality status, in the sense of their having true or independent self-existence. It does not refer to conventional greed or attachment, although of course if one appreciates the non-duality of things, one will naturally be freed from conventional grasping as well as from grasping at a duality status.

The third verse focuses on meditation, which he speaks of as being "...clear blissful absorption in the perfect mystic mandala."

One could also say that the first two verses condense all the general teachings of the Buddha, and that the third verse condenses the Buddha's tantric teachings.

The fourth verse describes the context in which the first three spiritual applications should be engaged. In other words, the practices of universal love (i.e., action), wisdom of emptiness (i.e., view) and absorption (i.e., meditation) should always be conducted from within the sphere of "an energy flow always beneficial to others," like a "grey wind blowing forcefully through space." In this way the three applications are safeguarded against ever becoming artificial or contrived exercises, and are stabilized as true, authentic spiritual undertakings.

The fifth and final verse is his dedication. He directs his song to the benefit of the world.

◆ *Emptiness, Meditation, and Action*

An image of a sun enthroned in the heavens,
Radiating one thousand beams of light:
Were one to shower bright rays of love upon all living beings,
How excellent.

An image of a kingly eagle gliding high in space:
Were one's mind to glide without grasping
In the space of truth itself, clear and void,
How excellent.

An image of fresh, white clouds,
Bright, pure, and drifting freely:
Were one to build clear, blissful absorption in the perfect
    mystic mandala,
How excellent.

An image of a gray wind flowing forcefully through the sky:
Were one to maintain an energy flow always beneficial to others,
The best of spiritual practices, never artificial,
How excellent.

An image of the vast sky everywhere free of obstruction:
Were this song on emptiness, meditation, and action
Without hindrance to benefit the world,
How excellent.

Song Rapidly Invoking Power

The colophon to this poem states, "In the Year of the Water Dog, Kalzang Gyatso visited Ganden Monastery. Inspired by the extraordinary vibration pervading the place, and filled with awe at the kindness and power of omniscient Tsongkhapa, who had founded Ganden, he was moved to compose this song."

Ganden Monastery was founded by Lama Tsongkhapa in 1409, and is located about thirty miles east of Lhasa. It's physical location is one of the most beautiful of any monastery in Tibet, built as it is on the ridge of Nomad Mountain, with a circumambulation path around the cluster of buildings looking out over the Kyichu River and the valleys of the region that feed into the Kyichu. Below the circumambulation path the mountain drops almost straight down for well over a thousand feet.

In the early days Ganden served as the head monastery of the Gelukpa school, but from the time of the Second Dalai Lama was eclipsed in importance by Drepung. Nonetheless, over the centuries it remained—together with Drepung, Sera, and Tashi Lhunpo—one of the four principal Gelukpa monasteries. Its two main colleges are Shartsey and Jangtsey, and all former abbots of the Gyumey and Gyuto tantric colleges are placed on a list of succession leading to positions called "Dharma Masters" (i.e., Chojey) of Shartsey and Jangtsey. The post of Ganden Tripa (literally "Ganden Throne Holder"), or Head of the Gelukpa School, rotates every seven years between the "Dharma Masters" holding the Shartsey and Jangtsey thrones. The present head of the Gelukpa school is a monk from Drepung Loseling who previously held the post of Jangtsey Dharma Master, so the next head will be the lama presently holding the post of Shartsey Dharma Master. Thus the three most important seats in the Gelukpa all use names associated with Ganden, to symbolize the importance of this monastery in the early days of Gelukpa history.

Tsechok Ling quotes this poem in full in his biography of the Seventh Dalai Lama, although he doesn't say much about it other than the information that is provided in the colophon as given above. The piece was written spontaneously, and not at someone's request. The Seventh Dalai Lama obviously was deeply moved by the natural beauty of Ganden, and saw it as an embodiment of the spiritual depth and power of Lama Tsongkhapa, its founder. Anyone who has ever visited Ganden can easily appreciation his infatuation, for indeed it is a most remarkable site. At the time of its construction Tibet was under the rule of the Pagmo Drupa clan, an aristocratic family associated with the Kargyu school of Tibetan Buddhism. Although Tsongkhapa was from Amdo, Eastern Tibet, he had come to Central Tibet for higher education when he was sixteen and spent the rest of his life studying, meditating, and then teaching between the Lhasa, Yarlung, and Dvakpo areas. The Pagmo Drupa family from the Lhasa area eventually became his principal patrons. Two of the princes in the family were disciples of Tsongkhapa, and it was at their request that Tsongkhapa wrote his famous commentary to the Six Yogas of Naropa, one of the principal lineages coming into the Gelukpa from the Kargyu school. They suggested that he build a monastery in the Lhasa area in order to house and preserve his teachings, and offered to help with the necessary funds. He agreed to consider the proposal, and engaged in dream yoga methods to determine the suitability of the concept. Over the following days, he experienced numerous auspicious dreams. In one of them he saw Nomad Mountain; it was clothed in monastic buildings, and served as a training ground producing hundreds of enlightened masters. He therefore consented to the request of the Pagmo Drupa princes.

In all probability, the princes were somewhat shocked at the site indicated in his dreams, for it was remote and not easily accessible. Nonetheless, the building project succeeded, and Ganden Monastery soon came into being. Tsongkhapa himself never took up a long-termed residence in it, however, and instead put several of his senior disciples in charge of the training program there. He preferred to continue his life as a wandering teacher, living in caves and hermitages as he traveled, and only visiting Ganden on occasion in order to teach, do retreat, or give initiations. He died in Ganden, and his body was mummified and placed inside a reliquary. All later heads of Gelukpa were also mummified and their bodies kept in reliquaries in Ganden. These were all destroyed by the Red Guards during the 1960s.

According to tradition, even though Tsongkhapa attained enlightenment, after his death he transmigrated to Tushita Pure Land, where he came into the presence of Maitreya Buddha. It is prophesied that there will be 1,000 buddhas of this auspicious aeon who perform the twelve deeds of a universal teacher. Shakyamuni Buddha, the founder of the present Buddhist tradition, who lived 2,500 years ago, was the fourth of these. Maitreya will be the fifth. He will remain as "the lord of Tushita" until the time comes for him to descend and perform the twelve deeds. At that time, he will pass his crown on to the ascended master prophesied as the sixth universal teacher. This legacy will continue until all 1,000 masters have fulfilled their prophecies. It is said that Tsongkhapa will be the eleventh in this illustrious line, and until then he will remain in Tushita overlooking developments in the world, occasionally sending emanations whenever these are required. As part of the process of fulfilling this destiny, he named his monastery Ganden, the Tibetan equivalent of the Sanskrit name Tushita.

His building of the monastery, and the name he would give it, was prophesied by Buddha Shakyamuni himself, who said, "In the lands to the north, on a mountain called Nomad, in the area between Dri and Den, a monk will come who will perform great deeds for the benefit of Dharma and of living beings. His monastery will be called Joyful, and will be the source of thousands of buddhas." Ganden means "possessed of joy." The First Dalai Lama, as one of Tsongkhapa's chief disciples, played an important role in the continued success of Tsongkhapa's lineages, as have all subsequent Dalai Lama incarnations.

The Seventh Dalai Lama visited Ganden several times during his life in order to teach and meditate there. His visit during the summer of 1742 seems to have been the most powerful for him, though, if we are to judge from his emotional intensity in this poem. In it he generally refers to Tsongkhapa by the much warmer and more intimate name of Jey Rinpochey, or "The Precious Master."

♦ *Song Rapidly Invoking Power*

Above, in actuality pristine awareness
Manifest as a radiant buddha-mandala,
Lies the Pure Land of Tushita, the Joyous Abode
Blessed by buddhas past, present, and future.

Mountains of herbs blanketed in sweet aromas,
Flowers blossoming morning, noon, and night,
A forest of leaves with turquoise trees:
Reminders of the physical presence of Jey Rinpochey.

The murmur of a river flowing swiftly,
The stirring songs of birds,
The magnificent sound of a Dharma teaching:
Reminders of the gentle voice of Jey Rinpochey.

The blue sky freely hovering,
Clear, white clouds scattered surreally,
The young sun casting beams everywhere:
Reminders of his wisdom, compassion, and power.

Body adorned with the marks of a Buddha,
Speech raining down vast and profound Dharma,
Mind seeing all things in the sphere of clear light:
I recollect Jey Rinpochey, Lobzang Drakpa.

Fulfill your vow to benefit beings;
Descend, grant protection and power.
To you I offer an ocean of all-good things:
Enjoy them within your great bliss.

On the mighty Nomad Mountain, quiet, easy,
A land made good with goodness and power,
Stands Ganden Monastery as prophesied by Buddha,
A monastery producing limitless Awakened Ones.

Your mind absorbed in bliss and void inseparable,
The flow of life appeared as a rainbow.
One body now sends endless clouds of emanations
To set this world ablaze with joy.

Your profound teachings bridging the sutras and tantras
Are jewels for those truly seeking liberation.
Even the words you used are perfect,
Nakedly pointing the way for the ripe.

O Jey Lama, because of your infinite kindness,
We can understand all sutras and tantras as precepts,
Have a clear map of the entire path leading to perfection,
And transcend all delusions and mistaken understandings.

O Master, merely hearing tales of your deeds
Can place a person on the enlightening path.
With thoughts of your greatness, with heart trembling,
I fix my mind upon you.

Invisible father, gone to bliss,
Listen to this plaintive song
Of a child still in samsara's quicksands,
Of an ill-fated son cut off from his refuge.

In terms of external appearances,
A monk can easily be proud of his life,
But if his thoughts are only on the transient,
Are his attachments not worse than those a of layman?

The masses revel in dark actions
And through harmful means gain their ends.
Flashes of a degenerate age
Crash in the depths of my soul.

How glamorous and exciting to go
Through the motions of practicing Dharma,
And to hear the profound teachings:
But the mind, hard as wood, is slow to improve.

The spirit, weak and uncontrolled,
Staggers with the three psychic poisons
Whenever an object appears to it:
A golden vessel filled with shit.

Precious humanity, the chance to be a buddha—
But instead we create only misery with it

And throw away all hope of ever
Benefiting either ourselves or others.

I, born so late, unfortunate,
Pass my time amid negativity and confusion.
Fatherly lama, look upon me and
Hold me on the hooks of your compassion.

In this life, the bardo, and future lives,
Pray, be my guide.
My refuge, forsake me not;
Omniscient One, be with me always.

Care for all beings as a mother for her son.
Spiritual father, to we who are children
Directly reveal the mandala of your mystical presence,
Magnificent with every mark of perfection.

Bestow upon us the oral teachings
Which render every experience meaningful.
Bless us to make our minds of one taste
With great bliss and ungrasping vision.

Life is impermanent, like the setting sun,
Wealth is like dew on the morning grass,
Praise is like wind in a mountain pass,
A youthful body is an autumn flower.

Help me to understand the shortcomings
Of constantly turning on the wheel of samsara
And to fix the depths of my mindstream
On the path leading to ultimate knowledge.

Bestow upon me transforming powers to fill
My mental continuum with love and compassion,
To see the beings of samsara's six realms
As mothers who forever have helped me.

Bestow upon me transforming powers
To realize quickly the-way-things-are,
To understand images viewed by the mind
As paintings created by the mind itself.

Help me to attain enlightenment in this very life
Through the yogic methods of tantra's two stages,
To see external events as the sport of the buddhas
And to satiate the mind with bliss and the void.

And when, in order to fight delusion, meditation's enemy,
I retreat to a cave on a distant mountain,
A place giving birth to serenity and joy,
Help me to penetrate the innermost profundity.

Grant me powers to swiftly eradicate
All inner and outer negative forces,
And power to cleanse the stains of having dwelled
Far from the limits of Dharma's three bonds.

O Manjushri, bodhisattva of wisdom, who emanates magically
In peaceful, wrathful, and protective forms,
May your auspicious deeds reach fruition,
Pray, remain a constant refuge to the world.

Bestow upon me the powerful blessings
Of your mysterious body, speech, and mind,
That my every physical, verbal, and mental
Movement may only benefit beings and the teachings.

May the thunder of the sutras and tantras shake the earth;
May the sun of Tsongkhapa's practice lineage rage;
May all trainees attain realization
And all sentient beings fulfill their wishes.

Images

The Dalai Lama did not provide a colophon to this poem, but Tsechok Ling's biography describes the circumstances in which it was written: "While at Ganden Monastery that summer [1742, the Water Dog Year] His Holiness gave a transmission of the complete works of Tsongkhapa to an assembly of over a thousand monks. Between sessions he would often take walks in the mountains and enjoy the natural beauties of the place. Wildflowers were in bloom everywhere, and the abundance of nature brought with it a host of insects. He observed the bees as they sang their way from flower to flower, and also the other insects as they went about their various activities. He was inspired to write the following song."

♦ *Images*

O guru inseparable from Manjushri and Consort,
Whose blessings fulfill all needs
And grant every mystical attainment,
Bestow upon me your transforming powers.

Hundreds of flies gather
On a piece of rotten meat,
Enjoying, they think, a delicious feast.
This image fits with the song
Of the myriads of foolish living beings

Who seek happiness in superficial pleasures;
In countless ways they try,
Yet I have never seen them satisfied.

The bee of golden stripes
Flies from flower to flower,
Never pausing but for a moment.
This image fits with the song
Of the people of this degenerate age,
Who, powered by impure mind,
Change from friend to enemy in a moment;
I have never found a reliable one.

The turquoise fly of splendid hue,
Fills its stomach with excrement,
And then takes its load and wings proudly away.
This image fits with the song
Of those who polish and flaunt with pride
Their body-sack punctured by holes for the senses
And filled with bone, blood, pus, and urine.

The song of the fly, the boring buzz,
For a moment is sweet to the ear,
But, empty of meaning, it can please not for long.
This image fits with the song
Of how praise and the sound of one's own name
Please the mind for a brief moment
And then fade to emptiness.
I have never seen them have lasting effects.

The six-legged wasp is proud in summer
To fly for a moment in merriment and pleasure,
But soon he will die from the cold.
This image fits with the song
Of the young man, handsome and robust,
Who stands strong, confident, and bold,
Not thinking that death soon will come
And lead him helplessly away.

The bee with its bee-perception
Seeks not medicinal plants
But follows the perfume of ordinary flowers.

This image fits with the song
Of how most people of the present day
Turn away from saints and holiness
And, deluded, prefer to follow
Worldly men of wealth and power.

The bee, which depends on the flower,
Drinks its fill of nectar
And then shamelessly flies away.
This image fits with the song
Of how the people of this age
Use the sages and spiritual masters
Who love and work for them;
And then they abandon them as enemies.

The young, freewheeling bee ties himself not
With attachment to places or friends;
He flies happily wherever he likes.
This image fits with the song
Of how those not bound by clinging
To the sensory objects of the world,
From the depths of their hearts aspire
Only to practice meditation and yoga
In peaceful, remote forests.

It is the last month of summer now;
Red and yellow flowers are in bloom.
A hot mid-day sun hovers above;
The flies and bees, friends of melancholy,
Dance and play before me
In a scene of honey revelry.
I, a vajra who opens in melody, watched them
And wrote this song of straight lines.

A Song of Erroneous Ways

The colophon to the next poem reads, "During one of my retreats I was saddened at how much of my early life had been lost to distraction, mental wandering, and superficiality. Thinking that to outline my own mistakes in spiritual practice might be of benefit to others, I used the periods between meditation sessions to write out this song."

The Seventh Dalai Lama made numerous short retreats every year, usually of somewhere between a week and a month in length, and I was not able to discover in which of these he wrote this piece. Its placement in the collection suggests that it was during the short Migtsema retreat he undertook during his Ganden visit of 1742, but this may not be correct. After returning to Lhasa he undertook several more short retreats in order to do mantras associated with tantric mandalas into which he had been requested to give initiation.

He puts his poem in the structure of the Lam Rim trainings, taking a dozen or so of the Lam Rim themes and looking at how one can practice these badly. He begins with how guru yoga can go wrong, and then gives a few verses for each of the three levels of the Lam Rim training, finishing with the principal points of the tantric path.

By this time, of course, he had achieved realization, so he isn't writing about personal spiritual mistakes in the present tense. However, being a lama is not an easy job, and this is even more true for a Dalai Lama. Every day he would receive dozens of visitors, each of whom would tell him of the ups and downs in their spiritual life, ask him for advice to improve their practice, and hope that he would solve their problems. In addition, people would often write to him from all over the country, usually asking for some sort of spiritual advice.

The present Dalai Lama has much of the same lifestyle and personality as the Seventh. Perhaps the political turmoil characterizing both of their times contributed to this. At one period during my twelve years in Dharamsala, I would go to his office several times a week in order to translate Tibetan texts with one of his secretaries. The window of the room in which we worked looked out onto the patio of the Dalai Lama's reception room, and we would see his visitors as they came and went. Usually His Holiness would come out to the patio to receive them, walk them back into his reception room, and then, when the audience was over, walk them out again. We could overhear the gist of much of what was said during the audiences (even though we tried not to eavesdrop), for the room in which we worked was only a couple of dozen feet from his reception room, and he kept his door open for the fresh air, as he didn't like air conditioning. Usually, the visitors would ask questions concerning spiritual training—what retreats to do, how to solve problems that had come up in spiritual practice, and so forth. His Holiness would always listen closely, and then respond with carefully considered advice. He received everyone from great scholars to yogis who had been in retreat for years, and from somewhat new Western Buddhists wanting to discuss simple issues to Chinese and Japanese Buddhists with Buddhism in their blood for centuries, and thus who had much more sophisticated questions to ask. Then there was the host of non-Buddhist visitors, from Christian monks to Hindu sadhus, who came to him for blessings and advice. He was very much the patient sage of the mountain, and no problem was too large or too small for his consideration.

No doubt the Seventh Dalai Lama had much the same flow of visitors, albeit less international, and they probably had much the same type of questions and problems to discuss. Hence, he would have seen every possible way of taking Dharma in the wrong direction, and have considered every solution.

The poem that follows, then, can best be understood as a list of the most common mistakes made in spiritual practice, together with his advice on how to avoid them, prevention being more valuable than cure.

♦ *A Song of Erroneous Ways*

O kind guru who fulfills all wishes,
Wondrous jewel reflecting all perfections,
Master who abides in the stillness of clear light,
Pray, care for me forever.

This precious life now in hand
Easily becomes a slave to the eight worldly concerns,
Then every day works against truth.
Look at the fools carried away in nonsense.

Coming too close to and seeing as mundane
The compassionate guru, matrix of all power,
Stunts the growth of profound devotion.
The root of attainment is thus lost.

Wasting oneself in a mere show of practicing
The profound teachings revealed by the guru,
Brings no significant benefit to the mind.
The methods which refine the spirit are thus lost.

Studying and contemplating the sutras and tantras
Solely to amass knowledge and win personal esteem
Produces no understanding of Buddha's thought.
The path which benefits eternally is thus lost.

Dharma clothing is beautiful to behold,
But if one heedlessly transgresses the precepts
They do not help to purify the mind.
The road to higher being and liberation is thus lost.

It is said that sensual indulgence is vain;
Yet still we lead coarse, samsaric lives
Because of our attachment to riches and fame.
The chance of undying happiness is thus lost.

One may generate a little compassion in meditation,
Yet if waves of anger creep up from within
When one meets with the aggression of cruel beings,
The seed of the Great Way is thus lost.

Reciting prayers for the welfare of others
While holding selfish thoughts deeply within
Is not even facing the Bodhisattva Way.
The aspiration which fulfills everyone's wishes is thus lost.

Searching for the ultimate mode of existence
But continuing to fall into "I"-holding delusions
Yields not the slightest progress on the path.
The sword which cuts samsara's root is thus lost.

Taking ripening initiations into various mandalas
Merely to win an egotistical number game
Does not fulfill the sacred tantric oath.
One parts from the yogas which please the yidams and dakinis.

Meditating on the tantric view of the world as mandala,
Yet letting the mind wander aimless and uncontrolled,
Does not lead toward the state of a buddha.
Hope for enlightenment in one life is thus lost.

Anyone can recite a prescribed number of mantras,
Yet the purpose of tantric retreat is not accomplished
If mantra is not accompanied by clear meditation.
The link to the yidam's essence is thus lost.

If one always takes note of faults in others,
One does not notice that one's own every moment
Passes in blindness to one's own inner faults.
One parts from all hope of any spiritual progress.

One can engage in the profound meditation techniques,
Yet if one allows negative karma and delusion to prevail,
Not one single session finds its way to the heart.
So with that, O samsara, I bid you farewell.

Song of the Tantric Path

The next entry in the Seventh Dalai Lama's collection is very tantric in nature, and therefore makes use of a specialized and esoteric language. I suspect that some of it will float over the heads of non-initiates. Nonetheless, as the Tibetan saying goes, "If you don't have any teeth, at least you can work on it with your gums." For those with a background in tantric literature it perhaps will be appreciated as one of the most profound and powerful pieces in the volume.

Unlike most of the works in the collection, this entry actually has a lead-in. It reads, "A melodic song, entitled 'Essence of All-Beneficial Ambrosia,' on the key points of the sutra and tantra paths in general, and on the system of the five-deity mandala of the Indian mahasiddha Gantapada in particular."

In other words, it is a verse work expressing the tantric experience in the language of a particular mandala cycle.

The Buddhist tantras are divided into four categories, with each of the four having numerous mandala cycles. Each of these has its original tantric text coming from the Buddha, its lineage of transmission through the Indian and then the Tibetan masters, and its structure of practice. The highest of the four tantra classes is known simply as highest yoga tantra. In the Gelukpa school a dozen or so of these are preserved, but the four principal ones are Guhyasamaja, Heruka Chakrasamvara, Vajrabhairava, and Kalachakra. Here the Seventh Dalai Lama dedicates his song to the stages of the enlightenment path in accordance with the structure and language of the Heruka Chakrasamvara cycle. That tantric system in turn has three main lineages of transmission coming from India to Tibet: those from the mahasiddhas Luipa, Gantapada, and Krishnacharya. All three have similar language and yogic structures, but have several important differences in details. The Seventh Dalai Lama uses the linguistic environment of the second of the three Chakrasamvara transmissions, that from Gantapada.

The colophon explains why. It states, "The great Changkya Rinpochey, a supreme illuminator of the Dharma, a man of unsurpassed knowledge and wisdom, wrote to me with the request that I compose a spiritual song, easy to comprehend and chant, expressing the essence of the two stages of tantric practice in accordance with meditations of the Indian mahasiddha Gantapada's lineage of Heruka Chakrasamvara, with its five completion stage yogas. In response, the Buddhist monk Kalzang Gyatso wrote this, entitled 'The Essence of All-Beneficial Ambrosia.'"

Thus the Seventh Dalai Lama wrote it at the request of one of his disciples, Changkya Rinpochey. Better known as the third incarnation of the Changkya Tulku, this extraordinary lama is mentioned several times in Khetsun Sangpo's biography.

The First Changkya, whose ordination name was Drakpa Ozer, had been born in the Changkya region of Domey, and became a monk in Gonlung Jampaling Monastery. When in his mid-teens, he was sent to Central Tibet for higher studies in Drepung Gomang. However, the name of his birthplace stuck with him, following him throughout his life and thereafter being prefixed to the names of his subsequent reincarnations. His immediate reincarnation, Changkya Lobzang Choden by name, was born in 1642, the same year that the Fifth Dalai Lama rose to become the spiritual and temporal head of Tibet. He became a monk at a young age, and when he was twenty years old, went to Central Tibet and received higher ordination from the Fifth Dalai Lama himself. That Changkya passed away in 1714, when the Seventh Dalai Lama was six years old. His reincarnation, who eventually became famous under the name Changkya Rolpai Dorjey, was born three years later, and was to become not only a close friend of the Seventh Dalai Lama, but also his main spiritual heir.

Rolpai Dorjey was recognized at the age of four as the reincarnation of the Changkya Lama. His predecessor, the Second Changkya, had been a guru to the Manchu emperor, and consequently the Manchus took a keen interest in the young reincarnate lama. When he was eight years old he received an invitation from Emperor Yungting to come to Beijing. Here the Manchu emperor showered the boy in gifts and gave him an honorary court name, which translates as "Omniscient Lama, Lord with Love and Compassion Towering Over Living Beings." (It sounds smoother in Manchurian.)

In 1720 the Manchu Emperor sponsored Changkya to travel to Central Tibet with the young Seventh Dalai Lama, so that he could participate in the Seventh's enthronement in the Potala. The two lamas remained close friends from that time on. Both also became close disciples of the Second Panchen Lama. When the Seventh returned to eastern Tibet between the ages of nineteen and twenty-seven, Changkya traveled with him. Toward the end of their stay in the east, the Seventh gave him all the Chakrasamvara initiations.

Later, Emperor Chinlung sponsored Changkya to put together and oversee a team of lamas charged with translating the Tibetan Buddhist canon known as the Tengyur ("Translated Words of the Indian Masters"), with its three thousand books, into Mongolian. Under Manchu patronage Changkya also built numerous monasteries and temples in Beijing as well as elsewhere in China. Changkya's visits to Beijing were always sponsored by the Manchu emperor. As well as giving many Dharma teachings and tantric initiations to the Manchu ruler and his family, he even taught the Emperor to read and write the Tibetan language. Later the Emperor sponsored Changkya to form a team of lamas and translate the entire Tibetan Kangyur ("Translated Words of The Buddha") into Manchurian, again involving well over a thousand books.

Changkya and the Seventh Dalai Lama remained close over the years, and the Seventh passed most of his tantric transmissions to him. Therefore, in the lineage prayers of several of the main Gelukpa tantric systems, the name of Changkya Rolpai Dorjey appears immediately after that of the Seventh Dalai Lama. The Gantapada lineage of the Heruka Chakrasamvara Tantra is one of the most important of these.

When the Seventh passed away in 1757, Changkya Rolpai Dorjey was put in charge of the search for his reincarnation. He also served as the Seventh's official biographer.

In this song the Seventh Dalai instructs Changkya Rolpai Dorjey in the essence of the tantric yogas associated with that lineage. Changkya, in turn, took the text of the Seventh Dalai Lama and chanted it daily for the remainder of his life as part of his meditations. Eventually he manifested enlightenment, and passed his lineages on to his own disciples. The process continued, with the transmission passing from master to disciple, until the present day. Kyabjey Trijang Rinpochey, the Junior Tutor to the present Dalai Lama, was the main lineage holder of the Gantapada lineages to escape from Tibet.

Thus, the practice and realizations associated with the transmission, so well expressed by the Seventh Dalai Lama in his poem to Changkya, comes into the present day intact.

♦ *Song of the Tantric Path*

Homage to Jey Rinpochey, a second Buddha,
Manifestation of Vajradhara, lord of all buddhas,
In whose body reside the awakened ones past, present, and future,
As well as their retinues and buddhafields.

Homage to the feet of my own root guru;
Who is in true nature inseparably one with
Father-Mother Heruka,
The wheel composed of all objects of knowledge,
Whose essence is great bliss, clear as the autumn sky.

In the hands of one's spiritual master
Lie the roots of every mystical experience.
All happiness and suffering from now until enlightenment
Are his responsibility alone.

See the physical world as the guru's body;
Take sounds as the guru's teachings;
Mix thoughts and memories with his bliss and insight;
Rely on this practice, king of all paths.

Fortunate are they who meet with the doctrine
Of all-kind incomparable Tsongkhapa,
Who showed as precepts all sutras and tantras.
Fortunate indeed—an opportunity obtained but once.

Yet breath, like mist, is delicate;
And life, seemingly strong, is ever near to passing.
Quickly pluck the essence of Dharma,
For definite it is you will die at the hands of the great enemy Death.

Have not the three doors stood open to negativity?
Then the inconceivable misery of the lower realms

Certainly will fall upon you,
And, if still weak, you will not be able to bear them.

Some look, and see; in the innermost way they turn
To a *guru-deva*, an embodiment of Buddha, Dharma, and Sangha.
With attentive concentration they focus
On cultivating the white and dispersing the black.

Reveling in objects of greed and attachment
Is drinking poison mistaken for nectar.
The luxuries, securities, and comforts of the world
Are like dramas enjoyed in a dream.

No lasting happiness can be found
In any samsaric position,
And how foolish to sit complacent
In a hole filled with misery.

Turn the horse of the mind upward,
Rein him with the three higher trainings,
Strike him with the iron whip of fierce effort,
And cut unto the open road of liberation.

All beings, mothers who lovingly have nurtured us,
Are floundering in the seas of confusion.
The son who cares not for their anguish,
Are the waters of his heart not bitter?

Wholly discarding selfish thoughts,
Hold close the ways that better the world
And strive to live the six perfections
That yield buddhahood, ultimate benefit for all.

Sever the mind from chaotic wandering;
Fix it firmly on its object with mindfulness,
Without falling prey to agitation or dullness:
Train in meditation blissful and clear.

The manifold things we perceive
Are deceptive projections of deluded thought.
When we search for their ultimate essence,
Emptiness free of an essence appears.

The things that manifest also fade
And only footprints of names remain;
The other side of this is called dependent arising.
What else need be known?

The teachings of Nagarjuna and his disciples
Aryadeva, Buddhapalita, and Chandrakirti
Were thus by Jey Rinpochey understood—
A most wondrous view free from extremes.

Having first trained in these foundation practices,
Seek out a tantric master, embodiment of Buddha Vajradhara,
Lord of the Paradise Beneath None;
Gain the four ripening initiations
And enter into the mystic circle.

The body transforms into a great vajra-mandala,
And, in the inconceivable mansion of joyful repose,
The real deity—the subtle mind held between the
Kiss of the male and female drops—
Manifests as the blood-swilling Father-Mother.

The dakas and dakinis dance a blissful dance
In the mystic channels and secret drops;
Mundane perception is severed from consciousness
And all emanations become ultimately pure.

Visualize yourself as Heruka with consort,
Luminous yet void, body empty,
Energy channels of three qualities vibrating within;
At your heart a Dharma wheel with eight petals

Bears the indestructible drop in the form of *HUM*
Between the sun of method and the moon of wisdom.
Mind firm on this, tremulous misconceptions are cut,
And the clear light, sheer as the autumn sky, arises.

The outer consort, in nature fire,
Melts the life-drops that course
Through the 72,000 channels,
Bringing them into the central channel,
Giving rise to the four ineffable joys.

Outside, all sensory movement of mind and energy ceases;
Inside, mundane views, ignorance, and darkness disperse.
Thus by yoga even sleep is transformed
Into the nature of Dharmakaya's clear light.

By cultivating these yogic methods,
We can in general see through all distorted appearances
And in particular know the body as dreamlike,
Thus building the dancing form of an endowed deity
And maintaining the according emanations.

By mentally reciting the secret mantras of the vajra dharmas
Of entering, resting, and dispersing energy at the heart
While controlling the life-drop made of five clear essences,
The knots of ignorance are easily untied.

The tip of the vajra is placed firmly in the lotus
And mind as the syllable *HUM* is brought into the central channel;
One drinks and drinks the essence of nectars
And goes mad with innate joy unmoving.

By thus settling the mind in the subtle vajra letter
And bringing the drop to the four *chakras* and sensory gates,
One directly sees all aesthetic objects
Found throughout the three worlds.

Thus one opens the windows of the six miraculous powers,
Sees the faces of innumerable deities,
Masters the meanings of the words of the teachings
And gains the delightful company of an immortal lover.

In the tip of the vajra between the eyebrows,
The light of the sun, moon, and stars swirls in the drop.
By bringing mind and energy to that point,
The white bodhimind is forever increased.

Then with the fine brush of samadhi paint
A masterpiece incorporating all beauties of life,
One gains the aid of a fully qualified consort
And one's experience of the blisses blazes higher and higher.

Mind fixed on the bliss and *mudra* of the consort,
A rain of innate joy pours down.

Again and again seducing the beautiful one,
Symbol of the mind embracing reality itself,
One melts into the sphere of spontaneous bliss.

From the center of the navel chakra where meet the three
        energy channels,
Shine lights from white and red pyramids.
Looking through the nucleus of five drops therein,
The mind's nature is seen as five buddhas.

White and yellow energies shape into a vase
And the all-destroying fire rages.
The letters *AH* and *HAM* flare, fall, and vibrate,
Transporting one to the end of the primordial path of great
        bliss and wisdom combined.

Lights from the mystic fire flash into the hundred directions,
Summoning the blessings of buddhas boundless as space.
Once again the five natures of mind arise as sounds,
Releasing a rain of ambrosial knowledge.

The apparitions of people and things
Dissolve into light, and the waves
Of misconception are stilled.
No longer is the radiance of clear light obscured.
Even post-meditation mind maintains immaculate view.

In the sphere of semblant and innate Mahamudra,
Empty images appear as rainbows.
Flawless method emanates phantom circles,
Erecting the perfect mandala of deities and abodes.

The illusory body merges with clear light
Like clouds dissolving into space.
The fires of innate wisdom arise
And consume the seed of grasping for self.

This great union of the radiant vajra body
With the vast clear light of mind
Is called "the samadhi moving magnificently,"
A stage not touched by the ordinary intellect.

This consciousness, purified of all transient stains,
Gazes clearly and directly at the sphere of truth.
Like a magic gem it manifests the Beatific Body
Of Heruka Chakrasamvara for the sake of others
And sends out countless emanations,
Each in accord with the needs of the world.

Thus in this age of short life span,
Buddhahood is swiftly and easily attained
By turning lust for sensual objects
Toward the friend who instills great bliss.

Think: "By studying, contemplating, and meditating
Upon the flawless Vajrayana teachings,
The highest path, the esoteric way of all tantric
Adepts of the past,
May I in this very lifetime attain with ease
That point most peerless and supreme.

And if in this life ultimate power is not found,
At my death may the dakas and dakinis protect me
And lead to the rainbow palace of Vajrayogini
In the pure land Kajou Shing, there to enjoy clouds of
      transcendent offerings.

May I and all practitioners of this tantra
Soon complete the esoteric path of secrets
And, within ourselves ever perfecting the practices
Of the sutras and tantras taught by the Buddha,
May we master this mysterious way.

Until then, may the mighty dakas and dakinis
Who dwell in the twenty-four Heruka grounds
Care for us in every time and situation
As a mother watches over her only child.

A Song of Essential Precepts

The colophon to this entry states, "Written at the request of Goshri Ngawang Tenpel, who from afar requested a song of advice on how to benefit this life and the next." Goshri Ngawang Tenpel was also a disciple of Changkya Rolpai Dorjey, the lama who requested the previous song of spiritual advice. He does so "from afar," meaning that he sent the request in writing, probably with a group of pilgrims visiting Lhasa, who while in the holy city would receive an audience with the Seventh Dalai Lama. Until today, Tibetans prefer to send their private letters by hand, feeling that the personal touch it adds to the communiqué will create a stronger impact. In this case it worked, and the Seventh Dalai Lama responds to the request with a Dharma song.

The advice that he gives to Goshri Ngawang Tenpel on how "to benefit this life and the next" is a personalized reformulation of many of the spiritual teachings of the great masters of India, especially Nagarjuna, Aryadeva, Shantideva, and Atisha. As always, it comes with the freshness and edge that the Seventh Dalai Lama brings into all his writings. One of my favorite of his great lines is in this piece: "If, in this life, you do not become a sage,/ You are as stupid as a sheep!" Unfortunately, too many people in the world fall into that category.

The Seventh here writes in a clear, simple language of the spirit. His message rings as true today as it did 250 years ago. Anyone who can take what he says to heart indeed will see benefits in this and future lives.

◆ *A Song of Essential Precepts*

Homage to the guru, whose kindness is incomparable,
Who in nature is the Buddha Akshobhya,
Emanator of the various mandala deities
That arise in the myriad forms.

If one does not rely with utter clarity
Upon a perfect master, a wish-fulfilling jewel,
The rain of *siddhis* does not fall;
With profound concentration, devote yourself.

It is possible to misunderstand one's teacher,
Manifestation of the perfect buddhas,
By projecting faults into his sublime ways;
Of all negativities, this is the worst.

It is also possible to practice Dharma intensely,
And to apply oneself to its profound techniques
With the shallow motive of worldly gain;
This is the mistake of mistakes.

And it is possible to return empty-handed
From the jewel island of life
Because of having ignored spiritual matters;
This is the great deception, cheating oneself and others.

Working and struggling for the things of this life,
Neither body nor mind find a moment's freedom.
Look to that which benefits eternally;
Ask yourself if the spiritual quest has been fulfilled.

Squandering almost every moment of each day
In senseless diversions and escape tactics
Brings not the slightest Dharma realization;
What have you so far accomplished with life?

Recollect the various friends you have known—
High and low alike, are they not dying around you?
Do you not think of your own oncoming death?
Have you attained immortality?

Where will you go after death?
What you will become? No certainty!
Not having the strength of a realized mind,
Will death not terrify you?

To sit in the darkness of negativity
While clearly knowing the difference between good and evil
Surely leads to the black dungeons
Of the sufferings of the lower realms.

There is no way to hide hypocrisy
From the mirror of black and white actions.
Turn the mirror of Dharma toward your mind now,
And see what is good, what neutral, and what weak.

Do what you will to nourish and pamper
The flesh and bones of your body,
Soon they will go to the earth, or to flames, or to dogs and birds,
And all your pampering ends in nothing.

Even the things you greedily acquire
Are of no benefit at the time of deepest need,
When alone you wander to another world;
Regard your possessions as belonging to others.

Relatives, friends, admirers, and servants
Bring only attachment and anger,
And with the smallest provocation they disappear;
In the long run, they are no different than enemies.

In general, no worldly attainment is trustworthy,
No samsaric project ever ends,
And there is no time in worldly living for the mind to know peace.
Invoke a spiritual awareness now.

If one does not stop the mind
From unconsciously wandering to sensory objects,
There is no hope of gaining lasting happiness.
Control your thoughts with mindfulness and alertness.

If, in this life, you do not become a sage,
You are as stupid as a sheep!

Focus discerning awareness upon reality
And decipher just what is happening here.

Drink and absorb the essence of the teachings
From a true teacher of the Great Way.
By contemplating and meditating upon their meanings,
Discover the nature of your own mind.

Body seen as the body of a buddha,
Speech incessantly reciting the vajra mantra,
Mind absorbed in bliss and wisdom conjoined:
Pursue this meditation and satiate your spirit.

The elixir which turns all efforts of body, speech,
And mind into practices of the Great Way
Is the bodhimind, the enlightened attitude;
It is the one force benefiting both self and others.

The wealth and property you now possess
Will not belong to you forever.
Therefore you should be easy with them
While you still have the power.

The flowers of the high paths and spiritual stages
Do not grow on the dead tree of a mind
With the roots of self-discipline decayed.
Live the ways entailed by your practices.

The enemies or troubles one encounters
Are the ripening fruits of our own deeds
Done in this or in previous lives.
Meet them with patience, not anger.

It is impossible to accomplish anything meaningful
With actions governed by a fluctuating mind.
Maintain a calm, steady effort
That flows as irreversibly as a river.

By the ambrosial nectars of these useful precepts,
May the stains of your faults and obscurations be cleansed;
May you attain a buddha's three perfect kayas
And be filled with a wondrous glory.

Song to Build a Link with the Lama

The following piece is a prayer written as a poem for one of the Seventh Dalai Lama's disciples, intended for recitation as part of the disciple's daily prayers. The compiler included it in this collection of poems and songs, rather than place it in the various collections of prayers and liturgies found in the Seventh's collected works, due to its many references to the Lojong and Lam Rim meditations.

The colophon to it reads, "Written at the request of Khenpo Hotuktu Mergen, who made an offering of memorizing Jey Rinpochey's *Great Stages on the Path to Enlightenment* (Tib. *Lam-rim-chen-mo*) and *Great Stages On the Mantra Path* (Tib. *sNgags-rim-chen-mo*), as well as Nagarjuna's *Fundamental Treatise on Wisdom* (Skt. *Prajna-mula*) and Shantideva's *A Guide to the Bodhisattva Ways* (Skt. *Bodhisattva-charya-avatara*). He successfully recited these texts before Choden Angkor, and offered the effort to His Holiness Kalzang Gyatso, requesting that His Holiness write him a prayer that would always keep him linked with and cared for by His Holiness. Kalzang Gyatso responded by spontaneously composing the above for him."

The first name of the person who requested the composition, "Hotuktu," is a Manchu title, and identifies him as a Tibetan lama who had served as a guru to the Manchu court. The second name, "Khenpo," means abbot; it is likely that he was the abbot of a monastery in Amdo, from where so many of the Hotuktu lamas were drawn. Tsechok Ling mentions him in his biography of the Seventh, for he requested several teachings and initiations from the Seventh in Lhasa in the mid-1740s.

What is most impressive about the colophon is the list of texts that Khenpo Hotuktu Mergen memorized and "offered the effort" to the Seventh when he made his request. The first of them alone, Tsongkhapa's *Lam Rim Chenmo*, is 522 folios, or 1,044 pages in length. The second, Tsongkhapa's great treatise on the four classes of tantras, is over half that length. The third and fourth texts are two of the great Indian classics to be translated into Tibetan. To memorize even one of these four texts would be something of a challenge, let alone memorizing all of them. The Seventh Dalai Lama, always a practical man, had his assistant Choden Angkor accept the offering for him, knowing that it would take Hotuktu Mergen several days of rapid chanting to complete the recitation.

The text that the Seventh writes for him is a guru yoga liturgy, a common genre in Tibetan literature. Several other works of this nature are found later in this volume.

♦ Song to Build a Link with the Lama

Jetsun Lama, king of all buddha families,
Wishing-fulfilling tree possessing four kayas,
Cloud raining down the millions of siddhis,
I offer you my spiritual aspirations.

When the parched grass of negative karma
Tosses in the scorching winds of attachment,
The flames of misery rise higher and higher—
O Lama, light rain that pacifies.

On the desolate plateau fenced by attachment,
Barren of the waters of calm, clear Dharma,
The heat of anger blazes ever on—
O Lama, thick white cloud that cools.

In life upon life, aeon upon aeon,
The heart has always by ignorance been pained;
I, one with the most chronic illness—
O Lama, great life-saving doctor.

In this dark dungeon, difficult to escape,
We are tortured by the instruments of the three miseries;

I, weak and protectorless—
O Lama, Dharma King bestowing refuge.

To we who are now destitute and without hope
Ever to know the precious wealth
Of ultimate or even temporary joy,
You are the jewel fulfilling all wishes.

From the clear mirror of your sublime wisdom
Come millions of rays of unfading light
To embrace the flowers of knowable things:
The sun heralding an ocean of good fortune.

O lord of the mandala manifest as a rainbow
Of five wisdoms painted in the dharmadhatu sky,
An infinite circle of infinite wisdom
Formed by peaceful and wrathful buddhas beyond number.

Essence of compassion never cold,
Who gives power to those both near and far,
Synthesis of Sugatas past, present, and future,
A sacred ocean of good fortune.

In this age unfolding with five erosions
We walk a cliff dropping to pain.
You, who are more kind than all buddhas,
Come and guide me with your rope of compassion.

I recollect the unrepayable kindness of you
Who were prophesied by the Buddha in both the sutras and tantras.
O venerable ocean of good fortune,
With fierce emotion I look to you.

Repository of the secrets of all buddhas,
No matter what falls upon me
In this life, the bardo, or thereafter,
I visualize you sitting on the crown of my head.

By the force of infallible dependent arising
Of sowing the seeds of relying upon a guru,
And practicing hearing, contemplation, and meditation,
In all my lives may the holder of Compassion's Lotus

Sit with pleasure on the crown of my head,
Upon a lion throne studded with jewels,
And may you rain down an unending flood
Of Mahayana teachings upon those who are ripe.

Bless me so that when this life stops
I may meet with the Bodhisattva of Compassion and his retinue,
And that without hindrance I may reach
Quickly and safely the Pure Land of Joy.

The things that out of greed are amassed,
Like the honey of a bees, one day fall to others,
And the closest friendship at any moment
Can turn from affection into the deepest hatred.

Not one of the cherished samsaric addictions
Ever brings anyone the slightest good.
They allure, like a dancer fast as lightning,
And like luxuries known in a dream.

The possessions or positions one may gain
By nature are things destined soon to be lost.
Help me now to win liberation
From this cyclic pain embracing the world.

Bestow upon me transforming powers to see
Every living being as my own parent,
And, in order that I may eradicate suffering,
Help me to know the ways of the wise.

Help me to make myself into a jewel
Able to satisfy all needs of the world
And to gain the power always to manifest
As best suits each and every occasion.

The things that falsely appear as solid
From the start have had no inherent existence;
Help me to reach this kingly view overlooking
Ultimate reality free as the sky.

Help me to understand bliss and wisdom united:
To see all forms as the guru's body,

To hear all sounds as the guru's mantra,
And to know all thoughts as his vajramind.

Direct a rain of your auspicious blessings
In a steady flow to the life-drop at my heart,
Quickly to open the laughing lotus
Of my every temporary and ultimate fulfillment.

Song of the Four Mindfulnesses

The four mindfulness meditations, or *satipattanas*, constitute a major phase of training in ordinary Buddhism, where they refer to cultivating an accentuated awareness of body sensations, feeling-response tones, mind-flow patterns, and outer phenomena. These four trainings are used as preliminaries to tantric practice.

The four mindfulnesses that here are the subject of the Seventh Dalai Lama's composition, however, are not these same four. Rather, they are four special yogas associated with tantric Buddhism.

In his colophon, the Seventh Dalai Lama states, "This song was written by the Buddhist monk Lobzang Kalzang Gyatso in order to lay instincts of a centered vision upon his own and others' minds. It incorporates the four mindfulness meditations given as special oral instructions by Manjushri, the Bodhisattva of the Wisdom of Emptiness, to Lama Tsongkhapa, a mighty king of doctrine." The text also has a lead-in that states, "A Guide to Centered Vision, entitled *Song to Release a Shower of Siddhis*." From these comments we learn that the Seventh wrote the piece spontaneously, and not at the request of a disciple.

The important phrase in both the colophon and the lead-in is "centered vision." This refers to the "middle view," or centralized position of experiencing things. The Tibetan expression is *uma ta-tri*, which literally translates as "a guide to the middle view (or centered vision)." It refers to a genre of Tibetan literature, and there are hundreds of Tibetan texts with this subtitle.

On the existential level, "middle view," or "centered vision," refers to how all things are free of the qualities of truly existing and truly not existing. They are free from eternalism and nihilism. They have a "mode of appearance," which is their conventional nature, and a "mode of being," which is their void, non-dual nature. In experiential terms the centered vision refers to seeing things in their nakedness, without imputing anything extra onto them or overlooking (i.e., blanking out) something that is there. On the conventional level this vision means appreciating both the void nature of the objects of perception and also their illusory, mundane, operational nature.

In subjective terms, the middle view is the centered vision that simultaneously enjoys both the infinite aspect and the finite aspects of a phenomena. Ultimately, all human unhappiness arises from the fact that we do not have this well-centered posture in dealing with the various facets of our life. We either don't appreciate their infinite aspect, and instead see them in the light of a duality status, or we don't appreciate their finite aspect, and develop unrealistic relationships with them. In the Buddhist sense, our highest priority in life should be to establish a well-centered view that simultaneously appreciates both the finite and infinite poles of the objects of experience. As the First Dalai Lama puts it in one of his Lojong commentaries, "This is the ultimate protection against dissatisfaction and suffering."

Tibetan Buddhism is rich in oral transmission teachings (Tib. *man-ngag*). These are special teachings formulated by a great lineage master, based on his personal meditation experience, in which the 84,000 teachings of the Buddha are boiled down to their essence and then repackaged in a manner that the master feels renders enlightenment most easily accessible for the generations to follow. Oral transmission is, if you will, Buddhism's way of continually revising and updating itself. For example Atisha, who brought the Lam Rim and Lojong teachings to Tibet—both of which are oral transmissions—also brought numerous other oral lineages from his Indonesian guru Serlingpa. Once Atisha was asked, "What is the best approach: To engage in a vast study of the teachings, or to apply oneself to an oral transmission teaching?" He replied that the latter produces the most rapid enlightenment.

Lama Tsongkhapa received and also formulated many oral transmissions. His "Three Principal Paths" is one of his most famous formulations of this nature. Another is his transmission of "Guidelines to the Middle View," of which there are two: one for the Sutrayana, or general Buddhist approach, and one for Vajrayana, or tantric approach. The Seventh Dalai Lama's poem is inspired by the second of these.

According to this transmission, in order to achieve quick enlightenment we need to accentuate four principal presences in our awareness: (1) awareness of the guru, (2) awareness of universal love and compassion for all living beings, (3) awareness of a disciplined ego-identification process, and (4) awareness of radiant emptiness.

Intensifying awareness of the presence of the guru introduces the subject of the four gurus from which we learn and grow. These are: (a) the living guru, that is, advanced beings with whom we study and train, (b) the instruction guru, meaning the words of all the great masters of the past, as preserved in oral and written teachings, (c) the guru of our own ordinariness, which means the little voice within, through which we learn by digesting the essence of what we experience on a day-to-day basis, and (d) the guru which is our own ultimate nature, meaning attunedness to the depths of our being. When we access these four at all times, we travel quickly along the path to enlightenment.

The second awareness—unconditional love and compassion for all living beings—is heightened by applying the appropriate contemplative techniques during formal meditation sessions, and then sustaining this atmosphere between sessions by maintaining that perspective in every situation.

As for the third awareness, that of yogic ego-identification, here the Seventh Dalai Lama says, "In the inconceivable mansion of great bliss joyful to know,/ Sits the pure aspect of one's body and mind as the yidam." What he means is that the body (including the world experienced through the bodily senses) and mind form the basis on which we create an ego identity. "Yidam" is a tantric term referring to the mandala deity with which a tantric practitioner identifies. The word literally means "supreme mind." The idea is that, because of the habit of the duality syndrome, people create ego-identification with whatever arises in the flow of their lives, such as body qualities, job, family, mental attributes, and so forth. This reified ego has nothing to do with the infinite aspect of being, but is a mere conceptual construct based on passing aspects and distorted by the duality syndrome. Yet it is taken as the "real me."

Tantra bypasses the construct by providing a conceptually manufactured alternative, one that is more in tune with the authentic nature of being. It establishes the ego-identity not on this or that ephemeral aspect of being, but rather on the ground of natural joy, radiance, and spaciousness, thus providing the practitioner with a model that can move without hindrance through all spheres of experience. One of the reasons tantric practice is dangerous, of course, is that playing with the ego-identification process is something of a delicate matter, and thus in tantric Buddhism strong emphasis is placed on sustaining an effective working relationship with a qualified guru.

The next two verses address the topic of final nature, or authentic being. This is the awareness of ultimate reality, or emptiness. It does so first from the subjective perspective, the clear light mind, and then from the objective perspective, the reality of non-duality as an omnipresent factor in all things.

As the Seventh Dalai Lama says in his colophon, this fourfold formulation of tantric practice originates in the visionary experiences of Lama Tsongkhapa, the root guru of the First Dalai Lama. The Seventh Dalai Lama takes the four principal elements of that transmission and translates it into a tantric song, based on his own training in the teaching. His quintessential text achieved instant popularity, and since then has been used as a teaching tool by lamas training their students in the methods of cultivating the four mindfulnesses within themselves.

◆ *Song of the Four Mindfulnesses*

On the throne of unchanging method and wisdom
Sits the kind guru, synthesis of all objects of refuge.
See him as a buddha both transcended and realized;
Not thinking he has faults, with pure vision turn to him;
Not allowing negative thoughts to arise,
Turn to him with devotion.

In the dungeons of limitlessly painful samsara
Wander the six types of living beings bereft of joy.
See them all as parents who have cared for you with love;
Not holding partiality, meditate upon love and compassion;
Not allowing negative thoughts to arise, turn to them with
    compassion.
Generate unletting mindfulness and hold it in the realm of
    compassion.

In the inconceivable mansion of great bliss joyful to know,
Sits the pure aspect of one's body and mind as the yidam.
See yourself as the yidam of three indivisible kayas;
Not holding ordinary views, practice divine pride and clear
    manifestation;
Not allowing negative thoughts to arise, turn to the deep and clear;
Generate unletting mindfulness and hold it in the realm of the deep
    and clear.

In the mandala of knowable things appearing and evolving,
The sky of clear light, ultimate reality, everywhere pervades.
See everything in this indescribable light of reality;
Not holding intellectual fabrications, look to this immaculate
    emptiness;
Not allowing negative thoughts to arise, turn to the face
    of emptiness;
Generate unletting mindfulness and hold it in the realm
    of emptiness.

At the junction of manifest objects and the six consciousnesses,
The chaos of duality, a baseless fabrication, is seen.
See the drama, the illusion, the magical creation;
Not thinking it to be real, look to the face of emptiness;
Not allowing negative thoughts to arise, turn to appearance
    and emptiness;
Generate unletting mindfulness and hold it in the realm of
    appearance and emptiness.

A Daily Prayer to the Guru

The next piece is another "prayer to the guru," and thus is in the same genre of Tibetan literature as "Song to Build a Link with the Lama."

The colophon states, "Written at the request of the monk Lobzang Tsering from the Shang Gyatso Dechen Meditation Center, who asked for a daily prayer focusing upon his guru."

Shang is a district in Amdo, populated mostly by Mongolians who intermarried with local Tibetans. Lobzang Tsering, who requested the Seventh Dalai Lama to write him a verse work on guru yoga, was a monk who hailed from a small meditation center there. Most probably he had met the Seventh Dalai Lama during the latter's childhood years in Litang and Kumbum, or later when the Seventh moved back to the east between the ages of nineteen and twenty-seven to avoid the civil conflicts that had erupted in Lhasa between various aristocratic factions. During both of these phases of his life the Seventh traveled extensively through Kham and Amdo, giving blessings, initiations, and Dharma talks in the temples and monasteries on the routes through which he passed. Again, the compiler included the piece in this collection of songs, poems, and verses of advice given by the Seventh, rather than in one of the other sections of his collected works, because the prayer in it requests blessings to achieve the realizations of the Lam Rim and Lojong paths.

After two opening verses to the guru, the Seventh writes seven verses that focus on what in Tibetan is known as "the seven-limbed devotion": (1) prostrations, (2) making offerings, (3) acknowledging failings, (4) rejoicing in goodness, (5) requesting the enlightened beings to turn the

Wheel of Dharma, (6) requesting the masters to remain in samsara until all beings achieve enlightenment, and (7) dedication of merits. This classic devotional structure, probably originating in the *Avatamsaka Sutra* with the *Mahayana-pranidana-raja*, became very popular with all schools of Tibetan Buddhism, and in one form or another finds its way into almost all Tibetan liturgical practices. After the seven-limbed devotion, the Seventh Dalai Lama dedicates one verse each to turning actions of body, speech, and mind to the spiritual path, another verse to love and compassion, and then concludes with a prayer to Lokeshvara, the Bodhisattva of Compassion, for blessings in achieving final spiritual fulfillment.

This kind of prayer is generally used in conjunction with a visualization. One imagines the guru as seated on a lotus above the crown of one's head, and recollects that he or she is the embodiment of all the compassion, wisdom, and power of all buddhas past, present, and future. One then meditates on the many ways in which the guru benefits trainees, and the correct ways of relating to him or her both physically and mentally. Only when this vision has been well established and the appropriate emotional state induced does one proceed to chant the guru yoga prayer.

At the end of the session, the guru shrinks to the size of a thumb, descends into one's body via one's crown aperture, comes to the center of one's heart chakra, dissolves into light, and absorbs into one's body, speech, and mind. These become one with the compassion, wisdom, and power of the guru, and the objectives of the prayer are accomplished.

Many Tibetans perform a meditation and liturgy of this nature several times daily, every day of their lives.

♦ *A Daily Prayer to the Guru*

Above my head, on a precious lion throne,
On a seat made of a lotus, the sun, and the moon,
In the form of Vajradhara, all buddhas in one,
Sits my guru, an ocean of good fortune.

You who are all lamas, all yidams,
All bodhisattvas, arhats, and protectors,
Fulfiller of wishes, most precious of jewels,
Sit with joy above the crown of my head.

Visualizing all sentient beings as
everywhere surrounding me,
I emanate bodies numberless as the heavens,
Which bow to you with body, speech, and mind,
And offer you a boundless ocean of praise.

Intriguing one, who brings eternal joy,
I fill the skies with precious things
Held up by immortal goddesses
Created through the force of my samadhi.

I collect together all good things
Of the humans, nagas, and gods
Of a hundred million world systems
And offer them to please you.

In the blissful expanse of stainless emptiness,
My confused mind brings itself pain.
My every negative karma I now face,
Regret, and vow never again to enact.

The positive energy created by myself and others
Is the seed of happiness of all the world.
Lama in whom I always rejoice,
Turn the wheels of sutra and tantra
In accordance with the predispositions of beings.

O master with birthless and deathless vajra body
Appearing in human form for the good of the world,
Until the day samsara is emptied
Stay with us unwaveringly.

The pure waters of past, present, and future goodness
I direct now to wash away the obstacles
To the temporary happiness of higher rebirth
And the ultimate joy of gaining the three vajra kayas.

This human life of measureless potential,
Until now in narrow paths has been lost.
Show me the powers of your mystic vajra form
And inspire me to turn to spiritual ways.

The working of breath giving birth to speech
Has produced only words idle and harsh.
Show me the power of your mystic vajra speech,
Every sound of which is sacred vajra song.

This mind, long tempered by conditioning,
Is welded to attachment, hatred, and ignorance.
Show me the powers of your mystic vajra mind
Absorbed in the yoga of conjoined bliss and void.

Here, in the ocean of beginningless existence,
Again and again I am cut by pain.
Take me in your boat of limitless compassion
Beyond the violent waves of birth and death.

The countless beings have all been our mothers
And have given up their bodies and lives for us.
Inspire me to practice only as brings benefit
And happiness to each and every one of them.

Master, who dwells on Mt. Potala, grant your blessings
That I may never be separated from my spiritual masters
And my wishes to study and practice the great Way
To utter perfection reach final completion.

Song to Contact the Guru from Afar

The following entry is another guru yoga liturgy. The colophon states, "Written at the request of Lama Ngawang Drakpa, who asked for a prayer with which to contact his guru whenever they are widely separated."

Ngawang Drakpa was another of the Seventh's disciples from the east. He requests the Seventh to write him a prayer that he can include in his daily chanting practice. Again, this piece is in a genre of its own, known as "contacting the guru from afar," and there are thousands of liturgical practices of this nature in Tibetan literature. The collected works of almost every great lama contains one or more. It is, I suppose, the Tibetan mystical equivalent of a telephone, without the technological trappings. The Seventh Dalai Lama must have developed a reputation for liking the format as a vehicle of his poetic expression, and there are several hundred of them scattered throughout his collected works. Four of these are in this particular collection, namely, those that utilize the language and structure of the Lam Rim and Lojong transmissions.

◆ Song to Contact the Guru from Afar

O enlightened one protecting living beings,
The thought of whom dispels all sorrows,
The sound of whose name grants freedom from the terrors
     of the lower realms,
Come as a jewel to the crown of my head.

I see you, O my guru, as a matrix of all powers,
Source of the goodness and happiness
Of the beings of ten million worlds;
Bestow upon me blessings of body, speech, and mind.

I see you as a tantric mandala deity emanating
In myriads of peaceful and wrathful forms
From the oneness of unobstructed dharmadhatu;
Bestow upon me powers magical and supreme.

I see you as the Buddha, Dharma,
And Sangha, above all obscurations
And made excellent with every realization;
Help me to progress and attain liberation.

I see you as the dakini, the fountainhead
Of the wisdom of voidness and radiant bliss
Far beyond the descriptive power of words;
Arouse innate joy within me.

I see you as a magnificent vajra protector
Who, with a dance of infinite patterns,
Tramples to dust all demons and interferences;
Release your enlightened karma and fulfill my spiritual hopes.

In this life, the bardo, and all future lives,
Whether I am high or low, happy or sad,
I need look for perfection to no one but you.
Out of mercy, care for me.

Confused by the complexities of this life
And anxious with thoughts of my oncoming death,
I turn to you now, infallible refuge;
All-knowing guru, gaze on me kindly.

Bless me so that I may control with mindfulness and alertness
This, my mind, root of both good and evil;
Bless me so that I may direct it from the forces of blind passion
And turn it onto the road of truth.

With veneration I recollect you, O master;
Help me correctly to practice the yoga

Which looks for the face of the guru
In every experience, even those that entangle the mind.

Kindly protector, like a parent to sentient beings,
Never forget this one of sad fortune;
Care for me in all times and situations
And help me quickly to gain highest realization.

A Song for a Friend

The background of the next entry is explained in the colophon, which states, "A letter in verse form, written at the request of the Buddhist monk Lobzang Tenpai Gyaltsen, throne holder of the Megen Lhakhang Temple." In other words, the piece was requested by the head lama of a small Tibetan monastery. Presumably this is the same monastery of the lama who requested "Song to Build a Link with the Lama." In all probability the monk again is among the many with whom the Seventh developed spiritual connections during one of the two periods in which he lived in the east, both of which lasted just under a decade. His tenure in Kumbum seems to have been especially important during this phase of his life, and many of the lamas who gathered around him at that time remained close friends throughout his life. Most, of course, also became his disciples in his later years.

The spiritual advice that he gives to Lama Lobzang Tenpai Gyaltsen is straightforward and clear, and perhaps as well as any other piece in the collection sets forth the essence of the Seventh Dalai Lama's spiritual message to his people.

♦ *A Song for a Friend*

Homage to Buddha Vajradhara, creator of all mandalas,
Who trains living beings in this age
By manifesting as the guru, radiant as a new moon,
To bestow everlasting joy.

From the tongues of the gurus, the real prophets,
The gently smiling masters, come
The purifying teachings of the Buddha;
Take up this rosary strung from their words,
Which show how to be happy in every situation.

If we use this life born of a hundred virtues
For nothing but material purposes,
In truth we are no better than animals,
Who also sense not higher values.
This is my heartfelt advice to you.

When thought is powered solely by delusion,
Every move of body, speech, and mind is negative.
Rely upon spiritual alertness,
Or the depths of your heart will corrode.

Life ends in certain death,
And that death could befall you today.
What can the eight worldly dharmas do then?
Keep the mind in a realistic space.

No matter what possessions we may have,
Not one of them can help us forever;
And, at present, they bring just worry and work.
Satisfy the mind with things of the mind.

The friends and relatives surrounding us
Can be disturbing sources of anxiety and frustration.
The smallest cause can end your life!
Look to affairs deeper than worldly friendships.

Squandering the day in ceaseless talk
And blanketing the night in clouds of sleep,
Mind rests in Dharma for barely a minute.
Watch yourself closely and honestly.

If the objects that you acquire
Bind your mind in chains of attachment,
They ruin both this life and the next.
Do not be attracted to that which only harms.

From beginningless time the blind passions
Have constantly shadowed after the mind.
If you do not check them with spiritual forces,
Your practice is only a show for others.

The spiritual teacher who shows the Great Way
When approached fulfills one's every wish.
Do not be repulsed by ostensible faults;
Develop perfect trust and confidence in him.

Constantly visualize the guru on your head
And the circle of truth at your heart,
A practice always infallibly effective
In completely and thoroughly transforming the mind
Of this life, the bardo, and thereafter.

The joy and sadness seen in the people of this world
Are products of their own white and black actions.
With utter precision guard the practice
Of cultivating good and uprooting evil within yourself.

If you consider as kind the mother
Who carried you in her womb,
How can you dislike any being?
For in countless past lifetimes
All have been your mother.

Since the beginning are all things void;
Yet we grasp at reality in pictures created by the intellect,
And thus we make the world into a pit of sorrow.
Cut out false projections, the root of all delusion.

In brief, since the seed of all things—
Happiness and suffering, good and evil—
Is the mind itself, tame the mind
With mindfulness and steady alertness.

By my thus pouring the juice of core instructions
Into the stomach of an avid practitioner,
May the seed of happiness in this and future lives
Be thus firmly and irrevocably planted.

Advice to a Throne Holder

The following is one of two pieces that the Seventh Dalai Lama wrote for Gendun Drakpa, throne holder of the monastery in Oro Jungar. Both are in this collection; the first is in verse, and the second is a letter, which immediately follows. Tsechok Ling quotes both of them in his biography of the Seventh, indicating that he especially enjoyed them and felt that they represented the essence of the Seventh's personal character and spiritual teachings.

The colophon to this work states, "Gewai Shenyen Rabjampa Gendun Drakpa, throne holder of the monastery at Moro Junkar, wrote to me requesting that I send him some practical spiritual advice. Therefore the lazy Buddhist monk Lobzang Kalzang Gyatso wrote him this song."

The Seventh Dalai Lama mentions the place name as Moro Jungar (Tib. Mo-rud-jun-gar). Tsechok Ling spells it as Oro Jungar (Tib. O-rud-jun-sgar). In any case, the lama who requested the poem is a Buddhist monk of Jungar ethnic extraction, but in the spiritual lineage of the Gelukpa school of Tibetan Buddhism. He is the head lama—presumably the reincarnate head—of the Moro Jungar Monastery.

Tsechok Ling states in his biography that this lama first met the Seventh when he showed up with many of his countrymen to attend the public teachings that the Seventh gave at Ganden during the summer of 1742. I suspect that this poem was requested a number of years later, after the connection had matured. The Jungar are a Mongolian tribe, although at the time they were not part of the Central Mongolian Empire.

In fact, it was the Third Dalai Lama who had first opened the Mongolian regions to Tibetan Buddhism. During his visit to Mongolia in 1578, the Mongolians embraced Tibetan Buddhism as their national religion and the Dalai Lama incarnations as their spiritual head. The Third Dalai Lama spent much of the remainder of his life traveling, teaching, writing, and building in the north and east. It was he who constructed the monastery at Litang in Kham, near where the Seventh was born and in which he first became a monk; the Third also constructed Kumbum Monastery in Amdo (or at least extended it, if one wants to debate that the temple previously at this site was a monastery), where the Seventh later studied.

The Tibetans had mixed feelings about the Jungar Mongols, although this wouldn't have extended to the Jungar spiritual community. In 1703 Tibet had fallen to the Mongol warlord Aarsalan Khan. The Mongolians were upset over the young Sixth Dalai Lama's refusal to live as a monk, and claimed that a mistake had been made in his selection. They were strong supporters of Tibetan Buddhism, regarded the Dalai Lama office as their spiritual head, and weren't content to sit around and see a mess being made of affairs in this regard. The Tibetans, however, were devoted to the Sixth Dalai Lama; upset with the invasion, they formed an alliance with the Jungars to throw out Aarsalan and his armies.

In 1718 an army of 6,000 Jungar horsemen arrived in Lhasa, and the Mongols were sent packing. The ill-disciplined Jungar armies, however, frenzied by the many battles, went on a rampage. They not only looted much of Lhasa and its environs, but also proceeded to loot and destroy many non-Gelukpa monasteries. In particular, they looted and burned Dorjey Drak, a monastery that had been the home to many of the Nyingma lineages held and propagated by the Fifth Dalai Lama. The Tibetans immediately dissolved their alliance with the Jungars and formed a new one with the Manchus. The Jungars were soon beating a retreat.

Because of these events, relationships with the Manchus were especially strong during the Seventh's lifetime. The Jungars as a people, however, were not blamed for the excesses of the army of 1718, and Jungar children continued to be accepted into the monastic universities of Lhasa. In 1720 the young Seventh Dalai Lama was brought to Lhasa. By 1742, when Gendun Drakpa arrived to attend the Seventh Dalai Lama's teachings at Ganden, the Jungar fiasco had almost been forgotten.

In this poem the Seventh mostly gives private spiritual advice to
Gendun Drakpa, whereas in his prose letter the advice has more to do
with Gendun Drakpa's role as the head lama of the people of Oro
Jungar.

♦ *Advice to a Throne Holder*

The buddhas of the past, present, and future
Take ordinary form as human adepts, our teachers.
May those who are in nature four perfect kayas
Bestow their transforming powers upon us.

From an ocean of previous good deeds
Has precious humanity come into your hand.
Polish the mind with the sutras and tantras
And the clear light of mind will from mind appear.

What need to speak of my experiences
In dry, superficial words?
Yet with pure mind you asked that I write to you;
Therefore, I beg you, read closely.

For long have we wandered in samsara,
Yet, not to mention benefiting others,
We have not really helped even ourselves.
What have you to show for your efforts?

You with sacred human life,
With the opportunity to hear and contemplate
The teachings on discipline, meditation, and wisdom,
Make a concentrated effort to achieve something.

The gem that fulfills all wishes,
The source of siddhis magical and supreme,
Is the guru, embodiment of the Three Jewels.
Strive diligently to follow him closely.

That the King of Death shall not come
And stop life's breath this very day
Is a thing no man knows.
Be aware of death at every moment.

Friends, wealth, relatives, and admirers
Usually just push one further from peace
And bind one in chains of anxiety.
Look upon your attachments as enemies.

We pamper the body with food and clothes,
Yet soon it will turn old and ugly.
Look upon the body as a walking corpse,
A bag filled with excrement.

Any pain one ever experiences
Arises from imperfections of body and mind.
Turn your back on the enemy, imperfection.
See not the ugly as an ornament.

The highest god in the highest heaven
Sits in chains of mental distortion.
Soon he will fall to the flames of hell.
Hold no illusions about samsaric status.

Whenever your body or mind aches,
Generate compassion for all that lives.
Exchange selfish thoughts for universal love
That absorbs others' misery and shares others' joy.

The kindness of others is unimaginable!
Over infinite past lives they have again and again
Given up even their lives for us.
Seize the thought that hopes to repay them.

So many people lack the eye of wisdom
And stagger toward the precipice of pain.
Meditate upon compassion for these mothers
Bound so tightly in shackles of confusion.

Always, even until samsara is ended,
Hold firm the wish quickly to become a buddha,
Who has completed the path to spiritual joy
And spontaneously fulfills the needs of the world.

All things found in the world and beyond
Are illusions created by one's own thought.

Grasping at them but further distorts perception.
Give up grasping and see things as they are.

Dream objects are untrue, yet they still affect the mind.
In the same way, conventional truth is false,
Yet the laws of cause and effect are unfailing.
Therefore closely observe the "do's and don'ts" of practice.

Wherever you go, see yourself as a buddha
With an illusory body manifest and empty,
Abiding in an inconceivable mansion of wisdom;
Take sounds as mantra and thoughts as divine.

The undying heart-drop of mind and energy within you
Should be known as Buddha, Dharma, and Sangha.
Then one can freely enjoy food and drink
And transform them all into secret offerings.

When finally your life forces disintegrate,
Watch the elements of the body dissolve.
Then, like meeting once more with an old friend,
Eagerly greet the clear light of death.

Friendless and alone one enters
The dangerous path of the bardo.
At that time, turn to the gurus and tantric deities,
That they may direct you to the way of freedom.

During death, the bardo, and the rebirth process,
The impressions collected in this life
Will hold great power over you.
Transform them with the yogas of tantra's two stages
And discover a buddha's three kayas within.

Day and night examine the energies
Fusing in your body, speech, and mind.
Life is finally rendered meaningful by
The methods that tame one's inner stream.

While living in practices such as these,
Pass your time in altruistic ways
In order to plant pure, white seeds
In the soil of infinite sentient beings.

Think, "May my every movement
Of body, speech, and mind send out vast waves
Forever beneficial to beings and to Dharma."
Close every moment with this prayer.

By the merit of this song may the doctrine
Of the second buddha Tsongkhapa shine bright,
And may mother sentient beings endless as space
Gain his glorious state, possessed of three kayas.

Letter to a Throne Holder

This and the following work are the only items in the collection that are not written in verse. They were nonetheless included because their language is that of the Lam Rim and Lojong traditions.

This piece was written for the same lama as was the previous work, the Moro Jungar Throne Holder Gendun Drakpa. The verse work seems to have been written much earlier, as in this one the Jungar throne holder mentions having become old.

The text has no colophon, but has a lead-in that says, "A letter to the Moro Jungar Throne Holder and Abbot, Gewai Shenyen Rabjampa Gendun Drakpa, who asked for advice on various matters, but especially on how to prepare for the time of death." From this we learn that it has been written in response to a request for spiritual advice that he had received in a letter from the elderly abbot. In my note to the previous piece, I commented that Gendun Drakpa had come to the Seventh's teachings at Ganden during the summer of 1742. It is obvious from several of the passages in the Seventh's reply that Gendun Drakpa had long since returned to Moro Jungar. The Seventh takes the time to reply to him in considerable detail, and with the sense of personal intimacy characteristic of so many of his communications.

The closing passage in the letter states, "Along with this letter are enclosed some protection strings, three relic pills, a statue of Heruka Chakrasamvara, some hair from the Omniscient Fifth Dalai Lama, a yellow robe of a fully-ordained monk, and a monk's upper and lower robe." The little gifts that the Seventh included with his letter of guidance no doubt would have become sacred treasures of Moro Jungar Monastery. The hair from the Fifth Dalai was probably used as a blessing for placement inside statues, stupas, and other religious items.

✦ *Letter to a Throne Holder*

My spiritual friend, you have written to me saying that you wish to practice the Dharma and accomplish the significance of what you have learned, but that your power to effectively meditate has degenerated due to your old age. You have stated that conditions helpful to practice, such as environment, friends, personal freedom, and so forth, are rare in your life, that harmful conditions, such as negative influences from others, etc., are many, and that you sense that the time of your death is rapidly approaching.

You requested me to write a few words of advice that, as well as benefiting you, would help your people to grasp the principal methods of Dharma, such as what to study, contemplate, and meditate upon, and what disciplines to follow. I myself have not really accomplished much in this life, yet because you ask with sincerity I am sending this short reply.

You now possess the excellent opportunities afforded by a human body and mind, and you have met with the precious enlightenment teachings. As well, you have studied and contemplated the great texts of the ancient masters and know in depth the foundations of practice. This is extremely good, but you must also keep in mind the saying, "After you have studied a treatise on spiritual practice, accomplish its essence; that way, liberation from cyclic existence is easy." In other words, saturate your mental continuum with the material you have already studied, and then use it to win control of the mind and its faculties.

It is taught, "Having gained the prerequisite learning, one whose youth has faded should retire to a forest hermitage and pursue meditation." Therefore, leaving behind all familiar things, such as relatives, friends, attendants, disciples, patrons, and so forth, take your body to the distant mountains and keep it there as a victory banner of the sages. With your voice send prayers to the gurus and mandala deities, and chant the profound mantras. Keep your mind free of the dust of mental distortion and negative attitudes, and clear of the bondage of grasping at the transient. Do not mix the body, speech, or mind with negativities or failings. Be at one with Dharma. In these ways, practice is taken to its limits and one comes to know the meaning of peace. What goal could be higher? What could make human life more meaningful?

Dedicate all of your time to the vast activities of Dharma practice, for it is difficult to gain freedom from our present state of spiritual bondage. Immediately cut off all attraction toward possessions and worldly objects. Do not expect to remain alive even until tonight.

Consider that until now you have worked mainly for your own benefit, yet no ultimate benefit has ensued; whereas had you from the beginning held an altruistic aspiration for highest enlightenment, the state of a perfect buddha would already have been attained. Why are you not yet a buddha? Because in the past you dedicated your time to ineffective paths, to ways that do not get to the heart of spiritual life. From now on, constantly maintain the excellent thought that directs every action solely at gaining enlightenment as a means of benefiting others.

Constantly offer prayers that you may acquire such a noble attitude. With this thought—the bodhimind—as a basis, engage in the profound practices of the generation and completion stage yogas of highest yoga tantra. Especially, constantly maintain the divine pride of being a tantric mandala deity, and exert yourself at performing the appropriate mantra recitations and meditations. If this is well done, then no matter where you go or whether you are in solitude or not, the mind holds to the essence of the way.

It is more beneficial to maintain just one principal practice in these degenerate days than it was to maintain the entire foundations of practice in earlier centuries when Dharma was flourishing well. In the same way, it is more worthwhile to carry the burden of upholding the doctrine in a region where Dharma is scarce than it is to live in a great spiritual center where there are many gurus, spiritual friends, and Sangha members. Therefore, your fate [to live in Moro Jungar] is not in the least unfortunate, and I bid you to have courage and enthusiasm in your vast efforts there.

Encourage the lay people of your community to make themselves into proper vessels of Dharma by generating strong confidence in the Three Jewels of refuge. Encourage the monkhood to live in accordance with their *pratimoksha* vows and disciplines, as these are the roots of their every possible attainments.

You should teach the details of the methods of the enlightenment path—both the Bodhisattva Way and the Tantric Way—to proper vessels from amongst the monkhood and lay community alike. Nowadays it is very rare to meet anyone who really lives the teachings except in talk, so you should show your people how these things actually are to be practiced.

If anyone transgresses any of their trainings during the day, they should acknowledge their shortcomings to themselves and purify them by nightfall; if they break them at night they should acknowledge them by morning. For this it is useful to recite and meditate upon liturgies such as *The General Declaration of Failings*, *The Sutra to the Thirty-Five Buddhas*, and so forth, in front of images representing the Buddha, Dharma, and Sangha. Applying oneself earnestly in this way is very meaningful, for one is then able to maintain a pure mindstream and to abide in awareness of self-dignity and consideration.

Furthermore, you should encourage your people to study and teach the great texts and commentaries that deal authoritatively with the practices of the sutras and tantras. In order that they become able to put everything that they learn into practice, teach them the pointers found in masterpieces such as [Lama Tsongkhapa's] *Great Stages on the Path to Enlightenment* and so forth. Do not let them fall into superficial intellectualization or word games; have them follow methods that directly benefit their minds.

Do not ignore the lay community. On special occasions lead gatherings wherein they can engage in the twenty-four hour Mahayana precepts and the fasting rite. Encourage them to think constantly about the meaning of spiritual refuge, to practice prostrations and circumambulations, and to chant mantras, especially that of the female buddha Tara. Also, teach them the Migtsema practice, which calls up the essence of compassion, wisdom, and power. Give them discourses on subjects that reveal the nature of the laws of karmic action and consequence, such as *Tales from the Mind-Taming Scriptures*, *Tales of the Wise and the Foolish*, and so forth.

The root of all spiritual understanding lies in the earth of clear-minded enthusiasm in the powers of the Three Jewels and the laws of karma. Therefore, arouse this enthusiasm within your people and place them in the practices for transcending negativities and cultivating excellences of body, speech, and mind.

In these and other such ways you should strive tirelessly, exerting yourself in auspicious and meaningful works for the benefit of living beings and the enlightenment doctrines.

Along with this letter are enclosed some protection strings, three relic pills, a statue of Heruka Chakrasamvara, some hair from the Omniscient Fifth Dalai Lama, a yellow robe of a fully-ordained monk, and a monk's upper and lower robe.

Using Illness to Train the Mind

This, the second prose piece in the collection, has no lead-in or title. The colophon simply states, "Advice to a Drotsalwa; written in the Earth Dragon Year." Thus we can identify the year as 1748. "Dro" is the name of a region, and also the people of that region. "Tsalwa" indicates a traveler or pilgrim from that region. The Seventh Dalai Lama was famous for giving public audiences to the pilgrims who came to Lhasa, so we can speculate that the recipient of this piece was one of them. Generally the Dalai Lama would sit in his audience temple in the Potala, and the hundreds of pilgrims would stream through in single file to receive his blessings. Mothers would ask for names for their babies, and sick people would ask him to blow mantras on them to heal their illnesses. It was not uncommon for him to grab someone's hand or ear and ask them where they were from and why they had come, and thus engage them in a brief conversation. Whenever this occurred the line of pilgrims would stop until he had finished his conversation.

The present Dalai Lama continues the same tradition today. After the Kalachakra initiation in Bodh Gaya in 1974 the entire crowd of 150,000 went through in single file. I stood in line for three days before coming into his presence. As I passed before him he reached down, grabbed me by the ear and whispered a few words to me. Perhaps I read more into them than was there, but they seemed to sum up much of what had been on my mind throughout the entire two weeks of the teaching and initiation. On another occasion, and after another initiation, I had a very sore back, but was careful not to show it as I walked passed him in line. He reached down and whacked me on the very point of the excruciating pain. The problem went away instantly, and has never again returned.

In this letter of advice the Seventh Dalai Lama is addressing someone who is very ill. One of the key points in the Lojong teaching is the importance of learning how to take the difficulties that life throws upon us, such as sickness, harms from other living beings, loss, and so forth, and use these as training environments. The method is called "turning difficulties into aids on the path." The sense of the technique is that we can grow in every situation, not just pleasant ones. With pain and illness we do so through changing our inner perspective on our condition, and using the pain to intensify our meditative concentration.

In particular, the Seventh Dalai Lama recommends a Lojong practice known as *tong len*, or "taking and giving." This is done in conjunction with a breathing meditation. The Drotsalwa is advised to feel his pain and, as he inhales, to imagine that he takes upon himself the pains of other living beings, who have similar sufferings due to a similar karma. Then, as he exhales, he should breath out (and give) love, compassion, and healing energy to other living beings.

♦ Using Illness to Train the Mind

Whenever a physical illness arises, we usually multiply our suffering by worrying and by pressing mental anxiety on top of it. One should understand that the human body is a composite of elements and agents that constantly are struggling with one another. When these elements and agents fall into disharmony, or when external forces, such as negative energies, affect it, the various diseases quite naturally arise with intensity and for long periods of time.

Therefore one might as well face up to the fact that during the course of one's life a certain amount of disease is inevitable. When one does fall painfully ill, one should not be concerned with one's own situation; instead, consider the inconceivable sufferings of the hell denizens, the hungry ghosts, the animals, and so forth, whose anguish is infinitely greater than one's own. Ask yourself, "If they must bear such immense pain, how can I not bear this suffering which, in comparison, is so small? If I am so weakened by my suffering, how must they feel, whose anguish is so much greater? May their afflictions be alleviated by this illness of mine!"

Thinking in this way, visualize that you are surrounded by all sentient beings who endure every type of suffering. As you inhale, visualize that their negativities, obscuration, sicknesses, and pain ripen upon you, freeing them from all misery, and as you exhale, visualize all good things going to them in the form of white nectar, giving them happiness. Repeat this process again and again.

As the benefits of even one moment of this contemplation surpass the effects of any other positive action, any illness should be seen as an excellent opportunity to practice Dharma. Think, "Now, even if I never recover, I can continue to practice the meditation of taking others' sufferings upon myself and giving them peace, a powerful practice surpassed by no other. Therefore, I am perfectly happy to lie here with this illness."

If you can carry this advice into the depths of your heart, there is no doubt that you will be benefited in both this and future lives. Hence, keep it in mind.

A Plaintive Call

This brief guru-yoga liturgy starts with a colophon that states, "Written at the request of Erteni Achi Tunomohan from Dolunor, who asked many times for a prayer to the guru."

The lama at whose request the piece was written has a Mongolian name, with the Manchu title "Erteni" as a prefix. This title is the equivalent of the Tibetan "Panchen," or "Great Master." Several large Tibetan monasteries awarded the degree of Panchen to graduates of their training program, Tashi Lhunpo Monastery in Shigatsey being the most prestigious of them, and Kumbum Monastery in Amdo being another. Usage of the Manchurian version of "Panchen" usually indicates that the lama was a guru to the Manchu court in Beijing.

Presumably Erteni Achi Tunomohan is a disciple of the Seventh Dalai Lama who hails from the Dolunor region of Amdo, where names of this nature are common.

The text would have been used as a piece in the devotee's daily chanting, probably incorporated at the beginning of every meditation session. As with the earlier guru yoga works composed by the Seventh Dalai Lama, it reveals the classical attitudes to be held toward the guru by practitioners of tantric Buddhism.

◆ *A Plaintive Call*

O holy teacher and master,
In nature the three mysteries and undying vajras
Of all buddhas of the ten directions,
I beseech you, bestow upon me transforming powers.

O healer whose mind is most sublime,
Keeper of the essence of truth's elixirs,
The medicine giving immortality to the fortunate;
I beseech you, bestow upon me transforming powers.

The things of this life are like the peel of a fruit,
And we stupidly see them as the fruit's nectars.
O Jetsun Lama, bestow upon me transforming powers
To direct my mind toward meaningful ways.

Helplessly propelled by the three psychic poisons,
All of my time is lost to futility,
And I, a rock, must suffer the consequences.
O Jetsun Lama, be my refuge and guide.

Embodiment of the Bodhisattva of Compassion,
Forever be my spiritual friend.
Help this helpless one, an object of mercy,
To gain every siddhi both mundane and supreme.

Alphabetical Song II

This is the second of the two alphabetical poems included in this collection. The colophon to it reads, "Once when Demo Tulku was sitting with the Seventh Dalai Lama, he requested His Holiness to write him a short teaching. His Holiness paused for a moment and then spontaneously composed this song."

The line of Demo Tulkus is one of the most important incarnate lama lineages in Tibet, and all the incarnations have been very close to the Dalai Lamas. Two have served as regents in the minority years of a Dalai Lama.

The Demo Tulku incarnation for whom the following alphabetical poem was written is Demo Ngawang Jampel Delek Gyatso, who is the fourth in the line (or fifth, depending on how the counting of his early incarnations is done).

After the previous Demo Tulku passed away (i.e., Demo Ngawang Namkha Jamyang), the Seventh Dalai Lama oversaw the search for his reincarnation. He also then oversaw the enthronement proceedings of the young child who had been selected, and later lead the ceremony for the boy's monastic ordination. Over the years to follow, he closely supervised his education and arranged special seating for him at numerous teachings and initiations that he gave, in order to reinforce their spiritual connection.

When the Seventh Dalai Lama passed away in 1757, Demo Ngawang Jampel Delek Gyatso was requested to serve as regent of Tibet during the search for the Eighth Dalai Lama and during his minority. Naturally, he later led the enthronement ceremony for the young Eighth

Dalai Lama in 1762 and, in accordance with tradition, was the Eighth's first spiritual mentor. Demo Tulku continued to serve as regent until his death in 1777, fulfilling the Dalai Lama's dual role as temporal and spiritual head of Tibet.

Perhaps the song that the Seventh Dalai Lama here spontaneously composes for the young Demo incarnation can best be seen as a set of guidelines to the qualities that he expects the boy to embody, so that he will be able to meet the destiny that awaits him. Indeed, Demo Ngawang Jampel Delek Gyatso grew up to become a great and wise lama. His reign as regent is viewed by historians as one of the most successful of any of the regency periods.

◆ *Alphabetical Song II*

Ka: From the heart
of the golden lotus (*ka-ma-la*)
Kha: Comes honey
sweet to the mouth (*kha*).
Ga: But take note: the scent
of medicinal plants (*ga-bur-man*)
Nga: Is to be found in this
song of mine (*nga-gi*).

Ca: Do not give voice to
meaningless talk (*ca-co*), but
Cha: Only to words that yield
a measure (*cha-she*) of good.
Ja: Leave behind all
negative ways (*ja-ka-nag-po*),
Nya: And stay constantly radiant,
like the full moon (*nya-gye-da*).

Ta: Look not to the teachings
of the Buddha (*Tathagata*)
Tha: With superficial attitudes,
nor to the mere words (*tha-nya-tsig*);
Da: From now on (*da-ta-ne*),
practice the essence,
Na: And cross over the ocean filled
with monsters (*na-tra*) of suffering.

Pa: Learn the inner practices,
         the perfections (*pa-ra-mi-ta*),
Pha: And the systems of reason common
         to all philosophical systems (*pha-rol-mu-tek*);
Ba: Gain fame in them even
         to the western lands (*ba-shang-jou-ling*),
Ma: In order to tame the minds
         of all beings without exception (*ma-lu*).

Tsa: Even if your tantric practice
         is small (*tsa-ni*),
Tsha: Strongly face
         all trials and challenges (*tsha-trang-la-sok*);
Dza: Then when you call (*dza-she*)
         to the dakinis,
Wa: Their faces
         will naturally (*wa-ler*) appear.

Zha: Ah, Demo Rinpochey, Holder
         of the Yellow Hat (*zha-ser*),
Za: Do not think about
         food (*za*), clothing, or wealth;
A: Do not take pleasure
         in idleness (*aur*), but in
Ya: Practice, study, meditation, and contemplation
         as inseparable (*ya-trel*) activities.

Ra: Most people are as stupid
         as herd animals (*ra-luk*);
La: They discard sincere advice
         as if it were hard, coarse wool (*la-wa-tsub*).
Sha: Listen to the teachings
         so kind (*sha-tsa*) and helpful,
Sa: Wholesome like medicine, an ornament
         upon this great earth (*sa-chen*).

Ha: Like the fragrance of a
         sandalwood (*ha-ri-tsan-den*) forest
Ah: Are the wisdom teachings
         on the meaning of the sound *AH*.

Ha: Onto beings now covered
         in heavy (*ha-chang*) darkness
Ah: May they fall as a shower
         of divine nectars (*am-ri-ta*).

This song is noisily uttered by one poor in practice,
This I tell you plainly.
But I had an urge, a wish to contribute to the world,
And it yielded this song of letters.

O Demo Rinpochey, incarnate lama of the Ganden Order,
A tradition of countless accomplished masters,
I pray that you live long on earth
And release vast waves of enlightened energy upon beings
       endless as space.

Fundamentals of the Sutras and Tantras

The colophon to the next piece states, "This song on all the principal points of the path that combines the sutras and tantras was written at the request of the great Changkya Rinpochey, a supreme being who accomplished his own noble prayers and aspirations by safeguarding the Buddhadharma in this degenerate age. This work contains nothing not found in the song I wrote for him earlier, but because he persistently asked for another, I wrote it to silence his constant requests."

Thus it was written at the behest of the same lama who requested "Song of the Tantric Path." Changkya Rolpai Dorjey was destined to become the Seventh's greatest tantric disciple, and thus the heir to his many lineages.

The earlier work "Song of the Tantric Path," used the specialized language of the Heruka Chakrasamvara tantric system. The present piece is more general in its message, and its language is therefore less esoteric.

One verse in this song, perhaps better than any other in the collection, expresses the Seventh Dalai Lama's personal philosophy of life, and the approach he advocated to those seeking enlightenment:

> The pinnacle of aims is to follow this path:
> Body, speech, and mind kept stainless with pure self-discipline,
> Mind held in samadhi blissful and clear, and
> Wisdom seeing all realities of every situation.

If you forget everything else that the Seventh Dalai Lama has written on these pages, at least keep this one verse in you mind. It will serve you well.

◆ *Fundamentals of the Sutras and Tantras*

Homage to the all-kind spiritual guides
Who are inseparable from the Bodhisattva of Wisdom
And who are the primordial Buddha Vajradhara
Performing the dance of a human.

The spiritual guide, all powers unified,
At one taste with the beyond-samsara nature
  of all Buddhas of the ten directions,
Cannot be known by the intellect
Nor described in petty words.

For those of us born into this degenerate age,
He is kinder than all the buddhas;
For, like pushing gold into a beggar's hand,
He shows us the richness of the sutras and tantras
  and points to the path free of extremes.

A teacher of such great kindness
Should be approached with profound appreciation;
Look unflinchingly for the face of the true teacher
Who understands fully the ultimate nature of mind,

Whatever you want for yourself and others,
With a human form is easily attained;
Disengage yourself from meaningless efforts,
Strive to accomplish the highest of goals.

Because all things composite are impermanent,
Life changes and never abides;
That change is the basis of all suffering,
For the samsaric mind fills with frustration
On watching its creations continually fade.

This body formed from sperm and ovum
Emits foul odors from every hole.
It is not a thing to cherish;
Yet, due to the power of delusion,
We have become its servant.

Not to mention months or years,
We cannot be sure it will endure even until tomorrow.

If one is weak and facing death,
So what if the tree of wealth and friends is laden?

The higher you climb in samsara, the higher the cliff
     on which you perch;
The more things you own, the tighter you are bound.
The dearer you hold someone, the greater the chance
     he or she will hurt you;
The faster you subdue enemies, the faster their numbers increase.

This body is a thing borrowed for a moment,
And possessions are things stored for others.
Now we dally with them, but quickly are they lost,
And, misused, they end only as sources of misery.

Therefore, no worldly position
Is worth a struggle to gain.
Turn your back on that which only handicaps:
An unburdened mind is joy supreme.

The pinnacle of aims is to follow this path:
Body, speech, and mind kept stainless with pure self-discipline,
Mind held in samadhi blissful and clear, and
Wisdom seeing all realities of every situation.

The mother beings wandering in the six realms,
To me, their son, are pieces of my heart.
For many times have they soothed my troubles
And in infinite ways have they brought me joy.

These infinite beings, so kind, are covered by the fog of ignorance.
Constantly slashed by the whips of delusion,
They have no chance to lay down
The burden of misery from their minds.

Therefore, whenever you meet anyone,
Greet them with eyes smiling with love.
Why mention that you should not even consider
Holding harmful intentions or deceptive thoughts?

Aspire to practice purely and selflessly,
Not being discouraged even for a moment,

Exerting yourself in the bodhisattva ways
Just as does a bodhisattva of the ten stages.

The way people and things seem to be other than projected labels
Is a distortion created by the conceptual mind.
If we look at the root of things,
Emptiness is clearly understood.

And in the vast space of perception of emptiness,
Mental grasping for ultimates subsides.
Then, when one looks into the face of the world,
Everything is seen as being without a self.

Understanding interdependence, we understand emptiness,
Understanding emptiness, we understand interdependence:
This is the view that lies in the middle,
And which is beyond the terrifying cliffs of "is," "is not,"
        "neither," and "both."

The tantric master, he one with Buddha Vajradhara,
Must then stamp your mind with the four initiations,
Introducing you to the blissful path of the three kayas
And to the ultimate nature of body and mind.

Then one can bathe consciousness in the innate clear light,
Shape energies into the form of a tantric deity,
And abide unwaveringly in the deep, clear yoga
Which does not divide meditation from non-meditation.

All things that appear in the world are
Seen as an inconceivable site of wisdom,
And the endless beings dwelling therein
Are known to be an ocean of buddhas.

By the profound yogas of the secret path,
Such as taking food as ambrosial substances offered
To the dakas and dakinis who reside in the channels and energy
        forces of the body,
One's every action becomes tantric practice.

Outside, the dance of the consort captures the mind
And spreads into every direction;

Inside, one experiences the vast path of the union of bliss and void;
Pursue this practice as steady as the flow of a river.

And you who have mastered the tantric methods,
Heroes who have accomplished the yogic path:
Having totally separated your mind from obscuration,
    preconception, and grasping at life as mundane,
Do you not abide in constant joy?

Though practitioners at elementary stages
Are praised by the saints as supreme
For making the smallest meaningful effort,
The same deed, O great ones, would not become you.

Having committed yourself to safeguarding the
    enlightenment legacy,
Wear the armor of mental tenacity,
And with the four ways of benefiting the world,
Open a hundred doors of universal goodness,

May the sublime, joyous teachings thrive,
May the lineage holders live long,
And may living beings endless as space
Be moved to attain enlightenment.

To Shower Sublime Goodness

The next entry, which belongs to a genre of Tibetan writing known as
Lagyu Monlam, or "Prayers to the Lineage Masters," is also quoted in
full by Tsechok Ling in his biography of the Seventh Dalai Lama. According to Tsechok Ling, the Seventh wrote it when he visited the Olkha
region in 1756, a year before his death.

The colophon to the piece reads, "This prayer petitioning the present
and lineage gurus for siddhis, entitled 'To Shower Sublime Goodness,'
was written by the Buddhist monk Kalzang Gyatso at the request of
numerous disciples when he made pilgrimage to Lhading Nampar
Gyalwai Ling, the retreat site where Jey Rinpochey gained direct realization of emptiness, the ultimate nature of things."

The prayer addresses the three principal Indian lineages from which
the Gelukpa school is formed, mentioning some of the central person-
ages in each. It begins with a verse to the tantric lineages from the
Indian mahasiddhas, mentioning by name the illustrious yogis Luipa,
Ghantapada, Dombipa, Tilopa, and Naropa. It then dedicates a verse to
the Lineage of Vast Activity, mentioning the names of the Indian mas-
ters Maitreya, Asanga, Vasubandhu, Vimuktasena, and Shantarakshita.
Thirdly, it gives a verse to the Wisdom Lineage of the Profound Middle
View, mentioning Manjushri, Nagarjuna, Aryadeva, Buddhapalita, and
Chandrakirti.

The fourth verse introduces Atisha, "the crown jewel of India's five
hundred sages." This same verse mentions Atisha's chief disciple Lama
Drom Tonpa, and Drom's three chief disciples, popularly known as
"the three Kadampa brothers" (although they were not related by

blood). These are the early founders of the Kadam School that formed in the eleventh century, out of which the Gelukpa School was to emerge in the early fifteenth century.

The fifth verse is to Lama Jey Tsongkhapa, founder of the Gelukpa School, and also to the great accomplished lamas who followed in his wake. Thus it represents all the generations of Gelukpa lamas, down to the time of the Seventh Dalai Lama. The Seventh purposely has not written out the names of the Tibetan masters who came after Tsongkhapa, because there are many different lines of transmission. In addition to the mainstream lineage, there are the numerous lineages that passed through other of Tsongkhapa's chief disciples, and accordingly through the monasteries that they built to house their teachings.

The sixth verse, which begins, "Lama as Dharmakaya...," is to one's own personal teacher, who embodies the three kayas, or dimensions of buddhahood, and the realizations of all three lineages from India as transmitted through the Kadampa and Gelukpa masters of Tibet.

The remainder of the text is a prayer requesting the lineage gurus for inspiration and blessings, so that one might live in accordance with the enlightenment way.

◆ *To Shower Sublime Goodness*

All-pervading Buddha Vajradhara, lord of the three blissful kayas,
And those who with your blessings found highest siddhi—
Luipa, Ghantapada, Dombipa, Tilopa, Naropa,
And all gurus of the supreme tantric adept lineage—
Pray, bestow upon us waves of protecting power.

O Shakyamuni Buddha, leader of the world,
Maitreya, most splendid of Tushita's hundred buddhas,
And Asanga, Vasubandhu, Vimuktasena, Shantarakshita,
And all gurus of the Lineage of Vast Activity,
Pray, bestow upon us waves of protecting power.

O Lord Manjushri, manifestation of the wisdom of all buddhas,
Most noble Nagarjuna, the disciple Aryadeva,
Supremely attained Buddhapalita, illustrious Chandrakirti,
And all gurus of the Wisdom Lineage of the Profound Middle View,
Pray, bestow upon us waves of protecting power.

O Atisha, crown jewel of India's five hundred sages,
Drom Tonpa, incarnation of Lokeshvara, lama blessed by an
    ocean of buddhas,
The three emanation brothers who received your lineages,
And all gurus of the great Kadam tradition,
Pray, bestow upon us waves of protecting power.

O Lama Jey Tsongkhapa, Manjushri in human guise,
And the great accomplished lamas following after you,
Whose enlightened activity liberates beings limitless as space—
Lamas holding countless lineages and blessings—
Pray, bestow upon us waves of protecting power.

Lama as Dharmakaya, the great bliss free from all elaboration;
Lama as Sambhogakaya, with seven limbs of spontaneously
    born perfection;
Lama as Nirmanakaya, manifesting as most benefits disciples—
All-kind root guru, source of all siddhis—
Pray, bestow upon us waves of protecting power.

Should the days and nights of our life be lost to worldly
    indulgences,
We will be forced to enter the darkness of death
With the torch of wisdom still unlit.
O kind gurus, protect us, who have not the power
To be sure of remaining alive even through this day.

One shows kindness to others, yet gets enmity in return;
One strives for prosperity, yet it slips away;
One works for happiness, yet meets only with pain;
O kind gurus, help us forever escape
The flames of desire and expectation.

We are chained in the prison of karma and delusion,
Weighed down by the load of an imperfect body and mind,
And we ache with the diseases of birth, sickness, age, and death.
O kind gurus, help us forever escape
The miserable wilds of samsara.

Help us constantly to hold love and compassion
Toward all living beings, wish-fulfilling jewels,

A friendly gesture toward whom surpasses an offering
    to all the buddhas;
And help us to transcend seeing anyone as an enemy.

Give the light which nakedly reveals ultimate truth
To us, who blindly wander in clouds of ignorance.
Wrapped in confusion and bewilderment,
We do not see the very reality surrounding us.

Release a shower of omens foretelling the prosperity
Of the presence of the three higher trainings:
Supreme ethics, which bestows external and internal purity;
Calm, clear samadhi, which produces bliss day and night;
And radiant wisdom, which gives clarity now and forever.

O powerful dakinis and Dharma protectors,
Guard us against negative forces and hindrances;
Spread truth and harmony far and wide;
Carry joy into the ten directions;
Cover the world with signs of good fortune
And bestow mystical attainments with which
To fulfill the needs of self and others.

Four Rivers

The next entry was also written by the Seventh Dalai Lama during his 1756 pilgrimage through the sacred sites and meditational caves of the Olkha mountains. The colophon to it simply states, "Written by the Buddhist monk Lobzang Kalzang Gyatso, a holder of tantric knowledge." This is another of the Seventh's poems that Tsechok Ling quotes in full in his biography, again because he feels it reveals the character of his subject.

A key element in the poem is the play on the number four, a mystically significant digit in tantric Buddhism. Hence, in the first verse we have Mt. Kailash, the mountain in Western Tibet that is regarded by Buddhists and Hindus alike as the central power place on this planet, with its four sacred rivers—the Indus, Ganges, Brahmaputra, and Sutlej—all of which flow down to the Indian subcontinent. The "serpent king residing therein," mythologically the source of the world's wealth, naturally will benefit all the world. Verse two mentions the Buddha, son of King Suddhodana, from India "the land of four castes," who has but one job to complete: that of bringing benefit to the world. Verse three introduces the Unmoving Buddha, Akshobhya, who here represents the form in which the Buddha gave the tantric teachings, the essence of which is the four enlightenment activities: peace, increase, power, and wrath. By teaching beings to transcend ordinariness and embrace these four enlightenment activities as essential lifestyle perspectives, trainees are led to their own deeper nature, which is the inner guru.

The fourth verse shows how this is accomplished, namely, by relying on the outer guru. Here the "human form with four wheels so auspicious" refers to human beings born with four auspicious qualities: being born in a place where the enlightenment tradition thrives, having contact with a spiritual master or masters, having interest in spiritual matters, and being a vessel with a store of positive karma. Any human being in possession of these four qualities can achieve enlightenment, and without them enlightenment will not occur.

The fifth verse points to how the outer and inner gurus can be brought into synchronicity, which is by seeing the outer guru as the embodiment of the tantric mandala deities, and training accordingly.

◆ *Four Rivers*

Om svasti!
Four rivers flow clockwise
Down Mount Kailash and on to the ocean,
Bed of infinite treasures,
The serpent king residing therein
Wearing seven snakes as a headdress.
Why should he not benefit the world?

On the vast plateau of Vulture's Peak,
In the navel of the land of four castes,
Sat the incomparable Gautama Buddha,
Illustrious son of King Suddhodana.
Why should he not give refuge
To beings endless as space?

A circle of light which bestows the four actions,
The pure sphere of the Unmoving Buddha,
Where mind and energies emanate as five buddhas:
There sits the ultimate refuge, the inner guru.
Why should he not dispel the sufferings of
Practitioners of good fortune?

This human form with four wheels so auspicious,
By the waters of Dharma ever is nourished.
O my guru, whether my aspirations be true or false,

You alone have power to know.
Powerful master on whom I rely,
Never leave me behind.

Lama who reveals the three supreme mysteries,
I see you as mandala deity, daka, and dakini.
Hear this prayer always kept in my heart
And rain down siddhis mundane and supreme.

Song to Jey Rinpochey

The poem that follows is again one that the Seventh Dalai Lama wrote on his pilgrimage to the sacred meditation sites of Olkha, where Lama Tsongkhapa had made his long retreats and accomplished realization. It is the last entry in the collection that was actually signed by the Seventh Dalai Lama; the remaining five items are attributed to him, but do not bear his signature.

The colophon to this piece reads, "Written by the knowledge holder and Buddhist monk Lobzang Kalzang Gyatso." It does not give a date or place of composition. However, Tsechok Ling identifies these factors in his biographical account.

The poem is important in that it identifies, in the first six verses, the six factors that the Seventh Dalai Lama considers to be the *kyey cho*, or "unique qualities," of the lineages coming from Lama Tsongkhapa and his disciples. Although these are clearly stated in the verses, it may be useful to list them in a less poetic language: (1) academic excellence coupled with spiritual practice and realization from the Sutrayana side of the Buddha's teachings, (2) embodiment of tantric knowledge from the Vajrayana side of the Buddha's teachings, (3) being a lineage that draws into itself the complete system of 84,000 teachings from the Buddha, and not merely some facet or other of the tradition, (4) having a presentation of the emptiness doctrine (of the Sutrayana schools) that is free from all constraints, (5) having a presentation of the Mahamudra teaching (from the Vajrayana schools) that takes physical pleasure and mental radiance as its supports, and (6) being a way that does not compromise itself in the face of the world, but rather holds to the enlightenment way and prevails under all circumstances.

In the concluding verse the Seventh Dalai Lama celebrates the spiritual knowledge and joy that he achieved through the practice of the lineages from Tsongkhapa, and expresses the conviction that those who read his poem and appreciate its meaning will achieve similar results.

◆ *Song to Jey Rinpochey*

Ah Jey Rinpochey, in nature wisdom, compassion, and power,
    whose legacy is not a stack of dry words,
Whose successors, having won all realizations,
Hold the transforming powers that bestow insight:
Ah-ho-ye, what a legacy, what a legacy.

Ah Jey Rinpochey, embodiment of Buddha Vajradhara,
Not an exponent of shallow or false theories,
Guru who is a supreme mahasiddha
Outshining all other masters:
Ah-ho-ye, what a guru, what a guru.

The oral transmissions of the Ganden patriarchs
Contain not a fraction but all of Buddha's teachings.
Core instructions on all theories and practices,
They take the essence of every sutra and tantra in hand:
Ah-ho-ye, what core instructions, what core instructions.

Your spacelike yogas, free from philosophical extremes,
Reveal not something invented by mind,
But are the pinnacle of visions into the way things are,
A way divorced from the dusts of "is" and "is not":
Ah-ho-ye, what a pinnacle, what a pinnacle.

Your Mahamudra lineage, blissful and beyond intellect,
Cannot be reached by mere samadhi, but
Only by the meditation on bliss and radiance
That reveals the ultimate nature of one's own mind:
Ah-ho-ye, what a meditation, what a meditation.

Your methods, sure and in harmony with the Way,
Are not a vain pretense aimed at impressing others,
But, keeping in mind what brings progress and what stagnation,
They aim solely at producing eternal bliss in trainees:
Ah-ho-ye, what an aim, what an aim.

And I, a laughing vajra who opens in delight,
Sing not babble devoid of purpose.
Some who see this will know joy,
A delight both to themselves and to me:
Ah-ho-ye, what a joy, what a joy.

NOTE FROM THE TIBETAN COMPILER

The remaining works of this collection were not written at the requests of disciples but rather are spontaneous creations of Lama Kalzang Gyatso's pen. They have neither dates nor names of places of their creation. Each of them was composed in a single session, and not one word of them was thereafter changed from the way they originally appeared.

Although somewhat different in style from the previous songs in this collection, there is no reason to doubt that they are indeed by Gyalwa Kalzang Gyatso. Small in size but profound in meaning, they are extremely useful for anyone interested in spiritual development, and therefore are included.

An Autumn Day

As the Tibetan compiler of this collection has said above, none of the remaining poems in the collection have either dates of composition or place names with which to identify them. Nonetheless all five are considered to be by the Seventh Dalai Lama.

The first and shortest of the five works in this section is a beautiful little poem, perhaps the greatest in the collection, that the Seventh wrote on the half-moon day while in retreat one autumn. He uses the natural imagery of his environment to express the spiritual feelings that are pressing upon him. He ends by saying how, even in the face of great beauty, the flow of inner thoughts still determines the quality of the experience.

◆ *An Autumn Day*

O kind root guru, Vajradhara incarnate,
Treasury of Mahayana teachings,
In nature Buddha, Dharma, and Sangha,
Pray, sit in joy on the lotus at my heart.

In the eighth day of an autumn month
In a year of meditation;
My mind flows aimless.
I try to control it—
It, not still; me, brought down.

The sky of unstained space,
I thought to blend my mind with it.
The center of fresh, hanging clouds,
I thought to touch their softness.

Like mist in the wind,
This mind yearns to drift.
Before the sun turns red and sets,
I would leave behind all squalor.

I thought to gain a stable mind,
A lotus pool in a field of bliss.
Mind looks everywhere;
Melancholy visions flow out from within.

A Song in Paired Verses

The second of the unsigned poems in the collection is a piece reminiscent in structure of two earlier works, "In the Twelfth Month of the Water Dog Year," and "Images." This is a classical Tibetan poetic style in which two verses are strung together as pairs, with the first verse presenting a natural image and the second associating a spiritual symbolism with it. In the first of the three poems of this nature he uses six-line verses coupled together to make twelve lines for each pair; in the second he uses eight-line verses coupled into sixteen lines; and here he uses four-line verses to form eight-line pairs.

♦ *A Song in Paired Verses*

The young tigerlike bee
Holds no great lust for sweetness;
Yet when the lotus flower has nectar,
To drink is that very bee's nature.

> The dakinis who fly below and above
> Have abandoned all ordinary hate and love;
> Yet when one's yogic practice has mystic discipline,
> The dakinis release great bliss essence.

The sun this world illuminating,
No sense of pride entertaining,
From high in the heavens is shining,
A result of the merit of beings.

Should the sun of wisdom and method
Throughout a pure, clear mind be spread,
Of arrogance and haughtiness there is none,
Yet unto the world is one a gem.

The bright white moon sweetly smiling
In actual size is not changing;
The sun's light makes it wax and wane
As sun, earth, and moon alter position.

    The guru, embodiment of all highest sages,
    Actually never improves nor degenerates;
    Yet as the disciple's negative karmas ripen
    He mistakenly understands the guru's three perfect dances.

The stars, jewel ornaments of space,
With one another do not run race;
Because of the earth's rotations,
They swing across the heavens.

    The gurus, tantric deities, and dakinis
    For ambitions have no yearnings;
    In accordance with a trainee's evolution
    They descend and induce liberation.

The fresh white clouds hovering above
For altitudes have no love;
Due to the nature of wind and heat
They are carried high, and high do sit.

    Those who strive, the good to accomplish,
    Have their minds set not on prestige;
    Yet as the wheels of karma slowly turn
    Their fires of honor ever higher burn.

The autumn sky sparklingly clear
Was not by an artist polished so fair;
When from transient shadows it is free,
Indeed it is a delight to the eye.

    The rootless, ultimate nature of things
    Is not the creation of some recent thinker;
    When at last highest truth is known,
    False essence fades to itself and is gone.

The rainbow with its radiance and play
Has no basis on which to rely;
From conditions and the workings of lights
Magically spring five colors so bright.

> The things that appear outside and in
> Have no self-nature to reveal.
> From the fantasies of an ill-taught mind,
> We know a reality with false images entwined.

Guru Inseparable

In this song, the Seventh writes to his gurus, expressing all the classical ideas on the guru-disciple relationship in tantric Buddhism. It is a highly personal piece, in which he expresses his hopes, fears, and spiritual aspirations. In it we see a young man coming to terms with the destiny that has been thrown upon him, with his yearnings to surmount his personal weaknesses and live up to the expectations that his people have of him.

♦ *Guru Inseparable*

Guru inseparable from the Dharmakaya,
Spontaneous light pure from the beginning,
Wisdom embracing all objects of knowledge,
Awareness beyond any sign of fault:
I turn to you for inspiration.

Guru inseparable from the Sambhogakaya,
Who, although formless in Dharmakaya's bliss,
Arises as the primordial Adibuddha Vajradhara,
A lord of the five buddha families, possessor of seven kisses:
I turn to you for inspiration.

Guru inseparable from the Nirmanakaya,
A magic stone, a wish-fulfilling tree,
Compassionate and deathless one

Manifesting infinite bodies for infinite trainees:
I turn you for inspiration.

Guru embodying all spiritual masters,
Who brings buddhahood to us of such poor fate
That all the countless buddhas of the past
Did not come near us to tame our minds:
I turn to you for inspiration.

Guru embodying all mandala deities,
Who abides in a vajra palace of wisdom
And, by means of emanating transcendental phantasms,
Shows himself in countless peaceful and wrathful forms:
I turn to you for inspiration.

Guru embodying all dakinis,
A thought of whom breaks open the wheel
of every samsaric preconception
And grants the rhythm of great bliss:
I turn to you for inspiration.

Guru embodying all Dharma protectors,
The playful one who performs a vajra dance
To crush the terrifying armies of demons
That bring chaos to a dark, deluded mind:
I turn to you for inspiration.

When the guru radiates lights of compassion,
The fog of ignorance instantly disperses
To reveal the seat of that to be known.
To the Jetsun, Lord of the Sun, I turn.

When the guru releases white beams of love,
One's every mental ache is soothed
And ambrosial joys arise from within.
To the Jetsun, Lord of the Moon, I turn.

When the guru is like a crown upon one's head,
The purposes of this and of future lives
Quickly and effortlessly are fulfilled.
To the Jetsun, the Wish-Fulfilling Gem, I turn.

When the guru showers a rain of Dharma,
The heat of mental distortions cools
And the healing tree of insight blossoms.
To the Jetsun, Lord of the Gods, I turn.

When the guru would remove a disciple's illness,
He applies the medicine of wise and effective means
To cure the disciple of aversion, attachment, and ignorance.
To the Jetsun, a Medicine Buddha, I turn.

When the guru would act as a hero to beings,
He generates the sword of wisdom within them
And has them sever the head of their own ignorance.
To the Jetsun, a true warrior, I turn.

His intellect, radiant with five wisdoms,
Rests in the taste of dharmadhatu awareness
And fills the universe with tantric emanations.
To the master, an ocean of good fortune, I turn.

Were I to search everywhere forever,
No refuge greater than the guru could be found.
O Lama, look upon me with compassion.
I rely upon you now and hereafter.

I was born a human with the potential of enlightenment,
Yet seldom do I really practice Dharma,
And life passes almost entirely to the futile.
O Lama, look with compassion upon this vain being.

Everyday I see old and young people die,
Yet, not thinking that death will come to me,
I will be unprepared when it falls.
O Lama, look with compassion upon this clinger.

I have heard about the lower realms,
Yet, not having experienced true understanding,
I casually walk a precipice dropping to them.
O Lama, look with compassion upon this endangered one.

I do not want even a small pain,
Yet, misusing my body, speech, and mind,

There is a danger that misery will ensue.
O Lama, look with compassion upon one who errs.

I wish to know unending joy,
Yet, living in opposition to the Dharma,
I have no real confidence in my future.
O Lama, look with compassion upon one bereft of hope.

The objects of spiritual refuge are countless,
Yet, unable to lift my eyes to them,
I am a corpse thrown to the dogs.
O Lama, look with compassion upon one without redemption.

I find myself as a human radiant with life,
Yet like a traveler in a rented room,
Soon, so soon, I must leave all behind.
O Lama, look with compassion upon this drifter.

One may find a treasure vast as the earth,
Yet, like honey collected by a bee,
It would be as wealth held for another.
O Lama, look with compassion upon this pauper.

Friends and relatives surround me,
Yet so easily they could come to hate me.
They endanger both themselves and me.
O Lama, look with compassion upon this lone traveler.

The more material comforts we acquire,
The heavier the anguish in our minds;
Rarely do we pause for spiritual joy.
O Lama, look with compassion upon this weakling.

I think to apply myself to Dharma,
But, constantly assailed by mental distortions,
Everything I do only helps the samsaric mind.
O Lama, look with compassion upon this lost one.

I have heard and contemplated the profound Dharma,
Yet have not strangled the mind of pretence, and hence
Not a fraction of real practice is ever carried out.
O Lama, look with compassion upon this egoist.

The commitments of the three bonds are countless,
Yet, because of my bottomless apathy,
I constantly break them, the roots of insight.
O Lama, look with compassion upon this hypocrite.

The basis of the Great Way is the bodhimind,
Yet, my heart is locked in hostile attitudes, and
The bodhimind is a thing very far from my heart.
O Lama, look with compassion upon this selfish one.

I have vowed to attain buddhahood,
But, not having lived the ways of a bodhisattva,
My time for progress has not yet come.
O Lama, look with compassion upon this lazy soul.

Nothing has ever really existed,
Yet my mind, lost in eternal fantasy,
Has not cut the root of confusion.
O Lama, look with compassion upon this fool.

I have ripened my mind with tantric initiations,
But, unable to maintain the Vajrayana precepts,
Have not pleased the gurus or mandala deities.
O Lama, look with compassion upon this lunatic.

The seeds of enlightenment lie within me,
Yet, not having integrated the oral teachings,
The thought of attainment seems hopeless.
O Lama, look with compassion upon this unfortunate one.

Until now everything I have done has
Been polluted by the eight worldly concerns,
And not the slightest progress has been made.
O Lama, look with compassion upon this fool.

All-knowing Lama, forever befriend me;
For though I have tried in many ways,
I have not yet won enlightenment
Nor even closed the doors to misery.

All-knowing guru, never abandon me;
Wherever in the six realms I may happen to wander,

Keep me wrapped in the arms of your samadhi,
For I am captured by karma and delusion.

All-knowing Lama, never forsake me;
I, one fallen into the waters of bondage,
Can look only to you as my refuge and teacher
Until the ocean of suffering is crossed.

Melancholy Visions

The Seventh Dalai Lama was not an idealist. He lived in a difficult era of Tibetan history, and witnessed several civil wars. Although Tibet as a culture placed great emphasis upon spirituality, meditation, yoga, and so forth, and every one of its valleys was adorned with several monasteries, temples, and retreat hermitages, he understood the difference between a general commitment to the enlightenment way and the specific situations of individual human beings. He admired the former, and sympathized with the latter.

This poem could perhaps be viewed as a list of all the inherent weaknesses in the human spirit, and all the possible ways that things can go wrong in spiritual life. He does not point the finger at others, however, but follows the old Kadampa saying, "Whenever you see a fault in others, attribute it to yourself. That way you will get the benefit, and will learn from other's mistakes."

The song is in three sections. The first of these is comprised of the two introductory verses, in which he relates the mental perspective from which he writes. The next thirty-four verses, all ending with the refrain "a melancholy scene," describe the pitfalls and weaknesses of mankind and the world in which he lives. The eleven concluding verses are thoughts to hold in the mind in order to navigate successfully through the treacherous waters of human existence and thereby to progress along the path to enlightenment.

I have found this little text to be quite useful as a contemplative tool. If read at the beginning of every meditation session, it helps to deflate some of the arrogance and elitism that sometimes comes from misdirected spiritual practice.

◆ *Melancholy Visions*

Rising sun who disperses dark ignorance,
All-kind guru in nature Manjushri-Vajra,
Lord possessing the five certainties beneath none,
Pray, rest on the lotus unfolding within my heart.

Watching how unskillful actions bring confusion,
And how non-Dharmic people masquerade as practitioners
And play games that create only unnecessary burdens,
My heart filled with sadness, giving birth to this song.

If this semblance of humanity born of good karma
Is bound in chains of continuous craving,
It finds no time for the joys of the soul:
A melancholy scene, oneself harming oneself.

The body of a youth with flesh and blood abounding,
By years, months, and days ever decays.
Look anywhere at the body or mind—youth ages:
A melancholy scene, life reflecting death.

The ferocious gorillas of various elements gathered
In the barren land of five lordless aggregates
Rush in to devour the slender thread of life:
A melancholy scene, a body fragile as a bubble.

From very birth, life pauses not for a moment
But races onward toward the great Lord of Death.
Life is a walk down a wide road to its own end:
A melancholy scene, a criminal being led to execution.

Since beginningless time one has walked in samsara,
Yet neither oneself nor others have arrived.
One has known every pain, but still has not learned:
A melancholy scene, a lunatic hurting self and others.

One has wandered from top to bottom of existence
And has owned houses and lands for flashes in time;
But these are things one can hold for but a moment:
A melancholy scene, a pilgrim attached to a rented bed.

In previous lives, one has owned jewels vast as the earth,
But riches, gathered with greed and unable to satisfy,
Soon fall into the hands of others:
A melancholy scene, an old dog guarding its master's house.

When wealth and fame come, friends and relatives gather,
But though one is good to them, with the smallest condition
They turn hostile and feel only enmity:
A melancholy scene, kindness left unreturned.

The ways of a disciple are charming and sweet,
Yet if mixed with the habit of seeing faults in the guru,
They become a broom sweeping away the potential of both:
A melancholy scene, a prisoner tormented by his keepers.

Day and night one feeds one's stomach,
Yet only bad karma, stress, and confusion ensue.
The body of fallible elements easily becomes an enemy:
A melancholy scene, being dependent upon a weak protector.

The restless mind, roaming like an angry wind,
Helplessly is drawn to the channels of the senses.
It runs mad, unable to pause for a moment on the useful:
A melancholy scene, a living being propelled by delusion.

Busily we collect the useless luxuries of this life,
But the more we get, the more we disturb self and others.
Hoarding wealth but provokes a flood of problems:
A melancholy scene, a small gain for a huge loss.

The person who always gets but never gives,
And consumes what people hold dear as their flesh,
Is a devil obscuring his own happiness:
A melancholy scene, thinking poison is medicine.

Countless tortures are suffered by the beings of the hells,
As molten earth and flames from red-hot houses of iron
Burn everything inside and out:
A melancholy scene, being used as fuel for hell's fires.

The ghost searches in vain for a million years,
His days and nights only cycles of misery,

Yet neither friend nor environment can help him:
A melancholy scene, everything seeming hostile.

The animal lives in a vicious and cruel world.
He suffers from enslavement by others, and
His mind is blind as a rock to spiritual potential:
A melancholy scene, having no hope of liberation.

In the realms of the lower gods, the possessions of others
Only kindle flames of jealousy and pierce the heart like a thorn.
The only difference between that and hell is altitude:
A melancholy scene, a life and death passed in vain.

The desire gods enjoy every pleasure,
But never for a moment know satisfaction,
And, to them, death is hell itself:
A melancholy scene, attachment to a child's toys.

In the form and formless realms born from samadhi,
One knows bliss sublime. But led by karma and delusion,
Again one must plunge to infinite misery:
A melancholy scene, a marmot imitating a meditator.

Now as the sun of Buddhadharma is setting,
Most practitioners live in complete opposition to truth,
All they do is kill time:
A melancholy scene, using Dharma for mere show.

Inexperienced lamas force dry words, never understood,
Into the ears of lazy, faithless disciples,
Who in turn throw Dharma into depths of pettiness:
A melancholy scene, teacher and student but acting out roles.

The law speaks of justice, but favors the powerful;
Citizens cannot use freely even what they own,
While everybody abuses everyone higher than themselves:
A melancholy scene, head and tail each worse than the other.

The karmic fruit of harming others bursts,
And covers our walls with every spiteful condition,
Inviting a swarm of evil men, gods, and spirits:
A melancholy scene, a man condemning himself.

That called samsara is a house of scorching iron
Blazing with misery in every room.
It seems so normal that it wearies the spirit:
A melancholy scene, wandering through savage lands.

Look at any man or woman, high or low—
They may differ in dress, character and strength,
But finally, enmeshed in misery, they are made one:
A melancholy scene, friends and relatives of equal ill-fortune.

One tries to practice and develop one's mind,
But, because of beginningless immersion in darkness,
The white mind of truth rarely is seen:
A melancholy scene, effort producing no fruit.

It may seem that one is following a spiritual path,
Yet if one's practice is tied to the eight worldly concerns
It is only a matter of calling samsaric activity spiritual:
A melancholy scene, everything going wrong.

Every experience of the cold waters of suffering
Is a result of one's own previous karma alone,
A product of one's own mistakes:
A melancholy scene, blaming anything on another.

If there is a way to become free from misery,
One should use each moment to achieve it.
Only the fool wants more pain:
A melancholy scene, knowingly eating poison.

The pup addicted to mindlessness should look
At his conduct, which lacks awareness of Dharma,
For he is swimming into the depths of a sea of turmoil:
A melancholy scene, not working for liberation.

The masses, propelled by the black wind of delusion,
Wander helplessly in ways as dangerous and rough
As a mountain pass, and the end is still far away:
A melancholy scene, the ripening of previous negativity.

The holy teachers discard as grass their own interests
And walk the path which always only benefits others,

Yet we look on them as cunning and malicious:
A melancholy scene, scorning the wish-fulfilling cow.

Pretending to show the path of freedom to another
When one's own mind is not at one with truth
Is merely a cause of exhausting the two:
A melancholy scene, deceiving self and others.

As this age of five darknesses ever deepens,
Duplicity and falsity everywhere abound.
And things just get uglier with each passing year:
A melancholy scene, mankind reaching the bottom.

O precious gurus, eradicators of misery, look
At how violence, evil, and confusion thrive.
Masters who developed the bodhimind for all beings,
Teachers, objects of refuge, never abandon the world.

Others have experienced the same sufferings as have I,
For all of samsara tosses in waves of pain.
May we be aware of the faults of lacking spiritual joy,
And never lose sight of the detached mind.

The practice of gentleness, free of hostility,
Brings happiness in both this and future lives.
Therefore, may we see as more kind than our parents
Those who harm us and thus give us the chance
To train in the mind of sublime patience.

The eighty thousand types of obstructing spirits that surround us
Are but teachers to propel us on the path of Dharma.
Therefore, may we see them as guru, tantric deity, and
     Dharma protector,
And exert ourselves even more for enlightenment.

When body and mind throb with aches beyond conception,
May we make a profound effort to visualize them
As friends who share our ripening black karma,
And thus may our thoughts abide in unmoving joy.

In brief, whenever any harm befalls us,
May we see our pain as the product of negative mind;

May we meditate on taking the world's misery upon ourself,
For thus are negative conditions turned into aids on the path.

Looking inside, one's own body and mind don't exist to be harmed.
Looking out, harmful agents are like a rope mistakenly seen as a
    snake.
Therefore may we understand suffering as the creation of a mind
That sees as true that which is mere mental fabrication.

Although one may receive the heart of Buddha's teachings
From the mouth of a fully experienced master,
Still, it is difficult to tame one's own mind,
For we have long been addicted to samsaric ways.

Suffering and pain pervade this entire world;
Therefore I pray we may shed it as a snake sheds its skin,
And quickly reach such abodes of perfection
As Sukhavati, Pure Land of Bliss, and Vajrayogini's Kajou Shing.

Having entered the sublime path of tantric yoga,
May we bring the scenes of a world polluted by ignorance
Into the focus of wisdom peerless and supreme,
And thus spontaneously become a circle of three kayas.

May we discover the firmness of perfect enlightenment
And then release activity manifesting effectively
For worldly beings tormented by ghosts of duality.
Thus may the name of samsara be erased.

A Hymn to Milarepa

The Lam Rim and Lojong transmissions that inspired the works in *Songs and Advice for Spiritual Change* are most comprehensively preserved in the Geluk and Kargyu schools. As the Tibetan compiler of the anthology included a number of hymns and prayers to Lama Tsongkhapa, founder of the Geluk School, I felt it would also be good to include one of the Seventh's hymns to Milarepa, forefather of the Kargyu school, found in another of the Seventh's many collections of verse works.

The colophon to the Milarepa hymn reads, "Written at the request of the saintly Hotuktu Mergan Khenpo Ngawang Lobzang Khetsun, who asked for a prayer to the great yogi Milarepa that would fulfill the sacred pledges of the five dhyani buddhas." This, I presume, is the same monk who requested "Song to Build a Link with the Lama."

Milarepa is one of Tibet's favorite poets and saints. The chief disciple of the eleventh-century master Marpa Lotsawa, he is always held up as the example of someone who, against all odds, achieved enlightenment. His father died when he was a child, and the family farm was stolen by his uncle. As a result he grew up in abject poverty. He vowed revenge on his uncle, and eventually killed him as well as over thirty of his uncle's friends. At this point in his life, Milarepa seemed to be headed on a path of negative karma and darkness from which there would be no easy return.

However, a series of events occurred that caused him to reflect on what he had done, and he repented of the murders he had committed. He went to the master Marpa and requested spiritual teachings. Marpa accepted him as a disciple, and placed him on an intense course of self-purification. After several years of this, Marpa introduced him to the highest yoga tantra methods, and sent him off into the mountains to meditate. Eighteen years later he achieved enlightenment.

Milarepa is most famous for his spontaneously composed mystical songs. In fact, he did not write anything himself, but disciples kept records of his songs, and eventually they were published as a book, the *Mila Gurbum*, or *100,000 Songs of Milarepa*, which became an immediate hit across Central Asia. Today, almost eight hundred years later, it seems there is not a single Tibetan who cannot quote passages from Milarepa by heart. The Dalai Lamas all read his biography and mystical songs, and quote freely from him in their writings.

The Seventh Dalai Lama was especially enamored of Milarepa, and looked to his life and deeds for inspiration and direction. He wrote several hymns to him. I chose this one for the collection because the concluding verses are inspired by themes from the Lam Rim and Lojong transmissions.

◆ *A Hymn to Milarepa*

High on the snowy peaks of Tibet
A yogi pursued intense meditation
And burned the forest of inner poisons.
Thus through skillful method, his wisdom
Soared in the sky of truth,
The way things are.

His name was Milarepa, the people's delight,
And Zhepai Dorjey, "the Laughing Vajra."
He was a mountain towering over all yogis.
At his golden feet I offer this hymn
To cause the vital energy of realization
To enter the drop of vajra life at the heart.

In the skies before me, the wisdom of bliss and void
Manifest as a field laden with precious jewels
And adorned with medicinal herbs,
Beautiful lotuses and kingly trees filled
With serene birds to delight the mind.

There on an antelope skin
Sits Milarepa, the Laughing Vajra,
At the mouth of a mountain cave
Radiant with lights of five colors.
His legs are in the half-vajra posture
And his body has a bluish hue.
From his lips a vajra song
Melodiously resounds far and wide.

He sits amidst a brilliant halo,
His white cotton cloth a web of light.
Countless dakas and dakinis dance around him
As he smiles with joy upon the world.

Lights burst forth from his heart
And summon a limitless ocean
Of peaceful and wrathful mandala deities
Who, dancing magical dramas,
Dissolve into his body.

Clouds of wisdom, compassion, and power
Appear in the sky and release
A rainfall of transforming powers,
A shower of inspiring blessings.

Wondrous yogi who attained the vajra body,
Whose speech had a buddha's sixty qualities
And whose mind was great bliss
Spontaneously aware of all things—
O marvelous guru, I salute you.

Golden bowls of crystal clear water,
Flowers tossed to earth by the gods,
Incense that pervades the universe,
Butterlamps bright as the sun and moon,
Exotic perfumes that invoke joy,
Foods of a hundred satiating flavors, and
Delightful songs to fill the skies:
These and all things real and imagined
In their outer, inner, and secret forms
I create with the force of meditation
And offer in the presence of the sages.

O venerable yogi who in one lifetime
Attained the state of perfect buddhahood
By practicing intensely day and night,
I rejoice in your most wondrous deeds.

Turn countless wheels of Dharma
That protect living beings from samsara and nirvana.
Release your magnificent vajra speech,
One sound of which brings liberation.

For as long as the sun and moon shine,
Send your enlightened energy to this world,
Mysterious emanations to dance
Into the lives of spiritually ripe beings.

More kind than all the buddhas
Who are complete in freedom and insight
Is one's own spiritual teacher.
O Milarepa, bestow your inspiring powers
That practitioners may meet perfect masters
And with pure thoughts may follow them.

A human birth with spiritual endowments
Is a fortune held but for a moment;
Inspire us to take life's essence
By avoiding the eight worldly concerns.

The evening of life approaches;
The shadows of dusk grow long;
Breath is lost like a passing stream.
Inspire us to always abide in wisdom
And to dedicate what time we have
To the practice of ways good and sublime.

Swept away on a raging river
Of negative karma and destructive ways,
Living beings are washed into the dungeons
Of the three lower realms,
Where anguish continues without respite.
Inspire us to live in detachment
From ordinary samsaric craving
Through seeing that the addictions of men and gods alike
Are but so much excrement.

Caught in the chains of grasping at an "I,"
The living beings, in many past lives my mother,
Boil inside with the heat of delusion
And outside are cut and are wounded
By the vicious weapons of misfortune.
O venerable Guru, inspire us to quickly attain
The perfection of the three perfect kayas
So that we may be forever be empowered
To free them from samsara's terrors.

Inspire us to cut the inner chains
Of the eight worldly concerns,
Which tie the mind to turmoil;
And that with single-pointed concentration
We may practice and accomplish the yogas
Of the Sutrayana and Mantrayana paths.

O gracious guru, grant inspiring blessings
So that throughout this life,
In the bardo and in all future lives,
We may never be parted from teachers of the Great Way
And we may help mature and free the world.

Glossary

acharya: (Tib. *slob-dpon*) A Sanskrit title indicating someone who has completed spiritual training.

aggregate: *See* skandha.

Akshobhya: As a Dhyani Buddha, Akshobhya represents the positive pole of the skandha of consciousness, the highest manifestation of the space element, and the wisdom of dharmadhatu. He is often used in a general sense to represent Buddha Vajradhara.

arhat: (Tib. *dgra-bcom-pa*) Literally "foe destroyer." One who has destroyed delusion. The arhat is the Hinayana ideal, whereas the Mahayana ideal is the bodhisattva.

arya: *See* High One.

Atisha: The eleventh-century Indian sage who brought to Tibet the Lojong teachings on which the poems of this collection are based. Atisha was one of the most important gurus ever to travel to Tibet, and his teachings have come to form major foundation stones for all sects of Tibetan Buddhism. He was the first Indian teacher ever to reunite all lineages coming from Buddha, and his work in Tibet saved Buddhism there from degeneration and extinction. His contributions to tantric thought are unequalled.

Avalokiteshvara: (Tib. *sPyan-ras-gzigs*) The Bodhisattva of Compassion, known in Tibetan as Chenrezig. Provoked by the endless suffering of living beings, he vowed to continue incarnation in the six realms of samsara until all creatures had attained enlightenment. The line of Dalai Lamas is considered to be his foremost incarnation at this time. Important earlier incarnations were King Songtsen Gampo, King Trisong Deutsen, and Lama Drom Tonpa. Buddha gave many of the sutras on the Perfection of Wisdom to Avalokiteshvara.

Awakened One: *See* Buddha.

bardo: Commonly refers to the state between death and rebirth, which has three phases: the bardo of the moment of death, the bardo of the visions of reality, and the bardo of becoming, or moving toward rebirth.

bodhi: (Tib. *byang-chub*) The first syllable of the Tibetan term refers to the cleansing of the two obscurations; the second refers to an expansion of mind to an understanding of the two truths.

bodhimind: (Tib. *byang-chub-sems*) The enlightened mind, or the Mahayana attitude, of which two types are identified: conventional and ultimate. The former is of two types: wishing bodhimind, which aspires to enlightenment as the best tool with which most deeply to benefit all living beings; and the actual bodhimind, which, on the basis of wishing bodhimind, practices the six perfections. Ultimate bodhimind is the experience of emptiness based upon the above motivation.

In the three lower classes of tantra, bodhimind is synonymous with samadhi. In highest yoga tantra, bodhimind is differentiated into red and white bodhimind, symbolized respectively by ovum and sperm. These are the essential female and male forces of Being, and they represent wisdom and method. When united, the red and white bodhiminds support the innate wisdom of voidness and great bliss.

bodhisattva: (Tib. *byang-chub-sems-dpa'*) One who possesses the bodhimind, that is, a Mahayana practitioner. Bodhisattvas are of two types: ordinary bodhisattvas, who possess the conventional bodhimind, and aryas, who have experienced the ultimate bodhimind.

Buddha: (Tib. *sangs-rgyas*) Historically this is Siddhartha, who 2,500 years ago attained enlightenment and became known as Buddha Shakyamuni. Philosophically, it is anyone who attains enlightenment. The first syllable of the Tibetan term means "purified of the two obscurations"; the second syllable literally means "increase," and implies the expansion of wisdom to the understanding of the two levels of truth.

Buddhadharma: *See* Dharma.

Buddhafield: The pure land, or paradise, created by a buddha's meditation and power, into which devotees of good fortune may take rebirth in order to continue their development toward enlightenment.

Buddhahood: (Tib. *sangs-rgyas-kyi-go-'phang*) The state of full enlightenment, wherein all obstacles are overcome and all knowledge and good qualities are attained. *See* Buddha.

Chenrezig: *See* Avalokiteshvara.

clear light: A tantric term for the ultimate nature of mind. This level of mind is experienced by yogins on the second level of samadhi, and also momentarily by ordinary beings during the transition between waking and sleep and at the moment of death.

compassion: Technically, the active wish that others be freed from suffering. It is not to be confused with *pity*, which is a lesser term, nor with *bodhimind*, which is greater.

consequentialists: (Skt. *prasangika*) The Madhyamaka followers of Nagarjuna, as interpreted by Buddhapalita and Chandrakirti. They originally gained this name because they did not formally present a separate system, but used logic to show that the beliefs of the other systems led to absurd consequences. They are also called Consequentialists because they claim that the experience of emptiness is a consequence of philosophical investigation,

conventional truth: (Tib. *kun-rdzob-bden-pa*) Literally "all-false truth." This pertains to all levels of being other than emptiness. It is called "all-false" because ordinary beings are deceived by it, but still is truth (*bden-pa*) because it is knowable by a Buddha (though not in a way comprehended by ordinary beings).

daka: The male equivalent of the dakini. The daka represents the active energy of wisdom, whereas the dakini represents the intuitive energy.

dakini: A female tantric deity embodying the creative element of wisdom.

Dharma: (Tib. *chos*) This has two levels of meaning: in a general sense, Dharma stands for any object of knowledge; more specifically, it means spiritual or religious knowledge, defined as "that which holds back the mind from states of suffering." Buddhadharma is the Dharma taught by Buddha.

dharmadhatu: Literally "the sphere of truth." Usually used as a name for emptiness, but sometimes used to indicate the consciousness perceiving emptiness.

Dharmakaya: The mind of a buddha. More generally, Dharmakaya is the highest level of manifestation within Being. *See also* three kayas.

Dharma protectors: There are two types: worldly, which are ordinary gods, mountain spirits, etc., that have been bound by a tantric master to protect Buddhism and its practitioners; and non-worldly, which are manifestations of various buddhas in wrathful forms, dedicated to protecting practitioners of specific tantras.

divine pride: (Tib. *lha'i-nga-rgyal*) The tantric practice of visualizing oneself as a buddha, the world as a mandala, and sounds as mantra.

Drom Tonpa: Lama Drom Tonpa, the main disciple of Atisha. Drom received most of Atisha's lineages, including the Lojong.

eight antidotes to the obstacles of meditation: Confidence, aspiration, enthusiasm, physical and mental pliancy, mindfulness, awareness, wise application of forces that oppose the obstacles, and skillful restraint in the application of them.

eightfold path: (Tib. *'phags-pa'i-lam-yan-lag-brgyad-pa*) The noble path of eight limbs. It is called "noble" because on a deeper level it is understood only by those with experience of emptiness. The eight limbs are: right understanding, right view, right speech, right action, right livelihood, right perseverance, right mindfulness, and right samadhi.

eight freedoms: (Tib. *dal-ba-brgyad*) Freedoms from the eight conditions that obstruct spiritual practice. Four apply to nonhuman and four to human conditions. The four nonhuman obstructions are being born as: a hell-being, a ghost, an animal, or a long-lived ghost. The four human non-freedoms are: holding very mistaken views, being a deaf-mute, being born in an era when no buddha has appeared, or being born into a barbaric society. Having freedom from all eight is to possess the eight freedoms conducive to spiritual practice.

eight-petal lotus: The Dharmachakra, or energy center at one's heart, where eight energy channels converge.

eight worldly dharmas: Concern with pleasure and pain, gain and loss, praise and scorn, fame and obscurity. When asked the dividing line between a religious and a nonreligious person, Lama Drom replied, "He not concerned with the eight worldly dharmas is religious; he concerned with the eight worldly winds is not religious."

emanation body: *See* three kayas.

emptiness: *See* shunyata.

energy channel: *See* nadi.

enlightened attitude: *See* bodhimind.

enlightened karma: (Tib. *'phrin-las*) The activities of a buddha. The term is also used for the activities of a daka, dakini, or Dharma protector because, although these beings may not be fully enlightened, their actions are largely inspired by tantric bonds (Tib. *dam-tshig*) with enlightened beings.

enlightenment: *See* bodhi.

esoteric path: (Tib. *thun-mong-ma-yin-pa'i-lam*) Literally "the uncommon path," this refers to the Vajrayana. It is called "uncommon" because it contains many practices not shared in common with the ordinary Buddhist path. It is also called "the secret path" (Tib. *gsang-ba'i-lam*), because its uncommon practices are not to be revealed to the uninitiated. The Dalai Lamas embody the fullest knowledge of the path containing both the Buddhist exoteric and esoteric practices.

exoteric path: (Tib. *thun-mong-gi-lam*) Literally "the common path," or Sutrayana, which is called exoteric because its practices are shared in common with and act as a basis for the esoteric Vajrayana.

extremes: In Buddhism, the extremes are the poles between which lie the middle path outlined by Buddha. Morally, this middle path lies between the extremes of yogically submitting the body to overly severe penances on the one hand, and sensual indulgence on the other. Theologically, it avoids the extremes of disbelief in life after death and belief in an eternal, unchanging soul. Philosophically, the Madhyamaka, or Middle Way, passes between the beliefs that things ultimately do or do not exist.

five aggregates: The five skandhas: form, feeling, distinguishing awareness, volitional formations, and primary consciousness.

five certainties: *See* Sambhogakaya.

five clear essences: The essences of the five elements of the body. The mystic drop is made of the subtlest forms of these.

five degenerations: Five very negative conditions of this degenerate (and degenerating) age: human life span is short, the era in general is pervaded by afflictive emotions, sentient beings are engrossed in their materiality, wrong views are the norm, and sentient beings need to contend with the fact of limited resources and the consequent struggle for survival.

five drops: Essences of the five elements of the body. By forming these drops into a nucleus and fixing the mind therein, the meditator's physical energy and consciousness become extremely subtle, thus permitting very refined meditation.

five eyes of knowledge: Special visionary powers gained on the basis of the first level of samadhi. The five are: (1) the eye of physical knowledge, which can see for hundreds of miles; (2) the divine eye, which can see the time of death of others; (3) the eye of wisdom, which understands emptiness; (4) the eye of Dharma, which understands the dispositions of others; and (5) the eye of a buddha, which is omniscient.

five heinous deeds: Killing one's father, one's mother, or an arhat, causing a schism in the Sangha, and drawing blood from a buddha.

five obstacles to meditation: Laziness, forgetfulness, lethargy or over-stimulation, non-application of the antidotes, and over-application of the antidotes.

five phases of the completion stage: Refining of the body, refining of the speech, the illusory body yoga, the clear light yoga, and the yoga of the great unification.

five poisons: Five distorted states of mind: ignorance, attachment, aversion, envy, and doubt.

five wisdoms: The opposites of the five poisons. The five wisdoms are: mirror-like wisdom, the wisdom of equality, distinguishing wisdom, accomplishing wisdom, and the wisdom of dharmadhatu.

four enlightenment activities: Four types of tantric activity: peace, increase, power, and wrath.

four noble truths: The four reality-factors perceived by the aryas, or Noble Ones: (1) unenlightened life is pervaded by suffering; (2) suffering is caused by karma and delusion; (3) there is a state beyond suffering; and (4) there is way for living beings to achieve that state, which is the reality-factor of the path.

four opponent forces: Four methods whereby the imprints of a negative deed are erased: contemplation of the negativity in order to develop a sense of remorse at having committed it; reliance upon the bodhimind and the objects of refuge as forces with the power to overcome the effects of negative karma; generation of a strong sense of resolve to turn away from recreating the deed in the future; and generation of counteracting meritorious forces, through recitation of the Vajrasattva mantra or the names of the Thirty-five Buddhas of Confession, meditation upon emptiness, etc.

Ganden: The name of the monastery established by Tsongkhapa, the founder of the Geluk sect and teacher of the First Dalai Lama. Ganden, a Tibetan translation of the Sanskrit term "Tushita," is also the name of the Pure Land of Maitreya Buddha.

ghost: (Tib. *yi-dags*) An inhabitant of the ghostly realm, one of the six realms of existence. A ghost is a product of, and is characterized by, craving. Tibetan demonology identifies more than fifty main types, some of which are helpful, some very harmful, and some ineffective. *See* six realms.

God of Wealth: (Skt. *Vaishravana*) "The king of the northern direction." Rituals focusing upon him are said to produce prosperity. There are many other deities of this nature, but Vaishravana is the most popular with Tibetans.

gods: (Tib. *lha*) There are two types: non-worldly gods, which refers to the buddhas and bodhisattvas; and worldly gods. The latter are of three main types: those of the realm of desire, who experience tremendous sensual delight; those of the realm of form, who are absorbed in meditation upon objects of ideation; and those of the formless realms, who are absorbed in meditation upon formless subjects. Of these three, the first is a product of virtuous actions, the second of form meditation, and the last of formless meditation. They are called worldly because when the force of their virtue or samadhi eventually weakens, they fall back to low, worldly states. I have alternatively translated the Sanskrit word *asura* as "fighting god," "antigod," and "lesser god." In Buddhist mythology the asuras are not grouped together with the three categories of gods, but are said to live lower on Mt. Meru and to be very jealous creatures who constantly make war on the gods, something like the Greek titans.

guru: *See* lama.

guru yoga: The practice of visualizing oneself as inseparably one with the guru, and, on a simpler level, of devoting oneself to the guru.

Heaven Beneath None: *See* Ogmin.

hell: The lowest realm in cyclic existence. Buddhist cosmology identifies twenty-two separate hell regions: eight hot, eight cold, four surrounding, and two proximate hells.

Heruka: (Tib. *bDe-mchog*) The wrathful form taken by Chenrezig in the female highest yoga tantra. The full name of the deity Heruka is Heruka Chakrasamvara. The Heruka Tantra is practiced by all four sects of Tibetan Buddhism.

High One: (Skt. *arya;* Tib. *'phags-pa*) That is, someone who has direct meditational experience of emptiness and consequently has gone above worldly states.

high rebirth: Rebirth as a human, a lesser god, or a god. These states are called "high" only because they occur above the hell, ghost, and animal realms, and because the level of happiness in them exceeds the level of suffering. However, although these states are good in that they are somewhat conducive to enlightenment, they are not finally beneficial. Therefore, rather than higher rebirth, the Buddhist seeks nirvana or enlightenment, the states beyond the world. High rebirth is sought only as a tool with which to work for enlightenment, not as an end in itself.

Hinayana: (Tib. *theg-dman*) The Lesser Vehicle. It is called lesser because: its motivation is personal liberation as opposed to the Mahayana motivation of full enlightenment for the benefit of all beings; its path is comprised of the three higher trainings, which lack the six perfections and the bodhimind of the Mahayana; its goal is nirvana, or the cessation of suffering, as opposed to the Mahayana goal of omniscient buddhahood; and its objects of abandonment are the delusions, whereas those of the Mahayana, are delusions and the innate tendencies of the mental structure to formulate a sense of ego. Hinayana is not a derogatory term, as is often stated by Western scholars; it is merely descriptive.

illusory body: (Tib. *sgyu-lus*) The subtle body created at the center of the heart by withdrawing the subtlest form of the vital energies from the extremities of the body and channeling them into the central nadi.

With the illusory body one can leave the ordinary body and travel to special buddhafields, where meditation is much more effective, and then return to the ordinary body at the end of the session. It is this practice that makes the Vajrayana such a quick path.

indestructible drop: The meeting point of mind and subtle matter. It is called indestructible because these two component elements separate only upon enlightenment. Symbolically, this is the drop formed by the combination of the sperm and ovum at the time of conception. The sperm and ovum, or white and red drops, come to be stored at the crown of the head and at the navel respectively. They are called indestructible because a breaking of their link means death. In tantric practice one brings the two to the heart and forms them into a house wherein higher meditation is performed.

Jetsun: An honorific title given to high mystics. The first syllable, *Je,* signifies "endowed with spiritual qualities"; *tsun* indicates one who is of high or noble status.

Jey Rinpochey: A popular name for Tsongkhapa, root guru of the First Dalai Lama.

Joyous Abode: *See* Pure Land of Joy.

Kadam: The sect of Tibetan Buddhism established under the Indian guru Atisha, who came to Tibet in 1042. Although during the fifteenth century the Kadam merged with the Kargyu, Sakya, and Geluk sects and therefore no longer exists as an independent order, its teachings are practiced now as much as ever, being preserved as a living tradition within these three sects.

karma: Literally "action" or "deed." Karma refers to the laws of cause and effect, whereby every deed is seen as a seed for future experience. Conversely, all experiences are seen not as coincidences but as the fruit of deeds done earlier in this life or in past lives. The doctrine is sometimes condemned in the West as being fatalistic. However, this is a misinterpretation. Although to a great degree the circumstances that descend upon us—such as whether we are born rich or poor, intelligent or not, etc.—are a matter of fate, or karma, we are free to use the positive and negative situations given to us to build a stronger future. And who can logically disprove the view that the man struck by a car owes his misfortune to some deeds done earlier in this or past lives? It seems a more reasonable hypothesis than the view that considers the event to be a causeless coincidence.

lama: The Tibetan rendition of the Sanskrit term "guru," or spiritual teacher. The title does not imply that the person is a monk; some lamas are monks, and although the lifestyle of a monk is conducive to spiritual experience, it is not a prerequisite. For example, Lama Drom, who received the Lojong lineages from Atisha, was not a monk. Also, the Sixth Dalai Lama gave up his robes at the age of twenty-one.

The word lama has two interpretations: "heavy," meaning heavy in spiritual qualities; and "without a ceiling," that is, of infinitely high qualities.

Lama-lha: (Skt. *gurudeva*) Literally "lama who is divine," i.e., a buddha. Regarding the lama as such is the tantric attitude toward the teacher.

layman: In the Buddhist use of the term, a layman is one who has taken refuge and least one of the five lay vows: not to kill, steal, lie, take the wives of others, or consume alcohol.

life-drop: *See* indestructible drop.

Lobzang Drakpa: The ordination name of Jey Tsongkhapa.

love: Technically, this is the wish that others abide in happiness and the causes of happiness. It is a prerequisite of both compassion and the bodhimind.

lower rebirth: Rebirth in the hells, as a ghost, or as an animal.

Madhyamaka: *See* extremes.

Middle View, Middle Way: *See* extremes.

Migtsema: The mantra and guru yoga practice associated with Lama Tsongkhapa.

nadi: Literally "vein" or "channel." The term can refer to the veins and arteries of the body, but more often means the subtle channels through which the vital energies flow. In ordinary people, these channels are knotted and blocked, resulting in an unbalanced flow. Tantric practice aims primarily at clearing and releasing the flow of energy, thus permitting higher meditation.

naga, Naga King: Nagas are mythological serpent spirits that live in water and trees, etc. Legend states that they control great wealth. The Naga King, who rules over the nagas, is fantastically wealthy.

Nagarjuna: The Indian sage of the second century who received the Wisdom Lineage from Manjushri. Legend has it that he lived for six hundred years, of which the last hundred witnessed his manifestation as a great mahasiddha.

nine steps to samadhi: *See* shamatha.

Nirmanakaya: *See* three kayas.

nirvana: (Tib. *mya-ngan-las-'das-pa*) The state beyond suffering; the extinction of delusion and therefore of karmically induced experiences.

Ogmin: The Heaven Beneath None, the pure land to which great yogis psychically travel in the last moments before enlightenment in order to gain their final realization.

practice lineages: The lineage of tantric practice given by Buddha in his manifestation as Vajradhara and passed through the various mahasiddhas. The line of Dalai Lamas embodies the combination of this lineage with the wisdom and method lines of Manjushri and Maitreya.

Prasangika: *See* Consequentialist.

protector deity: *See* Dharma protector.

Pure Land of Bliss: (Skt. *Sukhavati*) The pure land of Amitabha Buddha.

Pure Land of Joy: (Skt. *Tushita*; Tib. *dGa'-ldan*). The pure land of Maitreya Buddha. I have occasionally translated it as "the Joyous Abode" for purposes of meter.

Red Hat Sects: The Tibetan sects whose origin predate the Geluk, or Yellow Hat sect. *See also* Yellow Hat Sect.

refuge: The objects of spiritual conviction. *See* Three Jewels.

root lama, root guru: One's principal or most personal teacher. In some Tibetan sects, such as the Kargyu, one's root lama is he from whom one received the formal refuge ceremony. In the Gelukpa it is the lama who first turned one's heart toward the spiritual path.

samadhi: Generally this term refers to the ability of the mind to remain in single-pointed concentration upon an object of meditation. In certain tantric traditions it refers to enlightenment itself.

Sambhogakaya: (Tib. *longs-spyod-rdzogs-sku*) The beatific body, or ethereal facet of a buddha. It is endowed with five certainties: it abides always in a pure land; it is a pure, non-samsaric form endowed with the 112 marks of perfection; it is immortal; it has only high bodhisattvas for an entourage; and it speaks only the Dharma of the Great Way. *See also* three kayas.

samsara: The state of imperfect, unenlightened existence, wherein beings are prone to suffering and pain, birth and death, confusion and terror. Enlightenment ends samsaric experience.

Sangha: The community of spiritual aspirants. On one level this is the monkhood; on a deeper level it is the aryas, who have meditational experience of emptiness.

secret drop: *See* indestructible drop.

Secret Path: *See* Vajrayana.

seven kisses: Seven qualities of the stage of Vajradhara, the state of buddhahood attained through tantric practice.

Shakyamuni: Literally "Lord of the Shakya Dynasty." A name for the Shakya prince Siddhartha, who became Lord Buddha.

shamatha: A highly developed state of meditative concentration. To attain shamatha, the mind must first be ripened through proper instructions and by correctly following a teacher. Then one must go into an intensive retreat and progress through the nine levels of concentration until mental and physical ecstasy are experienced and, finally, shamatha is attained. At this stage, samadhi and clairvoyance are easily achieved. Then the real work in spiritual evolution can begin.

Shantideva: An eighth-century sage very important in the Lojong lineage.

shastras: The commentaries written by the Indian masters in clarification of Buddha's teachings.

shunyata: (Tib. *stong-pa-nyid*) Literally "emptiness" or "voidness." Shunyata refers to the deepest object of knowledge, the most profound level of reality. It has many synonyms: the ultimate mode of Being (Tib. *gnas-lugs*); ultimate truth (Tib. *don-dam-bden-pa*); things-just-as-they-are (Tib. *ji-ltar-pa*); thatness (Tib. *de-nyid*); suchness (Tib. *de-kho-na-nyid*); etc.

siddhi: Although siddhi literally means "spiritual attainment," it generally is used to connote the magical attainments of a tantric yogi.

six consciousnesses: The six awarenesses arising through the powers of the five senses and through the power of thought.

six miraculous powers: Six special abilities gained from samadhi and advanced meditation in the realm of form. The six are: (1) the ability to see ethereal forms; (2) the ability to hear all levels of sound; (3) the ability to subjugate the elements and to perform miracles; (4) the ability to remember one's previous lives; (5) the ability to read the minds of others; and (6) clairvoyance beyond samsaric delusion.

six perfections: Generosity, ethics, patience, joyous perseverance, meditation, and wisdom, all of which, to qualify as "perfections," must be based upon the motivation to gain enlightenment as a tool with which to best benefit the world.

six realms: The six dimensions of cyclic existence: hell, the ghost realms, the world of animals, the human world, the lower heavens of the fighting gods, and the realms of the three types of higher gods (the gods of the realm of desire, form, and formlessness).

six types of living beings: *See* six realms.

skandha: (Tib. *phung-po*) Literally "heap," "pile," or "aggregate." Skandha refers to the psychophysical constituents of which sentient life is comprised: form, feeling (response), distinguishing awareness, volitional formations (mental archetypes), and primary consciousness.

spiritual friend: (Skt. *kalyanamitra*) A synonym for guru.

suchness: *See* shunyata.

Sugata: (Tib. *bde-gshegs*) "He gone to bliss," that is, a buddha.

super-compassion: *See* universal responsibility.

sutra: (Tib. *mdo*) The scriptures of Hinayana and Mahayana containing all the non-tantric teachings of Buddha.

Sutrayana: The vehicle or path as outlined in the Hinayana and Mahayana Sutras. In the Tibetan tradition, the Sutrayana serves as the preparation and foundation for the Vajrayana.

tantra: (Tib. *rgyud*) The scriptures containing the Vajra teachings of Buddha. Tantra literally means "stream" or "thread," that is, the stream of truth pervading everywhere, linking each moment and every event. In terms of tantric scriptures, four main levels of tantra are taught: kriya, charya, yoga, and maha-anuttarayoga, or, respectively, purification tantra, action tantra, union tantra, and great highest union tantra (or simply highest tantra). Tibetans generally prefer to practice the fourth of these.

Tantrayana: The vehicle, or path, to enlightenment as propounded in the tantras.

Tathagata: (Tib. *de-bzhin-gshegs-pa*) Lit. "He thus gone." A synonym for a buddha.

ten directions: The four cardinal points, the four sub-directions, and the zenith and nadir.

ten endowments: Ten spiritual qualities conducive to enlightenment, of which five are personal and five impersonal. The five personal endowments are: (1) being born human and (2) in a central country (i.e., a country with a thriving spiritual culture), (3) being endowed with the purity of not having committed any of the five heinous deeds, (4) being in possession of all sensory powers, and (5) having faith in the objects of refuge. The impersonal endowments are: being alive in an era (1) when a buddha has appeared and (2) taught the Dharma, (3) when the Dharma is still thriving, (4) when there are many realized practitioners, and (5) having the supportive love and care of others.

ten negative deeds: Of these, three are physical: killing, stealing, and sexual misconduct; four are of speech: lying, slander, harsh words, and meaningless talk; and three are mental: attachment, aversion, and wrong view.

ten virtues: The opposites of the ten negative deeds. For example, instead of killing, protecting life; instead of stealing, giving; instead of sexual misconduct, refraining from more than five orgasms nightly; instead of slander, praising others, and so forth.

thatness: *See* shunyata.

three bodies of a buddha: *See* three kayas.

three bonds: The three types of vows. These are the vows for personal liberation (Hinayana), the bodhisattva vow (Mahayana), and the pledges and commitments entailed by tantric practice (Vajrayana).

three doors: The body, speech, and mind, which are the doors through which the forces of karma must enter into our stream of being. Thus, according to the karmic law, if one wishes happiness, all one has to do is let only beneficial actions in through the three doors, and close the doors to negative karma.

three energy channels: The three main nadis through which the vital energies must travel.

three higher trainings: The higher trainings in ethical discipline, meditation, and wisdom. These constitute the essence of Hinayana practice.

Three Jewels: The Buddha, Dharma, and Sangha. These have an outer and an inner interpretation. According to the outer interpretation, Buddha is the teacher who lived 2,500 years ago, Dharma is his teachings, and Sangha is the community of monks. According to the inner interpretation, Buddha is the spark of enlightenment within, Dharma is the all-pervading truth, and Sangha is those with profound experience of truth. In Vajrayana, the Buddha is represented by the lama, the Dharma by the yidam, and the Sangha by the dakinis and Dharma protectors.

three kayas: The mind, speech, and body of a Buddha, or the Dharmakaya, Sambhogakaya, and Nirmanakaya. When a yogi gains enlightenment, his body, speech, and mind transform into Dharmakaya, which then, for the benefit of aryas, precipitates the formation of a Sambhogakaya, and for the sake of ordinary beings, a Nirmanakaya as well.

Sometimes the Dharmakaya is subdivided into two: Dharmakaya and Svabhavakaya, or Truth Body and Natural Body. The former then becomes the twenty-one wisdoms and the latter becomes the void nature of the former. A further division into the Mahasukhakaya, or Great Bliss Body, is sometimes made, but the Seventh Dalai Lama has not mentioned the term in this text.

three mysteries: The body, speech, and mind of a buddha. They are called "mysteries" because they are fully understood only by other buddhas.

three psychic poisons: These are the three root delusions: attachment, aversion, and ignorance.

three sufferings: Immediate suffering, such as hunger; the suffering of change, that is, the inevitable transformation of happiness into pain; and the all-pervasive suffering, such as having a body which is dependent upon particular conditions for its well-being, and is therefore forced to meet the demands of continually having to strive for them.

transforming powers: (Tib. *byin-brlabs*) Often translated as "blessings." The first syllable of the Tibetan term means "power"; the second syllable means "to change" or "to transform." Therefore a literal translation is "the power to transform or improve." The term "blessing" fits as a translation, but is vague. I have used "transforming powers" because it is a more exact rendition and is more accurately descriptive.

Truth Body: *See* Dharmakaya.

Tsongkhapa: Literally "He from the district Tsongkha," that is, Jey Rinpochey, who was born in 1357 in Tsongkha of Amdo Province, East Tibet. He studied under forty-five teachers representing all sects of Buddhism in Tibet, and then formed the Geluk, or "The Wholesome Way," which came to be known as the Yellow Hat Sect because of the golden hat worn by its patriarchs.

Tushita Heaven: *See* Pure Land of Joy.

two stages of tantra: In the three lower classes of tantras these are (1) the yoga of symbols and (2) the yoga without symbols. In highest yoga tantra, the two stages become (1) the generation stage, that is, generating the vision of oneself as the mandala deity, the world as mandala and sounds as mantra; and (2) the completion stage, wherein, by control of the vital energies and the mystic drop, one completes the illusory body and clear light yogas to actualize the great unification state of enlightenment.

ultimate truth: (Tib. *don-dam-bden-pa*) Literally "truth of highest significance." *See* shunyata.

universal responsibility: (Tib. *lhag-bsam*) Literally "super-thought." The term refers to the attitude that is a combination of love and compassion developed to an unusually strong degree and characterized by an urgent sense of taking full responsibility for universal goodness. Technically, this state of consciousness is one step higher than love and compassion, and one step below the realization of bodhimind.

vajra: (Tib. *rdo-rje*) The diamond scepter, a mystic symbol of the immutable nature of enlightenment and of the tantric path.

vajra body: The form of an enlightened being. It is called vajra because it cannot be harmed and is beyond birth and death.

Vajradhara: Literally "Holder of the Vajra." In one sense, Vajradhara is the manifestation of Buddha Shakyamuni who taught the highest tantras and inspired the Buddhist tantric tradition. In another sense, he is the primordial state of enlightenment for which tantric yogins strive.

vajramind: The mind of a buddha, which cannot be adversely affected by any negative force.

vajra protector: *See* Dharma protector.

vajra speech: The immaculate wisdom/speech of an enlightened being.

vajrayana: *See* Tantrayana.

vipashyana: (Tib. *lhag-mthong*) or "special seeing." This term refers to penetrative meditation upon emptiness. I have generally rendered it as "mystic vision" or simply as "insight."

Vishnu: A Hindu god.

Wisdom Lineage: The lineage of teachings upon profound emptiness, which was given by Buddha to the Bodhisattva Manjushri. Manjushri gave it to Nagarjuna, and eventually it came to Atisha, who combined it with the Method Lineage of Maitreya and brought it to Tibet. Atisha passed the combined lineage to Lama Drom. In time it came to Lama Tsongkhapa and the line of Dalai Lamas.

Yama: (Tib. *gshin-rje*) The Lord of Death, a mythological figure who rules over the underworld and summons and judges sentient beings at their time of death.

Yellow Hat Sect: The Geluk sect of Tibetan Buddhism, formed in the late fourteenth century by Lama Tsongkhapa. All other Tibetan sects wear a pointed red hat, whereas the Geluk wear a yellow hat.

Legend has it that the early Indian gurus wore yellow hats. Yellow represents earth and the powers of increase. During one period of Indian history these gurus were losing many of their public debates with the Hindus, thus causing great embarrassment to Buddhism. Therefore the color of the hat was changed to red, which is the color of fire and also power. It turned the debate scene in their favor. When Buddhism came to Tibet, the use of the red hat came with it. In the Geluk, however, debate was used not to defeat others, but as an educational tool. Therefore Tsongkhapa changed the color of the hat back to yellow, the color of the increase of good qualities. It also symbolized his emphasis on a return to the Indian roots of Buddhism.

Philosophically, The Geluk were most strongly affected by the old Kadam school. But in terms of their tantric practices, they were closer to the Kargyu and Sakya sects. Tsongkhapa studied extensively in the main Drikung Kargyu monastery, there receiving the doctrines of the Guhyasamaja Tantra, the Six Yogas of Naropa, the five treatises on Mahamudra, and many other transmissions. From the Sakya he received Hevajra, Heruka Chakrasamvara, and many more systems that became important elements within the Geluk system. He also studied extensively with the Nyingma Sect, and many of the kriya, charya, and yoga tantras come to the Gelukpa from this source.

The Yellow Hat Sect has been Tibet's largest religious system for five hundred years, and has also been the largest religious system in both Mongolia and Ladakh.

yidam: Meditational deity or tantric meditational image. One meditates upon it, not as a form of devotion or worship, but in order to generate the sense of oneself being the yidam. A yidam is a symbolic form of enlightened mind, and by contemplating and identifying with it, the mind gains special powers and realization. Yidam practice (Tib. *lha'i-rnal-'byor*), or "deity yoga," is called the quick path (Tib. *myur-lam*), for through it one can gain enlightenment in as short a time as a year or two.

yoga: (Tib. *rnal-'byor*) The first syllable of the Tibetan term means "true" or "valid"; the second syllable means "path" or "union." Yoga is therefore a true practice or valid path. In the Tibetan system, yoga is essentially a mental tradition and is only physical or verbal in the sense that where the mind goes the body and speech follow. It does not connote physical stretching exercises, as is so often the case in its Hindu counterpart, but also does not exclude them. The term is usually used in reference to tantric practice, although in the Madhyamaka literature we see it used as an exclusive term for the experience of emptiness.

Bibliography

Geshe Ngawang Dhargyey. *Tibetan Traditions of Mental Development*. Dharamsala: Library of Tibetan Works and Archives, 1974.

Geshe Rabten and Geshe Ngawang Dhargyey. *Advice from a Spiritual Friend*. Translated by Brian Beresford. New Delhi: Publications for Wisdom Culture, 1977.

Geshe Wangyal. *The Door of Liberation*. New York: Maurice Girodias, 1973.

His Holiness the Dalai Lama. *The Buddhism of Tibet*. Translated and edited by Jeffrey Hopkins. Ithaca: Snow Lion, 1987.

His Holiness the Dalai Lama. *Opening of the Wisdom Eye*. Translated by Thubten Kalsang Rinpoche and Bhikkhu Khantipalo. London and Illinois: The Theosophical Publishing House, 1971.

His Holiness the Dalai Lama. *Universal Responsibility and the Good Heart*. Dharamsala: Library of Tibetan Works and Archives, 1980.

Jamgon Kongtrul. *A Direct Path to Enlightenment*. Translated by Ken McLeod. Vancouver: Kargyu Kunkyab Chuling, 1974.

TIBETAN SOURCES

blo-sbyong-dang-'brel-ba'i-gdams-pa-dang-snyan-mgur-gyi-rim-pa-phyogs-gcig-tu-bkod-pa-don-ldan-tshangs-pa'i-sgra-dbyangs (*A Meaningfully Arranged Collection of Songs and Precepts Connected with Spiritual Change, Including the "Song of the Immaculate Path."*) Gangtok : Dodrup Sangye, 1975

bLo-sbyong-brgya-rtsa (*A Hundred Fundamental Treatises on Lojong*). Dharamsala: Sherig Parkang, 1975.

bLo-sbyong-khrid-yig (*Commentary on Spiritual Transformation*) by the First Dalai Lama (undated manuscript).

Byang-sems-gnyis-sgom-tshul (*Meditation upon the Two Bodhiminds*) by the Second Dalai Lama (undated manuscript).

Lam-rim-gser-zhun-ma (*Essence of Refined Gold*) by the Third Dalai Lama (undated manuscript).

dBang-rjes-gnang-sngon-'gro (*Preliminaries of Initiation*) by the Seventh Dalai Lama. Drepung Edition, 1945. Historical Sources

HISTORICAL SOURCES

Bell, Sir Charles. *Tibet Past and Present*. Oxford: Clarendon, 1968.

Bell, Sir Charles. *The Religion of Tibet*. Oxford: Clarendon, 1931.

Richardson, H.E. *Tibet and its History*. New York: Dutton, 1962.

Rockhill, W.W. *The Dalai Lamas of Lhasa and Their Relationship with the Manchu Emperors of China*. Leiden, 1910.

Shakabpa, Tsepon W.D. *A Political History of Tibet*. New Haven: Yale, 1967.

Snellgrove, D.L. and Richardson, H.E. *A Cultural History of Tibet*. London: Weidenfeld and Nicolson, 1968.

Stein, R.A. *Tibetan Civilization*. London: Faber, 1972.

TIBETAN HISTORICAL SOURCES

Khetsun Sangpo. *A Biographical Dictionary of Indian and Tibetan Saints*, Vol. 1-6. Library of Tibetan Works and Archives, Dharamsala, India, 1975.

'Phags-pa-'jig-rten-dbang-phyug-gi-rnam-sprul-rim-byon-gyi-'khrung-rabs-deb-ther-nor-bu'i-'phreng-ba (*A Jewel Rosary Illustrating the Various Incarnations of Saintly Avalokiteshvara, the Bodhisattva of Compassion*). The Kugi Yigtsang: Dharamsala, India, 1976.